The Sense

of

Vocation

The Sense

of

Vocation

A Study of Career and Life Development

LARRY COCHRAN

State University of New York Press

Published by
State University of New York Press, Albany

For information, address State University of New York
Press, State University Plaza, Albany, N.Y., 12246

Library of Congress Cataloging-in-Publication Data

Cochran, Larry.
    The sense of vocation : a study of career and life development /
Larry Cochran.
        p.   cm.
    Bibliography: p.
    Includes index.
    ISBN 0-7914-0245-2. — ISBN 0- 7914-0246-0 (pbk.)
    1. Psychology, Industrial—Case studies.   2. Vocation—Case
studies.   3. Self-realization—Case studies.   4. Success—Case
studies.   I. Title.
HF5548.8.C565   1990
158.6—dc20   89-34226
                                                                        CIP

10 9 8 7 6 5 4 3 2 1

Contents

Preface

What is the nature of a sense of vocation as it is lived over the course of a life? To investigate this question, I studied over twenty life stories of persons who clearly had a mission in life, from founding experiences in youth to culminating events in old age. Based upon these narrative accounts, I constructed a common plot or story line that reveals the pattern of life for those with a sense of vocation. This pattern involves four phases of life, showing how a sense of vocation begins, how it is cultivated, how it is enacted in a life's work, and how it ends. The central aim of this book is to portray the common plot through a detailed consideration of these four phases, their distinctive characteristics and dramatic form.

Most generally, the book was written for humanistic psychologists, developmental or life-span psychologists, clergy members, teachers, intelligent lay persons, anyone interested in the question of what makes life meaningful. Rather than speculate on the meaning of life in the abstract, my approach was to examine concrete lives that were radiant with meaning, or at least with one kind of meaning. For those with a sense of vocation, life is shaped in a way that lights up one's existence in an elevated story the person lives. It is not the only kind of answer that can be offered to the meaning of life, but it does offer one rather substantial answer, from which others might follow.

More specifically, the book was written for counseling psychologists, personologists, occupational psychologists, and business scholars, those who are concerned with the topic of a career, of work and life. This book is concerned with establishing a paradigm case of what a career is at its best. Typically, topics are approached in two ways. First, one can test numerous piecemeal hypotheses, hoping that a whole can eventually be constructed through small building blocks. Second, one can form a speculative theory and test hypotheses that derive from the theory. In this book, a third approach was used, that of holistic construction. In this approach, one attempts to construct a coherent and reasonably well-founded whole to serve as a basis for further refinements, extensions, and revisions. It is taken for granted that the initial construction is apt to suffer from various errors of commission and omission, but, if done well, the first portrait establishes a guiding point of reference for future corrections. Its potential value is fruitfulness.

Introduction

John Stuart Mill (1969), in his late youth, was moved by accounts of the French Revolution, the splendor of its democratic principles that burned brightly for a short period some thirty years previously, and then like meteors, burned out, leaving but an insignificant minority who still held the vision. Somehow, it seemed to bring his stringent education to a point, and while still under the tyranny of his father's educational methods, he imagined himself as a democratic champion. However, he was not able to do more than engage in fantasy. As yet, it was unreal, a spring for imagination, not for action.

In the winter of 1821 his capabilities and sensitivities were brought to a more definite and enduring aspiration. He read a three-volume work that was to be a turning point for his future development. He felt taken up to such an elevation that he could "survey a vast mental domain, and see stretching out into the distance intellectual results beyond all computation (p. 42)." His reading allowed him to see clearly and broadly, and in this seeing, he also found a vocation:

> When I laid down the last volume of the Traité I had become a different being. The "principle of utility" understood as Bentham understood it, and applied in the manner in which he applied it through these three volumes, fell exactly into its place as the keystone which held together the detached and fragmentary component parts of my knowledge and beliefs. It gave unity to my conception of things. I now had opinions; a creed, a doctrine, a philosophy; in one among the best senses of the word, a religion; the inculcation and diffusion of which could be made the principal outward purpose of a life. And I had a grand conception laid before me of changes to be effected in the condition of mankind. . . . And the vista of improvement which he did open was sufficiently large and brilliant to light up my life, as well as to give a definite shape to my aspirations [pp. 42–43]. From the winter of 1821, when I first read Bentham . . .

1

I had what might truly be called an object in life; to be a reformer of the world [p. 80].

At age fifteen, Mill achieved a sense of vocation that was to endure throughout his life. He never ceased to be a reformer; he only varied in his view of what would constitute reform. Even five years later, in the midst of his famous mental crisis, his sense of vocation was not questioned so much as the adequacy of his vision and his personal suitability for the task. For the next fifty-two years, Mill would pursue his vocation, until his death in 1873.

In this book, vocation is not necessarily a matter of occupation, job, position, or profession. In ordinary language, there are uses that level work-related terms to a mere job reference. However, the subject of this book is not the cheapened sense of vocation, but the elevated sense of a life's calling. Everyone might have a work position, but not everyone has a vocation. It is an exclusive concept, indicating a special status of great value, at least to those who have achieved it. Let us consider Mill for a preliminary characterization of the psychological reality of having a vocation.

Mill felt elevated, as though something special had been given him to do. His work was sacred to him. An avowed agnostic, Mill was raised without religious belief. Mill's father would not allow it. Yet to describe his experiences, Mill often borrowed a religious terminology and used it to portray the psychological reality of his feelings and convictions. Somehow, his work was sanctioned, perhaps by the awe of his vision, and made holy (in a way). Devotion, sacredness, purity, holiness, or wholeheartedness are all terms that come naturally to a discussion of vocation. There is an aura of religious experience, although that experience might be devoid of religious content, similar in some ways to Maslow's (1976) peak experiences.

Elevation is not something one can directly accomplish. Partially, one can struggle for it indirectly in the same way one can strive to be happy by indirectly doing those things most apt to make one happy. Partially, persons simply give themselves to a sense of vocation when it arises. For an analogical example, one can check, thwart, and divert a sense of happiness when it comes or one surrenders to it. A sense of vocation is partially an invention, partially a discovery, partially deliberate, partially involuntary, partially in control, partially beyond control. It is within this psychological context that ancient human activities seem to come startlingly alive. The vision quest, prayer, pilgrimage, rite of passage—all come alive as peculiar answers to the question of how to achieve a sense of vocation. One cannot will a sense of vocation and it is futile to just hope, but what is it that one can do? Ancient practices offer various answers to this dilemma of being. *The Spiritual Exercises of St. Ignatius* (1964), for example, can be regarded as a vocational guidance program!

Mill also felt that his work was himself or that he was his work. Person and work were not two different things, but inseparable aspects of some oneness of being. Elsewhere (Cochran, 1985), I have characterized personhood as a regnant position that serves to order one's being into a composition. Mill, for example, did not have a job as a reformer; he was a reformer. "Reformer of mankind" was a metaphor for self that defined his regnant position. It was an order of being, not just a conception and not just a feeling, but both. Personhood is a unity of incompletion or desire, erecting a gap between what is and what ought to be. To be a reformer, for instance, is to yearn to accomplish reforms. The same term that characterizes a person also characterizes a person's work. In short, a reformer strives for reform. That is what he or she does. The relationship is not contingent but personally necessary, a relationship of being and doing, potential and actual. In work, one strives to actualize or make real one's potential or order of being. In one sense, one's work is practical and can be assessed for practical achievements. In another sense, one's work is symbolic, conveying a certain spirit or meaning. For one who has achieved a sense of vocation, person and work are united. A person could not change his or her work without a change in being. This, of course, does not mean that force of circumstance could not coerce a person into doing other kinds of work, but those other kinds of work would not be his or her work. And it is the sacredness of one's "true" work that could not be changed while remaining the same person.

Last, of these preliminary characterizations, the work of a vocation is a life's work. First, it is expected to endure throughout life and to be the very measure of one's life. To write one's life story would be to tell the story of one's vocational preparations, aspirations, and achievements. Second, it is the center of a life, pervading the multitude of activities that make it up. For one with a vocation, we neither expect nor find a radical division in life in which there are compartments bearing no relation to others. One bends all of life in service of a vocation, and what cannot be bent can only be endured. For example, Mill formed a devoted relationship with Harriet Taylor. His love for Mrs. Taylor was not separate from reform, but came to support his efforts in so many ways that he regarded her as an indispensable blessing. How much this characteristic and others can be softened while still claiming a sense of vocation, I do not know. It is a topic for exploration rather than pronouncement, for which these characterizations but serve as guides.

The field of counseling psychology has tended to neglect the strong sense of vocation in favor of the more encompassing concept of a career. In the broad way the term is used, everyone has a career. Following Super (1976), a career involves the sequence of work and work-related roles that make up a life. Indeed, a career includes life roles generally as they rise and fall in a person's pattern of self-development. There is an attempt to stress work, but also to keep in focus a total life pattern of self-development. Most authors have adopted Super's viewpoint, often altering it in various ways. For example, Tolbert (1980) defined a career as a sequence of occupations, greatly restricting the term. Norris, Hatch, Engelkes, & Winborn (1979) have expanded the term to include the "total composite of one's activities throughout life" (p. 6), not attempting to draw a firm distinction between work and nonwork activities. Given the broad view of career, the field of career guidance is breathtaking in scope (see the excellent textbooks of Healy, 1982; Herr & Cramer, 1979), virtually a guided preparation for living a more productive, satisfying, and meaningful life. Counselors attempt to foster career development, taking up one definition of it: "Career development is the process by which an individual formulates a career and continuously evaluates the choice, new opportunities, and personal goals in an effort to find the most meaningful life" (Norris, Hatch, Engelkes, & Winborn, 1979, p. 8). While the field is broadly defined, supporting enormous breadth in counseling practice, the common aim of the field seems to be to help persons to more closely resemble those who have a vocation and successfully pursue it. Yet studies of exemplary cases, of those with a sense of vocation, are seldom if ever conducted (none to my knowledge). It is just assumed that we know what an exemplary case is like. There are a variety of other reasons for the neglect of vocation, some of which will be briefly explained below.

One reason might be called 'misleading concreteness.' For example, a vocation is equated with a job, occupation, or work position. However, the actual job a person holds might bear only a peripheral relation to his or her vocation. For thirty-five years, John Stuart Mill worked as a clerk and secretary in the East India Company, preparing correspondence for outlets abroad. The only importance this occupation had for Mill was that it supported and did not interfere with his vocation. It earned a livelihood, was a rather pleasant rest from his intellectual labors, and gave practical experience that added to his theoretical efforts at reform. It is better to ask what a person's work is rather than assume one knows.

A second reason is the normative viewpoint taken in research, using large groups and preestablished variables. As one example, Holland (1985) has constructed an ingenious typology of six kinds of persons and six kinds of environments. At this level of abstraction, the best that one can say about the meaning of a vocation is that an artistic person, for instance, is apt to be most satisfied in an artistic environment. A social person is apt to be most satisfied in a social environment, and so on. Or one might hypothesize that a person who has a vocation resembles more purely one of the six types. Whatever one does within the theory, a vocation will emerge as a very abstract and impoverished phenomenon. It is simply not very illuminating to assert that an investigative person is apt to be most satisfied in an investigative environment. Mill, for example, was an intellectual and would undoubtedly have scored high on Holland's investigative type, yet this captures virtually nothing about the reality of his vocation. Holland's theory is admirable, elegant, and of great practical value in career counseling, but it is inappropriate for understanding a vocation.

Super's (1957) theory offers more promise. A vocational preference is a translation into occupational terms of the kind of person one is. In an occupation, a person seeks to implement and then to actualize a self-conception (Super, Starishevsky, Matlin, & Jordaan, 1963). There are problems with this viewpoint. For example, it assumes an independent self-conception and an occupation that are matched through translation. Presumably, a person who has a vocation would be one with an adequate self-conception, a clear translation, and a good match of self to occupation. Following an example from Starishevsky and Matlin, that one is intelligent, healthy, and broad-minded might translate into psychologist. Research indicates generally that self-ratings are more similar to a person's desirable occupations than undesirable ones (for example, Blocher & Schutz, 1961). Mill's self-ratings, too, would probably have matched his ratings of a clerk in the East India Company, yet this does not illumine the meaning of a vocation. For Mill, his personhood was constituted by a metaphor for self, which was his vocation. There was not translation so much as a shaping of himself in accordance with his metaphor.

While there are difficulties with Super's viewpoint, and promise as well, the main point here is that it was immediately transformed into group statistical designs of research that are uniquely unsuited for understanding the meaning of vocation as it is lived. At best, one can talk of a good translation, a good self-conception, and there one is left in abstraction. Like Holland's typology, Super's theory is rich and useful, but is strangely lacking in trying to understand a vocation.

As a last example, one of the central aspects of Super's work is his theory of stages. Persons progress through a series of five overlapping stages of life: growth, exploration, establishment, maintenance, and decline. Each stage is characterized by a set of life tasks that must be accomplished before progressing to the next stage. The extent to which these tasks are adequately done bodes well or ill for future endeavors. Consequently, stress is placed upon career maturity, or the adequacy of one's skills and attitudes in coping with life tasks. Research has identified various skills and attitudes that predict later success, and it is anticipated that research will eventually create an adequate map for practicing counselors to follow. That is, the tasks will be identified and the skills and attitudes for accomplishing them will be specified. A counselor would then make clients aware of relevant tasks and cultivate relevant skills to master them. The clarity of this frame, its potential to guide research and practice, the sheer feat of rendering a chaotic topic into a coherent form are difficult to match. It is an amazing theory, in many ways, for which Super has scarcely received the credit owed. Very probably, a combination of Holland's synchronic structure with Super's diachronic structure will eventually offer a reasonably comprehensive framework for career psychology. However, as it is currently being developed and researched, the theory is not likely to clarify a vocation.

To see its lack regarding vocation, consider the career of a house fly. There are four distinct stages: egg, larva, pupa, and adulthood. Each stage has distinctive tasks. For example, a larva eats, and if it does not eat enough, there will be a deficiency in adulthood, for adult flies are not built for eating. They can supplement their food store a little, but the energy of the adult fly is largely dependent upon its consumption of food in the larval stage. The career of a fly could be drawn out to parallel the career of a person, as conceived by Super, and the parallel is far more fruitful and exact than might be expected. For instance, a fly works, doing little but fly-work. However, what the fly does is done automatically by virtue of being a fly. A particular fly's work does not reflect itself, but reflects the kind of being a fly in general is. By contrast, humans have diverse purposes, ambitions, values, competencies, and the like. A person's work is expected to reflect the person, at least in a vocation that is intensely personal. If we want to generalize about the nature of vocations, we must do so by understanding what is common to particular cases, or we generalize too soon. If we begin, not with an individual, but with large groups and norms, and turn those norms back on individuals, we see only as much of a vocation as is held in common with persons generally, most of whom probably have no vocation. The topic is generalized from the start by incorporating a few characteristics of large groups rather than exploring many characteristics of a few cases (see De Waele & Harre, 1976). A fly career becomes difficult to distinguish from a human career, and this occurs despite attempts to incorporate generalized principles of individuation.

A third reason for neglect is that career psychologists have been initiated almost exclusively into a positivistic worldview. No matter how humanistic or phenomenological a theory appears, it is transformed in research practice by positivistic assumptions. In positivism, the world is make up of objects with properties that interact predictably in events. We know nothing beyond that we sense; and what we sense is the externality of objects, their shape, size, movement, and the like. There is no intrinsic content, much less individuality. Cause, following Hume, is a regularity between events. The aim of science is to chart the regularity of events and form these regularities into a hypothetico-deductive theory. Although psychologists actually use statistical generalizations rather than deductions, the picture is the same, one of "the hurrying of material, endlessly, meaninglessly" (Whitehead, 1967, p. 54).

Psychology began not with immersement in the subject matter and explorations of methods most suited to it. Rather, psychology began with a distaste for rich description and positive zeal to make the subject, whatever it might be, conform to an external philosophy of science (Koch, 1959–63). What did not fit easily within this worldview was removed by the odd expedient of denying its existence. Thus, consciousness, purpose, value, anticipation, and the like, have all been denied, and those who used the terms were ridiculed. One might well wonder what was left to study, so assiduous were psychologists in denying all qualities that suggested a human being rather than a mechanism. One engaged in respectable research by a kind of massive deception. As Whitehead (1957) quipped: "Scientists animated by the purpose of proving that they are purposeless constitute an interesting subject for study" (p. 9).

As time went on and the pretense became increasingly more difficult to maintain, banished terms were reintroduced, but with this difference. The terms were taken from the context (e.g., of human agency) in which they were meaningful and placed in the context of a positivistic research methodology. Thus, values and meanings entered as properties of objects. Meaningfulness became a variable as if it were a tangible property discernible by the senses. Like a tangible property, the only question one asks is a quantitative one: How meaningful? Some objects manifest high meaningfulness and some low meaningfulness; and this variable can be related to other variables. The result is a vision that is just as mechanical, lifeless, and senseless as the vision that preceded it. Still, what is investigated are properties of object, not meanings of subjects.

With a topic such as vocation, the moment it becomes an object with properties, we have lost it. For example, a person with a vocation is one with measurably high degrees of work motivation, work satisfaction, and work meaningfulness or significance. Or a person with a vocation manifests a higher degree of intrinsic motivation than extrinsic motivation. Or a person with a vocation shows strong commitment to work. To engage in this sort of exercise is to become imprisoned in an illusion of having said something. At best, one is naming a few likely attributes of what one knows little about. To go further with quantitative studies that relate these variables to others or that seek to increase a variable, merely compounds the illusion. One has straightjacketed the subject with presumptions rather than investigated it. To have a vocation in life involves the meanings of the person who has it. If one did not explore that person's experience of vocation as it was lived, it is questionable whether one would be studying a vocation at all. Rather, one has defined it away.

A final reason for the neglect of vocation is that most theory and research are geared toward current practice and current social arrangements. For example, it is virtually foreordained that a project or theory will eventually end up as a test that links a person to occupation. Current practice requires tests. But really, why should so much end in this way? There is no doubt that it is advantageous to gear work toward current practice, and I would not argue against it, but it is exceedingly narrow. Vocational guidance did not arise in this century. Quite the contrary, vocational guidance has existed for thousands of years and only took a particular form in this century. As one example, vocational guidance flourished in ancient Greece:

> Like the sages and sophists who preceded them, the earliest moral philosophers were primarily devoted to two sorts of tasks: recommending life goals and specifying ideals of personal excellence. Men of affairs, in their reflective moments, turned to men called wise to learn the secret of the good life—of ultimate purposes and the goods most worth having; and sometimes, though probably much less often, they inquired about the traits of character most worth cultivating—the sorts of persons most worth being [Feinberg, 1970, p. 1].

The great philosophies of living (hedonism, eudaemonism, stoicism) arose as attempted answers to problems of guidance in life, preeminent of which is the question of vocation.

Vocational guidance took a professional form in this century through the work of Frank Parsons (1909). While Parsons advocated a variety of methods, what endured was his "true reasoning" procedure. With a clear understanding of oneself and knowledge of work, true reasoning is an effort to relate two sets of "facts." Parsons's procedure is rational and open to a scientific basis. It has become the prototype of a matching model that led to a boom in trait-factor counseling, which has dominated practice ever since. The aim of Parsons's model, and advanced forms of it, is not to cultivate a vocation, but to create a satisfying match between person and occupation. Vocation, in the strong sense, is peripheral and scarcely noted.

Our social setting with its multitude of job possibilities and relative freedom of choice virtually demands something like a matching model. The value and suitability of this practice is not in question. However, it does make vocation rather tangential. Indeed, to speak aloud of a true vocation might be an embarrassment at the present time. However, the psychological reality of vocation still exists, and in other times and cultures, vocation held a more eminent placement in the social scheme, being connected to a right relationship with the invisible world. More importantly, methods existed that were intended to cultivate a sense of vocation. Yet these methods and the nature of vocation remain out of sight in focusing upon current practice.

Once vocation is brought more clearly into view, the value of the subject for career psychology and other fields is apparent. While there might be a great variety of careers, not all reflect what we fully mean by career. For example, the careers of a welfare recipient, an alienated worker, a disenchanted job changer, a floundering idealist, and the like are interesting, but they do not capture very well all that we mean or envision in a career at its best. Vocation stands to career, in many ways, like a consummate instance, and might well be regarded as the quintessence of career. In vocation, the great questions of career come alive and can be pursued through exemplary cases. What makes work so meaningful? How does meaning arise? How do circumstances facilitate or hinder a sense of vocation? What is the proper relation of work to life? What is a vocation and how does it alter the quality of life? If a vocation centers and integrates a life, how does it do so? The aim of this book is to pursue these questions through the lives of persons who can properly be said to have had a vocation in life.

1 *Repetition and Rhythm*

In the life stories of persons with a vocation, the most striking characteristic is repetition. Experiences are repeated not merely a few times, but a multitude of times. From the first memory to the last, life appears as one big experience or a series of the same kind of experiences. Any given experience of significance stands as a variation of past and future experiences. There is no exact repetition, or as Heraclitus phrased it, "you cannot step twice into the same river" (Wheelwright, 1959, p. 29). Rather, there is repetition with variation. No experience exactly duplicates another, but resembles it enough that it appears of the same nature. Appropriately, Leeper and Madison (1959) have referred to repetitions of experience as reintegrations.

Unlike traditional research in psychology, in which a presumably respectable methodology is imposed regardless of the subject matter, the aim here is to allow a method to emerge from the nature of the subject. In lives, the central characteristic is repetition of experience, and this characteristic ought, in my view, to require us to build a methodology suitable to it. For recent developments of life history approaches, see Bertaux (1981), McAdams and Ochberg (1988), Runyan (1982), Watson and Watson-Franke (1985).

Through an investigation, we want to make claims. The basis for claims is repetition and variation. Repetition is an analogue to reliability in statistical studies. A series can be judged for internal consistency, and claims can be made about what is consistent or enduring. By implication, if we grasp internal consistency, we can judge variations and determine when there has been a significant deviation. Related to consistency is coherence. Repetition of experience does not involve a single atomistic element, but a configuration of elements. Particular elements might be added or subtracted, and still, the same configuration might persist. Coherence requires a judgment about the form or organization of experience such that one can determine or understand the way elements fit together. We cannot determine consistency without coherence.

11

Natural Categories

To spell out the method in more detail, consider the analogy of a concept to an experience. A concept is used over and over, but features of meaning vary in use. For example, when the romantic lead in a movie says to the heroine, "I care for you," he does not mean quite the same thing as a neighbor who says, "Yes, I will care for your pet while you are on vacation." One case stresses affection or mattering; the other stresses responsibility for the well-being of something. Uses of the concept of care vary considerably. Of the various features of the concept, some are highlighted in one use and deemphasized or neglected in another use. A concept is like a family of possibilities rather than a single essence.

Traditionally, concepts have been viewed as well-defined sets, rigidly bounded containers of instances appropriate for logic. For example, a set of red, round objects is an attempt to categorize sharply according to the criteria of redness and roundness. An object either would or would not belong to this category, and each object would reflect the category as well as any other. In contrast, Wittgenstein (1953) and Rosch (1977) have shown that concepts of ordinary language or natural categories are fuzzy rather than sharply bounded. Membership in a natural category is a matter of degree, more or less rather than either-or. For example, a peach is a better exemplar of fruit than is a tomato. Instances that more ideally exemplify a category are termed prototypes or paradigm cases; they are exceptionally clear examples, manifesting the features of a category broadly, with appropriate emphasis and organization. A natural category is not unified by a few criterial features, since no feature might apply to all cases. In Wittgenstein's (1953) famous example, he found no feature that was present in all instances of the category of games. Rosch (1977) has found that instances of a category, however, can be reliably rated as to the extent to which they belong. Belonging is not a matter of fulfilling a few criteria, but more a matter of similarity to a prototype. A natural category is built around prototypical instances.

The relation among instances within a category is one of family resemblance, to use Wittgenstein's description. For example, two siblings might appear to share no common features, yet still be recognizable members of the same family in their resemblance to father or mother. There are no firm borders of a category, and instances might fit within two or more categories. Indeed, borderline cases abound, fitting more or less as categories merge. A category is most distinct as exemplified by prototypes, which manifest not only the features of a category most clearly, but manifest the features of similar or opposite categories the least.

Generally, to gain clarity, philosophers conduct a conceptual analysis of a concept. See Wilson (1963) for one of the simplest presentations. First, a number of instances are gathered. For example, persons talk of a career in medicine, a career over a lifetime, an interrupted career, and so on, all varied instances of the way the concept is used. Second, cases are examined to see what features of meaning are present or absent, pronounced or unstressed, in diverse contexts. By lining up cases, one can determine what they might have in common, what features seem pervasive and what features seem more tangential. Third, cases that seem exceptionally clear as instances are examined to see what it is that makes them exceptionally clear. For example, if one refers to the career of Napoleon, of Winston Churchill, or of Henry Ford, the concept seems quite clear, but why? Fourth, one examines borderline or deviant cases to see what makes them borderline or deviant. For example, the career of a welfare recipient is a borderline use, and it seems borderline because a welfare recipient is not defined by work (aims and accomplishments) but by consumption, among other things. A welfare recipient receives without production through work, yet might manifest a course of life on welfare. Last, one examines similar and contrasting categories to try to gain perspective on what makes a given category distinctive. For example, one might assess work, recreation, occupation, and the like, to try to understand a career better.

These simple steps are certainly not the only ones involved in a conceptual analysis. There is an open number of possibilities and different philosophers stress different methods. For example, White (1967) tries to see what the use of a concept implies, to discover the questions that could be asked of it, to examine qualifications that are relevant or irrelevant, to search for contradictions, and to note the situations in which it is used or not used. However, further explication would not advance the argument here.

The analogy of concept and experience seems straightforward.

Instead of a number of uses or instances of a concept, we have a number of similar experiences. There is a family resemblance among the significant experiences that make up a life. Every experience might not closely resemble every other experience, but they still appear as offspring of the same family. By lining them up, we can see what features are common, what features are variable; and there are paradigm cases within a life just as there are for a concept. Due to force of circumstance, among other things, there are also borderline and deviant cases that allow us to at least sense when someone is on course or off course. In general, the tactics of conceptual analysis can be applied without strain to the experiences of a life.

As conceived here, the application of conceptual analysis to lives does not differ significantly from phenomenological methods (Valle & King, 1978), hermeneutics (Palmer, 1969), particularly as influenced by Dilthey (Rickman, 1976), and life history methods generally (Murray, 1938), although each has distinctive contributions to make. For example, the hermeneutic circle is concerned with the way we come to understand. Given whatever preunderstanding a person has, one begins examining parts to grasp the whole, and using an understanding of the whole to grasp parts better. Cyclically, from parts to whole and back again, understanding clarifies and deepens. However, I am stressing conceptual analysis not necessarily because it is more adequate, but because it keeps the central characteristic of lives in clear focus. Experiences are repeated and it is upon this solid foundation that one can build, using quite a variety of methods.

What exactly is repeated? Any rounded experience takes the form of a complete story with a beginning, middle, and end. We live experiences as a story, aware of beginning, a middle, and a striving for closure. We recount experience in story form. We question and investigate using story as a way to make things intelligible. That is, puzzlements (such as the motive in a mystery story) typically indicate deficiencies that a more complete story would alleviate. While the reasons why we dramatize experience or experience dramatizes us are quite far-reaching, having to do with the kind of beings we are (see Bruner, 1986; Burke, 1969; Carr, 1986; Harré & Secord, 1973; Polkinghorne, 1988; Sarbin, 1986), the bald claim that rounded experience presents itself as story is so natural to us as to appear self-evident. If there were doubt, one need only read several autobiographies or listen to some life histories. When an experience is described, a story is told.

What is repeated in life, then, is a multitude of stories. While the basic structure of story is apparent to nearly everyone, much is perhaps tacit rather than explicit (Polanyi, 1966). For this reason, a few of the most important features of story will be presented. First, however, let us establish a more concrete point of reference. Below is a summarized story from a person's life, one that is not too simple, yet characteristic of the kind of stories that are told in a life history.

The Would-be Jockey

In his youth, the great muckraker, Lincoln Steffens (1931), had a brief love affair with horse racing. Exploring the area around old Sacramento, he discovered a deserted racetrack not far from home. There, he used to gallop his horse, pretending that he was a jockey. Imaginatively, he won races and walked his horse victoriously before a grandstand of cheering on-lookers. Then, one morning, he found real persons at the racetrack. Initially, they (grooms and jockeys) jeered him and tried to get him to leave, but he was befriended by a black jockey named Smoke. After hanging around for some days, trainers found a use for him. They had him trot their horses. While jockeys called him a fool for working for free, young Steffens was delighted to have a chance to be more of an insider. Further, the trainers encouraged him to work hard, to stay small and thin, and some day, he might become a jockey.

Steffens worked very hard, trotting four or five horses a day for four or five miles, straining back on the reins to keep the horses from breaking into a gallop. He practiced the language, behavior, and style of jockeys. At home, he fasted, occasionally breaking down to stuff himself, until his concerned father eventually set up a regular diet for him. He attended all the races, becoming a fixture at the racetrack, and as his involvement grew, he idealized more and more. To be a jockey appeared, no doubt, as just about the finest aspiration a person could have.

As an insider, however, he was informed about fixed races and how they were good because "those in on the know" could earn a lot of money on them through betting. Yet, they did not seem like good things to Steffens, nor to his friend Smoke. As he watched jockeys he liked hold back horses he loved and knew could win, tears would well up and his faith dwindled. In on the know, he suffered.

One day, Smoke was ordered to hold back a young horse they both loved, a "comer." Even a half-century later, Steffens would remember the details of that race, a struggle between a spirited horse and a dispirited rider. Smoke would pull and the horse would bob his head up and down to break free. Occasionally, the horse received enough slack to move easily to the front, only to be pulled back once more. Steffens found Smoke later in back of the stables, hiding and crying:

> It's all right. . . . It's good business for white Folks, an' a nigger don't matter much, but—de hoss! A hoss is a gen'leman, kid. It hurts him to lose a race, it breaks him—permanent—to sell a race. You ought to 'a' seen de look he done give me when I got down off'n him. I had to sneak out o' his sight, and I don't see how I kin ever look'im de face again [p. 39].

Steffens lost interest in horse racing. He wandered alone trying to figure things out. Occasionally, he talked with confidants. Nothing was as it seemed. How could persons he liked do what they did? Upon advice from his father, he maintained contact with the racetrack to learn all he could about horses, but not to be a jockey. Even this ended, however. In trotting horses for the owners, Steffens had an orgasm, such a startling event for a boy that he fell off the horse. Naively, he tried to describe what had happened, but when they finally got the drift, he was hooted by the jockeys. The trainer was enraged and convinced the other trainers that Steffens was no longer to be trusted. "I was a joke. I slunk off on my pony, humiliated and perplexed" (p. 40). Yet, he still hung around the stables.

More decisively, his contact ended with the fall of Smoke. The owners had agreed that Smoke had pulled his horse so well that he was required to pull other horses. "He who hated it the most had to do it the most" (p. 41). Eventually, he was investigated, caught, and banned from racing. He could have received a lighter judgment, but no one spoke up for him. Those who required him to do it, now did not want to get mixed up in the situation, even as they asked Smoke not to give them away. When Steffens last saw him, Smoke was bewildered and hurt, still wretched with shame for the betrayals of his horses.

Near his home, Steffens sat silently on a fence, thinking. When his father found him, and was informed about Smoke, he sat quietly beside him. Finally, his mother found and scolded him for thinking too much, like his father, and doing nothing. But what does one do about disillusionment other than try to figure things out?

Story Structure

A story or dramatic form is what Lakoff and Johnson (1980) have termed an experiential gestalt, "the complex of properties occurring together is more basic to our experience than their separate occurrence" (p. 71). Story is a holistic unit basic to our experience, yet as Lakoff and Johnson indicate regarding natural categories generally, a story is indefinitely analyzable. A story can be decomposed into characters, situations or scenes, plot, story line, pretext and context, and the like, each of which in itself is indefinitely analyzable. The question of what makes up a story is at once exceedingly simple (that is, everyone knows) and exceedingly difficult, requiring centuries of effort by foremost scholars to clarify various strands. The aim of this section is to stress a few basic ingredients that are of particular importance for understanding repetitive experiences in lives.

The Beginning: Defining a Gap

The beginning of a story has been variously characterized as a disequilibrium, an upset, or a disruption. Something is aroused or enters experience that sets events in motion. Since story in the present case involves a single hero, the disequilibrium refers to a state of the hero. The hero is incomplete or in want or lacking in some way. Incompleteness is the basic condition underlying such terms as desiring, yearning, needing, wanting, intending, aiming, and so on. The way one is at the time is off, unfinished, or not right.

Incompleteness is not necessarily a negative experience. For example, Steffens went to the racetrack regularly and playacted that he was a jockey winning races and receiving honors. Then, by making himself useful, he had an opportunity to perhaps become a real jockey. He did not experience this opportunity in a negative fashion, but idealistically with high hopes, soaring ambitions, and immense devotion. An experience of incompleteness can be intensely negative or intensely positive, but it still functions in the same way. When a sense of incompleteness is aroused in whatever form, a person is directed toward completeness. One seeks what will make one complete.

The gap between incompleteness and completeness is a gap between what is and what ought to be. A desired and sometimes ideal end is projected upon the basis of what is. In Steffens's case, this projection was easy. He wanted to become a jockey. More ideally, he wanted to become a heroic jockey. In other cases, the end is not so easily specified. Struggling through confusion and uncertainty, a person might gradually cycle through approximate ends until he or she can specify it clearly. We are not always able to clearly grasp the nature of our sense of incompleteness, and consequently , have difficulty setting a direction. As projected, an end is a fulfillment of one's lack, an appropriate closure.

In the beginning, a story line is bounded by two poles, is and ought to be. This gap defines an apposite or appropriate opposition. If one begins with low esteem, higher esteem is projected as an end. If one is fired from a job, getting a new job is apt to be the desired end. Usually, since the nature of the end is dependent upon the nature of the beginning, the desired end can be inferred from the beginning. However, as noted previously, the nature of one's incompleteness might not have achieved enough definition to make an exact projection. The beginning can be more or less definite, and it might be completed by more than one opposite. For example, what would complete an undesirable dependence on others, independence or interdependence? All that we can be sure of is that once the gap achieves some clarity of definition, it will involve two opposite poles.

The relation between beginning and end specifies precisely the relation between synchronic structure at a time and diachronic flow over time. The gap emerging from incompleteness defines a line of movement, a personal story line. All events, opportunities, situations, and characters gain definition, relevance, and significance to the extent to which they are related to the line of movement. If a character were irrelevant to the line of movement, he or she would be irrelevant to the story, not really a part of the story. Opposition serves as a rather precise criterion for judging what is relevant and significant. However, a projected story is not the real story that must unfold in real circumstances, filled with contingencies. Rather, the projected story defines the participation of the main character, enveloping his or her participation in a field of relevance. It gives direction, but direction that must be worked out in actual circumstances.

The Actual End: Completing the Beginning

The actual end is not necessarily the projected end. For example, Steffens sought to realize his idealistic devotion by becoming a heroic jockey, one who weds skill and courage in such marvelous proportion that he achieves victory after victory. However, he ended in disillusionment. Now disillusionment certainly finishes devotion, but not in a way that Steffens imagined. For any beginning, there is no one opposite. Rather there is a field of possibilities, only one of which will be realized in story.

If a story does not involve opposition, the story is incoherent, not really a story. For example, one could begin with a lack of responsibility and end with a sense of humor, but without further elaboration, this does not make sense as a story. With more elaboration, we might find that the hero began with an overserious sense of responsibility, so idealistic when applied to fallible humans that he continually felt irresponsible. Later, after relevant experiences, he learned to soften this unreal sense of responsibility with humor, born from greater wisdom of the human condition. Gradually, this is beginning to make sense, and it does so precisely because the beginning and end poles are moving toward a more apposite opposition. An opposite is required for completion.

An end brings to closure what was aroused in the beginning. We are beings who seek closure to experience, stamping the stream of life with impresses of meaning. The end, however, is never just our judgment. We have remarkable freedom to refuse the ends that events offer us. Even when circumstances are powerful or overwhelming, we can answer like the gangsters in B movies: "It ain't over yet!" But still, circumstances might indicate that it is over. We might seek to close experiences in a desirable way, but in story, the real end is what actually completed it. It is the actual end, not the projected end, that organizes a story. In Steffens's story, events become relevant and significant to the extent that they bear upon the movement from devotedness to disillusionment. For instance, the central figure is Smoke, and Smoke contributed little to becoming a heroic jockey. Smoke, or what happened to him, contributed to his disillusionment. If Steffens had gone on to realize his ambition, it is doubtful that Smoke would have had a prominent role in the story. Others would have become prominent.

The tension of a story is maintained by the convergence and divergence of two lines of movement, the movement between a beginning and projected end, and the movement between a beginning and actual end. The end is always in doubt. We never know for sure how things will turn out, but we usually have a sense of being on course or off course. Weston (1970) has termed these two movements the line of intention (when the hero is active) and the line of action. One is apt to be optimistic, happy, or satisfied when the lines of intention and action converge, boding well for an optimal end. One is apt to be distraught when the lines diverge, boding ill. In story, the hero meets challenge after challenge to stay on course, and this struggle is the very stuff of story.

Story: Embedded in an Actual Dramatic Situation

Steffens's story was embedded within the context of horse racing where competition or racing provides the focal opposition for the definition of roles and situations. The larger struggle that Steffens discovered was the drive to make money. Contexts exist within contexts with no hope for discrete isolation. From a competitive viewpoint, a jockey who pulls his horse is a scoundrel. From a business viewpoint, a jockey who pulls his horse might be regarded as a reliable or loyal associate. Definitions of situations and roles are peculiarly open, always subject to redefinition. For this reason, let us refer to the actual dramatic context as one that involves ostensive roles and ostensive definitions of situations.

Horse racing is a setting for drama, complete with ostensive roles and definitions. Persons are aligned and opposed in fulfilling the ostensive purpose of the setting. In short, a context or setting is a world in miniature, and to be a part of this world, one needs a role that is relevant to it. To become an insider, one who has a role to play, Steffens developed the role of an aspiring or apprentice jockey. It was a role that perfectly fitted his stance. To fulfill his stance was also to fulfill his ostensive role at the racetrack. Zealously, he copied the attitudes, gait, mannerisms, and speech of jockeys. He learned the insider lingo or way of talking and defining things. He practiced being a jockey imaginatively and physically. He took on the discipline of a jockey, fasting to keep his weight down. Given the ideals for this ostensive role, Steffens strove to make them a personal reality.

Story: Embedded in a Symbolic Dramatic Context

The role of jockey does not exist outside the context that gives it meaning. However, there is another context that populates a world with roles or kinds of persons and with definitions of situations. For example, as Steffens's disillusionment progressed, he became alienated from his ostensive role or any role within horse racing, which ended the story in that context. Yet, his very disillusionment stimulated further development of a symbolic dramatic context he already had, one in which devotion and disillusionment were defined parts, or coming to be defined parts.

Steffens was given to idealization. He expected an ideal world that reality seldom fulfilled. His investment in horse racing was but one of a series in which an imaginative, idealistic, and heroic vision was undermined by the reality of an actual situation. As this drama developed, roles and situations came to be defined and laid over actual situations. For example, there might be those in the know, suckers, innocents, fronts, and so on. Steffens's father was one who took the world as it seemed, not as it was. In one incident Steffens watched his father and his father's friends bet the favorite in a fixed race. He felt like warning them, but they acted as if they knew everything. So when the horses started, he simply told them which horse would win. Ignored at first, they asked him afterward how he guessed. He told them in the vernacular (not by pedigree and performance), but could not tell them why he did not warn them. He did not want to tell them that they were suckers. From his developing symbolic context, situations came to be defined quite differently than the ostensive situation.

Dramatization is world building in scope. For example, one can say that life is a competition just like horse racing. A particular context is simply the nature of life in a microcosm. Upon the basis of a particular drama, life might be characterized as a journey, a pilgrimage, a war, a business, and the like. The symbolic dramatic context a person develops is a worldview or one in potential. Unlike an actual dramatic setting, a symbolic drama is unlimited in scope, and as it begins to crystallize, it offers a person a repertoire of roles, from which a person can adopt one.

Consider a simplification. Suppose there were a delinquent whose view of the world is limited to two kinds of persons, those who exploit and those who are exploited. Basically, life evolves around a drama of exploitation, and this can be used to size up any actual setting. One cannot escape it. Thus, the delinquent has a choice. He or she can be a "wise guy" or a "sucker," one who takes or one who is taken. Given the slant of this dramatic vision of things, a person is unlikely to want to be a sucker. Indeed, a wise guy might seem admirable, and one might eagerly try to cultivate the ideals of the role, to make the structure of one's desire agree with the role. While this simplification distorts in various ways, it does convey the power of context. When a person develops an orientation, he or she takes a position within an intelligible context. There is no position without an actual and symbolic context. If one's context is limited, one's possibilities for position are also limited (see Cochran, 1985).

The Main Character: Continuous Throughout the Story

Since a story, in the present sense, is about one person who is the main character, the continuity of character is essential for story. Continuity does not mean that a person must stay exactly the same. Steffens, for instance, changed from devotedness to disillusionment, yet somehow he appears as a continuous subject throughout. Indeed, a character could be continuous in the way that he or she irresolutely changes. Most generally, a character is continuous as a center of experience, memory, and anticipation. Less generally, a character manifests enduring qualities over the course of a story. However, these rather generalized characterizations seem too remote to answer the question of essential continuity, and the reason they are is that they are defined outside a story, outside a meaningful context.

Within story, a character is continuous as long as the opposition or gap matters to the person. A story requires a main character for whom the drama matters. The main character might waver, become uncertain, cycle between passion and cool calculation, but if the gap becomes a matter of indifference, the story is over. There is no reason to set unrealistic criteria for continuity. Persons develop. The nature of a gap might be refined and developed. There might be interruptions. There might be all manner of difficulty and complication, but continuity is necessary for one basic reason. A main character lives a story structured by a gap, and if he or she shifts to another gap, an irrelevant gap, the person ceases living one story and embarks on a different story.

A Story: Explains Change from a Beginning to an End

Unlike static description, a narrative descriptive is an explanation. As description, a story should also convey the smack of life through rich and significant detail; but as narrative description, a story is a form of explanation. That a story explains is apparent on intuitive grounds. For example, when we get to the end of Dickens's *A Tale of Two Cities,* we do not ask why Sydney Carton exchanged places with Charles Darnay at the guillotine. The story has already explained Carton's act of self-sacrifice quite amply. If a story succeeds as a story, the end is explained. We might question an explanation, but it is apparent that one has at least been offered.

Danto (1968) has shown one way in which a story explains. The beginning and end constitute the explanandum. That is, given a story, we are not interested in explaining the beginning alone, nor the end alone, but the change of a subject from the beginning to the end. For example, Steffens was idealistically devoted at the beginning and disillusioned at the end. According to Danto, the middle of a story is the explanans. To provide the middle is to explain how a subject changed from a beginning state to an end state. For example, Steffens found that races were fixed and this picture of racing was incompatible with his idealistic picture of heroic competition. The middle does not ordinarily contain but one decisive event or experience; it might contain a lengthy series. "Changes are nested within changes, and stories require increasingly complex middles to explain the outermost change" (p. 241). While complexity makes an investigation more difficult, it does not alter the role of the middle in explaining change.

While Danto's account is convincing, there is no reason to limit explanatory possibilities just to middle events. In a tale of change from diversity to unity, for example, middle events would likely be highly important in explanation. However, in a tale of an already formed person enacting a series of tasks, we would be justified in placing more stress upon the state of the person in the beginning. That is, in the beginning, the person manifested a structure that unfolded over time. In this case, the middle involves means, but we need not place such a heavy causal weight upon them in an explanation.

Of Aristotle's four types of explanations (formal, final, efficient, and material), psychology has fixed narrowly upon a particular version of efficient causality. A cause is a little activator that spurs one to movement, usually ascribed to an event regarded as discrete. However, as Harré (1974) argued, little triggers or discrete stimuli are insufficient to account for the patterned form of complex episodes. For this reason, he has reintroduced formal explanation as a powerful particular, a real synchronic structure that is realized in a diachronic unfoldment. For example, a plan exists at a moment and can be realized in a pattern of action. Harré's contention is that an enlightened psychology would seek powerful particulars to account for a complex pattern. Harré does not ignore other types of explanation. For instance, final explanation or the end an agent has in mind is also prominent in his accounts. Rather, he seems to be working toward a synthesis of explanatory types, giving each a certain prominence of place.

Originally, Aristotle drew his four types of explanation from a story of a craftsman crafting a product. In order to understand an end product, we must know what material composed it (material explanation), who made it (efficient explanation—the agent has been reduced in current psychology to little agents or controlling stimuli), the purpose for making it (final explanation), and the form or vision the agent had in mind for the product (formal explanation). Next, these explanations were generalized to account for everything (Hanson, 1969). However, my interest here is that Aristotle began with a story from which he extracted parts that helped make an end intelligible. A story is not just an explanation, but a synthesis of explanations, which might account for the stress upon dramatic form that is prominent in Harré's work.

Rather than speaking of causes (an overworked and confusing term generally), let us substitute making something intelligible. To make something intelligible at a certain level of understanding, one might use causes, reasons, and purposes. My contention is that in human affairs, a complete story is what makes something intelligible. If a part is left out, we experience puzzlement and an explanation relieves that puzzlement. For example, in a murder mystery, if the detective leaves out motive, the solution to the mystery is experienced as incomplete. The murder is not yet intelligible. Perhaps no adequate catalogue of parts currently exists to help specify deficiencies in a narrative account, and consequently a complete explanation is undeterminable at this time. However, there are schemes such as Aristotle's types and Burke's (1969) dramatic pentad (scene, act, agent, agency, and purpose) that guide an assessment.

For the present, it seems better to recognize that we know more than we can tell, to use Polanyi's (1966) description of tacit knowledge, rather than to seek premature exactitude. That a story explains at a certain level seems apparent. But in a story, we often experience various puzzlements that a fuller tale would potentially alleviate. We can use Aristotle, Burke, or others to assess the intelligibility of stories and to clarify the synthesis of explanations within them.

Cycle of Experience

Let us review major points before the next extension. A story is bounded by opposing poles. This opposition defines a line of movement. For example, Steffens moved from devotedness to disillusionment. An opposition is also a dimension that establishes a criterion of relevance and significance. The ingredients of a story bear upon this dimension directly or indirectly, or they are out of place. For instance, a person, event, or personal characteristic that facilitated or hindered the line of movement would be directly relevant. If an element facilitated or hindered greatly, it would be of great significance.

Situations are defined in accordance with an opposition, and the scope of an opposition to organize experience is unlimited. When Smoke pulled the "comer," the event was pervaded by the keenness of disillusionment within it, at least for Steffens. In another drama, it could be a golden opportunity for those in the know to make big money. While the situation is normatively defined by horse racing and what makes it up, it is dramatically defined by the opposition of the story. Roles are framed in accordance with a dramatic opposition, and take on an organization and role ideals that support it. Roles are cast in relation to other roles, each having a role to play. While roles complement, extend, support, and dominate other roles in many complex ways, the general organization of roles in drama is the familiar agon, in which characters become protagonists and antagonists. Role opposition is fundamental to the movement of a story.

Bounded by two poles, a story is a field of opposition in which the beginning pole gradually shifts toward the end pole. For Steffens, devotedness gradually shifted toward disillusionment, idealism toward realism. Over the course of a story, there are shifts in the relative proportion or balance of the two poles. Aristotelian opposition is inapplicable for two reasons. First, the law of the excluded middle would exclude the middle of the story in which mixing or proportion is most prominent. Second, the poles are natural categories or ordinary language concepts (e.g., devotedness and disillusionment) and must be so, for persons define the poles of their stories. The central "insight, shared by phenomenology, action theory, and interpretive sociologies, argues that to understand a person we must grasp the person's meanings and understandings, the agent's vision of the world, his or her plans, purposes, motivations, and interests" (Manicas & Secord, 1983, p. 409). An Aristotelian-type category seems excessively idealized or unreal by comparison. There is a tendency to count as most real the pure abstraction that poor reality can never satisfy. The mixtures of experience become less real than the abstractions that are supposed to illumine experience. How can a category reflect well if mixture is denied? No doubt, there are philosophical positions on this point of contention that are beyond my range of competence. In lieu of an argument, I shall simply state my view. I am more inclined to believe that idealized abstractions are less real than the mixtures of experience.

In contrast to an Aristotelian view is Chinese opposition where opposites are not absolute but relative. Stated most familiarly, there is yin in yang and yang in yin, as depicted in the famous T'ai-chi figure. Opposites interpenetrate or blend together. In short, a Chinese category is difficult to distinguish from a natural category or ordinary language concept. From this perspective, a pure substance is unreal, an abstraction. Indeed, a category is a rather impoverished attempt to reflect what is, which inevitably distorts things as they are. Reality status is assigned more to that which is categorized (i.e., the mixes, blends, proportions) than to the categories themselves. Consult

Holbrook (1981) for a very extensive discussion of Chinese opposition.

Interpenetrating opposition is fully applicable to the opposition in stories. For example, Steffens did not experience a pure (unnatural) devotion with no doubt, uncertainty, or disillusionment in it. Before the horse racing episode, he had had similar experiences, enough to make him suspect that things were not as they initially appeared in his idealizations. Later, this expectation became blatant. Here, it is latent, almost a spur to the very excessiveness of his idealized devotion. As well, he playacted or vividly and imaginatively enacted the hero of quite different adventures. Plunging into horse racing was another of a series. Even at the height of his devotion, he knew it was partially just play. Nor was disillusionment, in any way, pure undiluted disillusionment with no devotedness in it. Indeed, some remnant of devotion seems required for disillusionment to matter. Perhaps there are cases that will call into question this account. However, in life stories and accounts of real experiences, relative opposition has been evident and absolute opposition has not been apparent at all.

If this conclusion is accurate, it follows that a rounded experience involves change in the varying proportions of the opposing poles. The beginning of an experience is dominated by one pole. The end is dominated by the opposite pole. The middle involves successive alterations in balance leading to the emergence of one pole and the submergence of the other. While this hypothesis stems largely from an examination of cases, it follows from the nature of relative opposition.

A quadripartite image or quadrimage (see Holbrook, 1981, upon whose work this description is based) depicts the varying balances of opposition in four parts. Major yin is mostly yin with the least yang in it. Major yang is mostly yang with the least yin in it. Both are like paradigm cases or prototypes. Minor yin is yin inside the yang while minor yang is yang inside the yin. Depicting varying proportions, minor yin is primarily yang and secondarily yin. Minor yang is primarily yin and secondarily yang. This characterization is, however, somewhat misleading as it suggests linearity rather than complex qualities in shifting balances. Perhaps the minor aspects could be better represented as borderline cases, deriving from each pole.

In Chinese philosophy, yin is characterized as matter (form, container), earth, feminine, passive (receptive), and worldly. Yang is characterized as energy, sky, masculine, active, and spirited. The two poles and their combination in a manifold continuum are regarded as a basic logos of the world, an analogical basis for grasping the order of change in divergent phenomena. For example, the four seasons correspond to a quadrimage:

Winter = Major Yin or mostly matter
Spring = Minor Yang or energetic matter
Summer = Major Yang or mostly energy
Fall = Minor Yin or materialized energy

Winter is characterized by quiescence. Trees are bare. Little grows. The earth seems to be in a period of incubation. Spring is characterized by first growth as the earth begins to warm and come alive. Summer is characterized by vibrant growth. The buds of spring come to fruition. In fall the earth seems to exhaust itself. There is dwindling energy as withered leaves take the place of growth. While this characterization is exceedingly brief (see Holbrook, 1981, for a more lengthy description), it conveys the general idea. Stories are a human version of natural cycles that are everywhere around us, and stories as well as cycles seem to manifest varying proportions of an opposition. However, there is also another cycle evident in stories.

Upon the basis of previous work (Cochran, 1986), stories can be divided into four phases of a cycle. The first phase is incompletion, as described previously. Something happens that gives birth to desire and the structure of desire is a gap between what is and what ought to be. One is incomplete and directed toward completion.

The second phase is positioning. Perhaps there are actions that do not require preparation or positioning, but they are not easy to find. Positioning is concerned with getting into position, moving toward a readiness to act or undergo. It might include practical preparation and psychological preparation.

The third phase is positing. Something is posited, bringing to culmination the positioning that preceded it. One acts from position to realize something. Positing involves an actualization or bringing into existence. if the hero is passive in this phase, something is realized from the actions of others, while the hero undergoes change. Positing involves both a practical achievement and a symbolic attainment. For example, in publishing a book, Mill both altered opinions and institutions, or hoped to, and he also enacted the symbolic vision of life that went with being a reformer.

The last phase is completion. Positively, positing completes the incompletion of the beginning, allowing a person to experience closure. For example, if a person removes a sliver, he or she might feel relief. However, there is no requirement that a story must end positively, only a requirement that it must end. The end brings closure of some kind to what was aroused in the beginning, and that closure can be intensely positive or negative.

With this characterization of the four phases that make up a story, consider Steffens's experience in horse racing. It is not a successful or positive story, manifesting the powers of an inspired agent. Steffens does not experience burning desire, position himself to realize that desire, enact position in a glorious race, and then bask in favorable attention. Quite the contrary, he becomes more inactive as the story proceeds. For this reason, it provides more complexity with which to illustrate the four phases.

The story begins with Steffens racing around the racetrack he recently discovered, imaginatively enacting a heroic drama of racing and winning. He invests the setting with a meaning that defines his boyish desire to be a hero. Heroism is embodied in the imaginative role of a jockey, if only for the moment. Through playacting, which he did a lot of, Steffens invigorated a rather enduring state of want. A hero is devoted to some endeavor, and through hardships and daring deeds, he succeeds to the admiration of all. Like other investments, this one might have dwindled until Steffens embarked on another imaginative adventure, filled with idealism. However, real persons entered the scene, and through the friendship of Smoke, a real possibility seemed to arise. For Steffens it seemed as though he were offered the possibility of realizing a dream.

With the possibility before him, Steffens took steps and accepted opportunities. For example, he had to become an insider to the racing crowd and learn his task. He had to mold himself to the role (for instance, by fasting). Through trials and tests, Steffens was making himself into a jockey, preparing for the time he would race. Positioning is not separate from incompletion like two stages. The very acts of positioning elaborate (extend, refine, revise) his incompleteness. For example, as he imitated the being of a jockey. his devotion grew. The imaginative buds of springlike play showed vibrant growth as opportunities opened to him. Positioning is rather a pervading quality, a balance or proportion that characterizes a dominant meaning.

In an ideal drama for Steffens, all his effort would have eventually culminated in a race. He would have enacted his position as a jockey. Being a jockey, of course, is not defined as a job role, but as a qualitative composition of being. In this more ideal type of drama, the hero posits both in practical deed and symbolic attainment. However, this was not to be. Steffens largely became a spectator on the destruction of his idealistic devotion to horse racing. The positing was done by others, and Steffens moved from vibrant activity to falllike passivity, a dwindling of engagement.

It began with jockeys riding to lose in fixed races and moved closer when Smoke was ordered to hold back the "comer." Steffens's idealistic devotion did not disintegrate all at once, but gradually. He maintained his routine, clinging to his vision even as events began to shred it. But with Smoke, he was not an outside observer; he was very much inside what Smoke was thinking and feeling as he "ruined" the horse. The experience was vivid and his devotion could not survive it. It culminated in disillusionment.

Although Steffens maintained some contact with the racetrack, due to his father, his involvement was essentially over. His humiliation at the track (when he fell off the horse) and Smoke's banishment marked a separation that was really already complete. The dominant quality of completion, in this instance, was disillusionment. He was filled with mournful questions. Why was nothing as it seemed? Why did adults take things as they seemed rather than as they were? Why is nothing what it is cracked up to be? He was left with a bewildering and discouraging set of questions, a winterlike bleakness. Here, Steffens is least active. He sits and thinks, occasionally discussing the problem with others. Yet, in his winter lethargy, the questions burned. Disillusionment is not a positive completion to devotion, but a completion nonetheless.

It is assumed that any story manifests incompletion, positioning, positing, and completion in order. This does not mean that there is no room for complication. After all, there are stories within stories, and numerous cycles might make up a larger cycle. There is no reason to sacrifice the complexity of reality for a form. Rather, the form should help us to distinguish that reality more clearly and coherently;

it should help us to see more rather than less. While this pattern is based upon an examination of numerous episodes and upon the nature of relative opposition in a story, it is best regarded as a hypothesis or working assumption. To disconfirm this form, all that is necessary is to find one credible instance where it is not manifested. That is, it might be shown to be limited in scope, in need of elaboration, divided into types, and so on. However, I have not found a disconfirming instance, but only complications of cycles within cycles.

Rhythm of Cycles

Recurrence is rhythmic, a periodic flow with a regularity in the rise and fall of stresses. In comparison to poetry or music in particular, the rhythm of recurring cycles is primitive in conception, yet there is no reason why it cannot be developed. Here, however, I intend to stick with rudiments. To convey the basics of rhythm in experience, consider another experience from the youth of Steffens, more briefly described.

The son of one of his father's friends stayed with them for some months. The boy, Charlie, was to serve as a page when the California Legislature was in session. In return for showing him all his "places" and how to ride a horse, Steffens would be shown the Legislature. Excitedly, Steffens read about government, asked questions, visited the Capitol, and turned his vivid imagination loose upon state government. But like horse racing, his experience was a revelation. "I saw that the Legislature wasn't what my father, my teachers, and the grown-ups thought; it wasn't even what my histories and the other books said. There was some mystery about it as there was about art, as there was about everything. Nothing was what it was supposed to be" (Steffens, 1931, p. 47). Everything was fixed. The beautiful speeches, the votes, the debates were merely performances of no substance; it was all fixed before by bribery and threat, stage managed by actors behind the scenes. Even Charlie's job as page was fixed, for which he was paid $10 a day! By comparison years later in Steffens's first job as a reporter in New York City, he was paid only $35 a week. Like jockeys, it paid to be close to those in the know. The experience generated more questions, agonies, and issues for Steffens. Once again, he went from exciting promise to disillusionment. Was anything what it was cracked up to be?

The California Legislature was an obvious variant of Steffens's experience in horse racing. And numerous other experiences could be cited. Steffens's early life is a virtual catalogue of the varied ways one can become disillusioned. What is rhythmic in these recurring types of experiences?

First, and most generally, the flow from incompletion to completion is regular, involving the same ingredients in different contexts. Regularly, Steffens began with an excess of idealism and enthusiasm. Regularly, he ended in disillusionment, agonized questioning. In short, the flow of quite varied experiences is patterned, with each cycle appearing as a variant of the general flow. Some cycles vary more than others, but rhythm is not made up of exact repetition, but of repetition with variation.

Second, each phase of a cycle is a story in itself with its own peculiar rhythm. For example, a musical composition depicting winter is quite different than one depicting summer. Similarly, the rhythm of completion is different than the rhythm of positioning, for instance. For Steffens, completion was winter. He was slow, inactive, heavy, or burdened by questions, while underneath, vitality was in incubation. Positioning for Steffens was summerlike. He was quick, active, and light in hopes and aspirations. Not everyone would manifest these particular rhythms, but each phase would have its own rhythm in a person's experience.

Third, and most important, the phases of a cycle have relative stresses. For Steffens, heavy stress is placed on the completion phase, with somewhat diminished stress placed upon the phase of positioning where his hopes were the highest and his activities were the most energetic. Lighter stresses fall upon incompletion and positing. Stress varies with the nature of the cycle. For example, if Steffens had gone forward in horse racing, there would probably have been immense stress placed on positing, his enaction of position. In series of recurrent cycles, there tends to be a similar stress placed upon the varying phases of experience. For example, in horse racing and in the California Legislature, stress is placed at the end, his disillusionment. In a cycle of experience, any phase might be stressed or unstressed.

Previously, the cycle of seasons was provided as an instance of a quadrimagic cycle. For centuries, the seasonal flow has been used as an analogue to human experience. For example, recently, a well-known book in the field of career development was entitled *The Seasons of a Man's Life* (Levinson, 1978). Usually, the seasonal flow is regarded as a fanciful or flowery way to describe a cycle. However, for reasons too complicated to recount here, there might be a more substantial basis for describing experiential cycles in this manner. For example, see Holbrook's (1981) alternative view of science and Frye's (1957) celebrated study of literature. What can be asserted here is that the flow of seasons seems to fit quite well the flow of experience.

There is no one-to-one correspondence between the four seasons and the four phases of experience. For example, in Steffens's story, incompletion manifested the qualities of spring. Positioning was his summer in horse racing. During positing, devotedness began to dwindle like the withering of leaves. Disillusionment was the winter of his experience. However, in other experiences, spring might take place in positioning, positing, or completion.

While the flow of seasons might vary in alignment with the flow of phases from incompletion to completion, there does appear to be a stable or most appropriate fit. Most appropriately, incompletion is winter, a time of incubation leading to spring in which new growths offer the promise and optimism of positioning. Summer with its excess of energy and growth resembles positing at its best, in which the person posits rather than receives the posits of others. In fall, the energy of the enactment dwindles with fading memories like leaves that wither and fall. Fall is a movement toward wintry incubation for the next enactment. This alignment is stable in the sense that one cycle prepares for the next, which resembles it in form. All other alignments are unstable. For example, Steffens's cycle from spring to winter is unstable; it is nothing to be content with, but something to strive to correct. Rather than gradually withdraw in perhaps satisfaction, Steffens was plunged into disillusionment. Also, the appropriate alignment is stable because there is a better descriptive fit among phases. The phase of positing, for instance, just should manifest the qualities of summer, growth, ripening, bringing things to fruition. For these reasons, let us regard the most appropriate alignment as a natural fit or prototypical case with all other alignments being regarded as unstable variations.

In Frye's (1957) archetypal criticism of literature, there are four generic plots or types of narrative: comedy, romance, tragedy, and irony. Each generic plot corresponds to the quality of one of the seasons. The rationale for these four types might be loosely summarized in this way. In human experience, there is a heaven and hell. For thousands of years, persons have believed in a literal heaven above and hell below. Earth or earthly experience is in between, a middle earth. Whether one believes or not, heaven is at least a model of perfection, and hell is a model of the opposite. As models of perfection and imperfection, good and evil, holy and unholy, they are not given to change, but rather stand as enduring points of reference. Consequently, the arena for change, cycles, or story lies more in the middle between these extremes.

Although Frye's cycle seems similar to the Chines cycle, there are differences. One of the charactatures of yang is indeed heaven, but yin is not hell. Yin is earth, and earth is not viewed negatively. The romance of Frye's scheme would correspond more to a proper relation of heaven and earth, heaven reaching toward earth and earth reaching toward heaven. Hell would correspond more to separation. However, still there is considerable overlap and Frye's exposition is compelling. Certainly, we have a strong sense as to whether our experiences are at a peak or a bottom, rising or falling. We have a strong sense of being more decisive or receptive, active or passive. In presenting Frye's cycle below, it is worth noting that his descriptions are a little different, a little more extreme than the Chinese cycle.

If we think of a cycle that rotates close to heaven, away from heaven, close to hell, and away from hell or toward heaven, we have the four generic plots corresponding to the seasons. Romance, the myth of summer, is closest to heaven. In romance, the hero is empowered, energetic, capable of taking effective action. Romance offers an idealized world or at least a world in which one can strive to make the world more ideal. The central aspect of romance is realization of design or making dream a reality. Life is a quest, requiring courage, determination, and the various qualities we expect of a hero.

Tragedy, the myth of autumn, is a movement away from heaven, a laboring under imminent downfall. The main character is still heroic, but fatally flawed, all too human. He or she combines greatness and smallness in a world that eventually grinds them both away. In the beginning, the hero is powerful, like a romantic hero, but slowly becomes ensnared inn the webs of fate, from which there is no escape. The hero strives mightily, but in the end, accepts his or her destiny. Idealization of the world is possible, but not for too long. In tragedy, one is confronted with mixtures of desire and limitation, excellence and weakness, magnificence and degeneracy. One strives not in sunshine, but under a growing shadow.

Irony, the myth of winter, is closest to hell. In literature, it is often given the name of realism. However, this title is too smug and presumptuous, as if one type of portrayal had a special claim upon reality. In irony, the main character is not heroic. Effective action is difficult if not impossible. There is a stress upon ambiguity, disorganization, defeat, confusion, and anarchy. Existence is stripped of idealization, and what comes into view are disintegration, obscenity, ruthless selfishness, pain, the horrors of existence. As romance concerns the dream or the desirable, irony concerns the nightmare or the undesirable.

Comedy, the myth of spring, is a movement away from hell toward heaven. Comedy rises while tragedy falls. Comedy has a sense of lightness, optimism, relief from threat, a conviction that all will end well. While ironic characters must make their way through the perplexities of ambiguous existence, comic characters also are prey to chance and circumstance. Effective action is limited, but possible. Comedies are filled with reconciliations, reintegrations, impending harmony, ostensible difficulties that can be overcome. There is folly and recovery. Characters strive under threat, but with a certain lightness afforded by anticipation of a happy end. While tragedy might concern the disintegration of power to idealize existence, comedy seems to concern the reintegration of power. Characters might lack heroic stature, but they muddle through and virtue is rewarded.

Each generic plot overlaps with those beside it in the cycle, and each is least like its opposite. For example, the early parts of tragedy resemble romance. The later parts resemble irony. And there is little sense of comedy, lightness, or optimism in tragedy. While it would be difficult to transide from tragedy into comedy, it would be much easier to transide from tragedy into irony, from irony (particularly via satire) to comedy, from comedy to romance, and from romance to tragedy. For this reason partially, Frye conceived of a metacycle or total quest-myth that unifies the four plots into a single plot.

In Frye's quest-myth, the hero begins in romance where the agon is a major theme. The hero then encounters catastrophe and descends to an endurance of hell, from which he or she rises triumphantly, restoring a new social arrangement or reconciliation. This alignment of phases (summer = incompletion, fall = positioning, winter = positing, spring = completion) is a drama of becoming, resembling the general structure of myth (Campbell, 1956) and rites of passage (Eliade, 1975; Van Gennep, 1960). However, as noted previously, it is still a deviation from stable form or a protypical alignment, and this is so for the obvious reason that it is a drama of becoming, change, or transition.

In life, there are stories within stories or cycles within cycles. In order to make one's way through this richness of material, it is necessary to have some conceptual scheme that imposes as little as possible, yet allows one to discern order if order there be. A complete experience can be conceived as a cycle from incompletion to completion. This is fixed. A complete experience can also be conceived through analogy to the flow of seasons or generic plots. This is variable. Steffens began with spring or comic optimism and ended in irony. Frye's quest-myth begins in summer and ends in spring. Each cycle has special qualities. For example, Steffens's cycle is distinguished by the stress it places upon desire or yearning. The hero ends not in contentment, but with burning questions. The cycle gives birth to yearning. Frye's cycle stresses transition, giving form to promise. It seems most appropriate for positioning as a whole. With these basic points in mind, let us turn now to larger episodes within which cycles of experience take place.

Rhythms of Life

A complete experience such as Steffens's horse racing experience takes place within the context of a larger episode. During a falllike episode, for instance, one might engage in a variety of relevant experiences. These experiences qualify the whole of the episode and, in turn, are qualified by it. Within a falllike context, the downward movement of tragedy is stressed, but also the adjacent plots of romance and irony might be stressed, elaborated, and prolonged secondarily. However, the spirit of comedy would likely remain unstressed, unelaborated, and short, for it does not fit well. Comedy exists within tragedy, but simply cannot be stressed, elaborated, or prolonged without altering the nature of the dramatic context. That is, too much comedy would upend tragedy. Similarly, tragic ingredients would be subdued in a comic context if that context is to remain comic. From the perspective of its opposite, any given generic plot is apt to appear grotesque, ridiculous, or appalling. From the perspective of irony, a romantic hero looks foolish, innocent, and difficult to fathom. It would be difficult to sustain romance with ironic perspectives intruding at every turn. By heightening and dampening features, a dramatic context influences the rhythm of experiential cycles within it (e.g., a tragic context would emphasize the tragic phase of a cycle of experience) and would also be influenced by these cycles, either heightening the sense of catastrophe or diminishing it.

A story is a story regardless of complexity or length of time. While length is apt to add to complexity, both a simple story and a long, complex story manifest a common form. If so, the same form that describes a complete experience also can describe the life and career of a person with a vocation. That is, a life can be viewed as a complete cycle of experience, beginning in incompletion and moving toward completion.

How a simple story and an enduring, complex story differ is in the organization of the person that is required. In a simple story such as getting a splinter and removing it, the continuity of the main character rest upon a feeing about having a splinter. The gap that matters to the person is minor injury and restoration of the injured part. A person is capable of taking an immense range of stances, and consequently, is capable of enacting an immense range of short stories. However, an enduring story cannot plausibly be based upon an isolated stance. To be in love for fifty years, for instance, requires a supportive organization of stances. For instance, it is implausible that a person would be hostile, impatient, selfish, and cruel, but still loving for fifty years. More plausibly, a person would be generous, patient, unselfish, and kind. A stance simply cannot stay alive in a person without a supportive context that nourishes it and makes it salient. In a longer story, then, the continuity of the main character rests upon an enduring composition of stances. Thus, part of this story would include how one achieved personhood or a unification of being.

In the chapters ahead, each phase will be considered in more detail. Here, as an advance organizer, let us consider some of the major features of each phase as a phase of life. What are the characteristics of each phase? What must be achieved to enter the next phase?

Incompletion

We begin life uncomposed, not yet persons. A child has many diverse tendencies that have yet to be organized into a composition, and organize one must to become a person. To the extent that one manifests divergent organizations of being in later life, there is no one person. Rather, there are many potential persons who have yet to become one (Royce, 1914). For a child, this divergency is perhaps not problematic. Children might not manifest inconsistency so much as rapidity of one desire following another. A short time perspective virtually eliminates inconsistency as a problem. However, as a child matures, incompatible diversity becomes increasingly problematic.

As events are repeated, we are able to discern patterns, and with patterns, expectations arise. We become aware of what is not, what did not happen, or what should have happened to fulfill an expected pattern. As patterns develop, time perspective increases, and it is here that inconsistency begins to create difficulties. More enduring patterns require a more enduring person! Not only do others begin to expect more consistency, but our plans and projects are based upon self-expectations of continuity. For example, if one plans to go to a baseball game in one week, the plan is tacitly based upon the assumption that the person who would now enjoy a baseball game will be about the same person in one week. We cannot function coherently in longer time frames if we remain a novelty to ourselves (Friedman, 1975).

Within a career, incompletion concerns the arousal and unification of an enduring structure of desire. From a scattered and fragmented diversity, one achieves a directed and coherent organization of one's incompleteness. If there were no desire, no unification of desire, and no endurance, there would either be no career or no one career. Without some enduring unity, it is difficult to speak of a single career or a single work of life. If one had two or more separate organizations of being, there would be many works of life and no one work of life, many plans and no one plan, or many lives and no one life.

No doubt, some persons or even a majority perhaps never emerge from incompletion. Throughout life, one might be fragmented by desires that never add up, overwhelmed by circumstances, or carried along by social expectations and convention. One's desires never unify or a central desire never transforms from a dream into a definite intention. In these cases, there is no full story to tell, but many different stories that do not progress to a larger form. The study of incompletion concerns how desire is given birth and achieves some degree of unity. But also, incompletion concerns how desire is transformed into a realizable possibility. Until a desire is transformed from merely a state to a condition of action, from a dream to an intention, one remains in incompletion. Before desire can be an adequate basis for action, one must form a general solution that one has a chance to realize.

Positioning

If a desire were immediately attainable, there would not be much of a middle. Most of what we recognize as personality, common humanity, or a human life probably arises from delay, our inability to satisfy desires immediately. The desire arising from incompletion is incapable of being satisfied immediately, at least in the cases I have studied. One must first get in position.

In short stories, positioning is most concerned with an adjustment of circumstances. For example, to remove a sliver, a person would have to set the stage (e.g., get a pin and tweezers). However, in longer stories, positioning is more concerned with shaping a composition of being. For example, Steffens developed skills, cultivated certain stances, and in general tried to take on the being of a jockey. Jockey was not the name of a job, but a metaphor of personhood, around which Steffens strove to unify his nature as a person.

Previously, personhood has been described as a regnant stance or position that composes other stances into a more or less harmonious composition (Cochran, 1985). When one becomes regnant, others crystallize around it (James, 1958). For example, consider three traits such as cooperative, intelligent, and persuasive. As isolated positions, they come into conflict. One's intelligence might allow a person to see things others do not, and voicing or acting on these insights might require uncooperativeness. Being cooperative might require the suppression of intelligence or persuasiveness at times. And one's persuasive power in courses of action might limit ideals of being intelligent. It is only when one position or harmonious cluster becomes regnant that coordination becomes possible. To stress intelligence means that cooperation and persuasion are put in its service, helping one to achieve ideals of intelligence. To put one stance in the service of another, though partially, means it can be compromised in that service. Picture in turn the radically different impressions that emerge when regnancy is shifted from one stance to another. Depending upon which term is regnant, different features of the other stances would be stressed and unstressed, just as features shift in diverse uses of a concept.

The achievement of personhood is no simple task; it is not as natural as growing up. Stances must be coordinated. Some stances must be subdued, others cultivated. The potentials of incompatible stances are always present, capable of throwing one out of position. What makes personhood such a difficult achievement is that it is indirect. One cannot think or feel into personhood. Rather, one must elaborate a "feeling about" that involves clarity of conception and invigoration of feeling, and this work is very indirect. For instance, we cannot directly make ourselves kindly. Indirectly, we can try to think, feel, and do things that will hopefully arouse kindliness. In the end, it is partially a product and partially a gift. When personhood is achieved, positioning reaches a culmination point and one moves to positing.

Positing

Positing is concerned with enaction of position. To act from position is to posit something in the world and to actualize the spirit or tenor of one's being. For example, St. Paul was an apostle, an advocate of God. John Stuart Mill was a reformer of humankind who strived for reform. Booker T. Washington was an educator who strived to educate his people in the wake of the Civil War. Advocation, reform, and education were their work, what was posited in the world that reflects their beings as persons. Work involves practical posits. For example, St. Paul established churches. Mill wrote books and initiated reforms. Washington erected and expanded educational institutions. The significance and variety of practical accomplishments can be investigated, but the most striking aspect of work is less open to direct investigation; it is the spirit or symbolic significance of work. There is a certain quality, vitality, or just spirit involved that is unmistakable. To grasp the symbolic posit of work requires not dead conceptions or general feelings, but an elaboration of a feeling about, an individual position within a dramatic context. To advocate, reform, or educate requires a worldview in which advocation, reform, and education make sense as something vitally important to do. They require a particular kind of person and a particular direction in actual circumstances. There is no definite end to an investigation of the personal significance of positing, but one can strive for a general understanding.

The relation between a person (as regnant position) and career is direct. To characterize the regnant position also specifies a regnant gap between what is and what ought to be. Enacting position is an attempt to bridge the gap. For example, an apostle advocates. A reformer reforms. An educator educates. Personhood is built upon incompletion. Originally a means or solution for the previous phases, a regnant position comes to be an end in itself, with incompleteness as its very basis. For example, a reformer is incomplete without trying to reform. The gap that is implicit in personhood offers a promissory definition of one's life story. How an actual life works out is subject to contingency, but it is given direction through a life-defining gap. The same term that characterizes a regnant position defines the ideal story line of a career.

Completion

Ordinarily perhaps, completion is not something to look forward to. To complete one's position is to end it. A position is formed in desire and one is centered in this lived gap, striving to bring the end about. But what if there were no more need to convert, reform, or educate? Suppose everything was as it should be. One would then be out of position, stripped of vital involvement in work. For this reason, it is perhaps best to die with one's boots on, so to speak, still striving. However, there are different kinds of completion. For example, for some, completion is more like depletion. For others, completion might be a pervading contentment or satisfaction, as one perhaps turns to other activities to round out one's life. For still others, completion might be a personal transformation. Ordinary personhood involves a unification of want. That is, one is formed upon the basis of incompletion and acts from fullness of desire. St. Paul was filled with apostolic fervor. Mill yearned for reform. Washington's zeal for education was intensive and extensive. They were formed and their lives took shape through a regnant gap between an "is" and an "ought to be." However, for those perhaps few who are completed in a fuller sense, they do not so much act from fullness of desire as from fullness of being. Something comes alive in them that is beyond desire. Joy, for instance, does not mark a gap. One in joy spreads joy, more like a gift that is shared than a desire that is realized. It is not the case that a completed person, in this sense, would never desire anything, Rather, it is as if a premise of existence had been reversed. Where desire was utterly dominant, it is now secondary. One now posits from a certain fullness within.

To integrate the various stands of discussion into a formal expectation, consider the type of enactment that would predominantly and ideally be manifested in each phase of life. These expectations can be spelled out as indicated in Table 1.

Pattern I is ideal for the incompletion phase of life, for it ends with winter, the period of receptivity, incubation, least activity, frozen form, and yearning. This pattern is given to the birth of desire.

Pattern II is the basic movement of a rite of passage, or transition from a lower state to a higher state. In the work of Eliade (1975) and Van Gennep (1960), the first part involves separation and conflict. One was firmly entrenched in a stable world of childhood, which is ruptured. Van Gennep refers to the middle as transition in which one wavers between two worlds, that of childhood, for instance, and that of adulthood. Through ordeals and tortures, instruction and revelation, one is ceremonially destroyed

Table 1. Patterns of Enactment

	Spring	Summer	Fall	Winter	Phases of Life
I.	1	2	3	4	Incompletion
II.	4	1	2	3	Positioning
III.	2	3	4	1	Positing
IV.	3	4	1	2	Completion

and cast into hell to be reborn. As Eliade (1975) noted, the basic logic of a rite of passage is that one must first be destroyed to be reborn or elevated to a higher level of existence. The two movements of the middle are catastrophe and loss as the old world withers, and the endurance of hell as the new self incubates. Often the imagery of a rite of passage involves being swallowed by a monster, digested, and later restored whole, but different. Initiates, for instance, might live in special buildings called the belly of the monster. There amid trials of various kinds to make one receptive, special instruction is given and new desires kindled. The final phase involves restoration to a prominent place, a reincorporation, usually involving ceremonies and licenses that indicate both a new role and a new social arrangement. During a rite of passage, the basic form of experience is repeated. Over and over, a person symbolically dies and is reborn. What makes up a passage is partially the overall form and partially that form enacted over and over, with the stress falling at the end in rebirth.

Pattern III is the stable form, ideal for the enactment of being. The stress of this form is on the enactment or positing with the energetic qualities of summer. This is the form for deeds, for constructing a work of life. It does not readily progress into another form without external influences, but rather is geared toward progressive construction.

Pattern IV is a form of dwindling energy perhaps or of energy in the phase of completion. Here there is growth or vibrancy in the sense of completion at the end. One might savor the satisfaction or contentment that was scarcely noted in the previous pattern, so intent was the person in the doing of deeds. In this pattern, energy for enactment might be less, but energy for completion might be more.

These patterns, briefly described here, will be elaborated more in the following chapters. As a narrative expectation, the rhythmic progression from incompletion to completion is common to all who have unified their lives in a vocation. Further, the dominant pattern of enactment for each phase is expected to vary uniformly such that pattern I characterizes incompletion, pattern II characterizes positioning, pattern III characterizes positing, and pattern IV characterizes completion. Each pattern names a kind of universal human condition that should help to identify commonalities in lives, if they exist.

Previous research has shown that persons dramatize work, that these dramas fit within a larger life structure, and that they constitute variations of significant dramatic scenarios evident in their life histories (Cochran, 1986; Chusid & Cochran, 1989; MacGregor & Cochran, 1988; McAdams & Ochberg, 1988; Ochberg, 1987; Osherson, 1980; Sloan, 1987). However, the majority of dramas that have been portrayed involve difficulties. Persons might feel split between or among contrasting dramatic possibilities with no resolution in sight. Some live negative dramas, are filled with lacks, oppressions, unrealized potentials, superficial performances, and the like. A study of persons with a sense of vocation does not differ from these studies in any significant way. Both involve the discovery of lived dramas. However, previous research has been concerned with self-deception, division, fragmentation, entrapment by routine and circumstance, and inauthenticity, among other things, in accordance with the content of the dramas investigated. In contrast, the present study is concerned with how lives look when things turn out well, offering perhaps a model portrait of dramas that are productive, positive, and meaningful. By the nature of the topic, this research differs in focusing upon such qualities as wholeness, fulfillment, and depth of meaning. In this way, the following portrait is offered as a complement to the rich work that has preceded it.

2 The Birth of Yearning: Rhythm of Incompletion

The period of incompletion is concerned with the composition of a unifying order of desire. A person begins with scattered, fragmented desires and ends with an organization of diversity into a unity. During incompletion, a person composes what is and projects what ought to be with more or less clarity and definiteness. The basic story line involves the arousal of a central or superordinate gap that bounds a life story, at least in potential. When this gap arises, one's life is given a general direction. The aim of this chapter is to describe major aspects of the way a life-defining desire comes into being, based upon the autobiographies of several persons who have achieved a vocation in life.

From Primitive Dramas to Dramatic Units

A primitive drama is a complete experience. In as much as childhood is the place of origins, and children's experiences are apt to be shorter and less refined than their adult experiences, these experiences of growing up are termed 'primitive dramas.' Sources of these dramas are many and diverse. Some dramas arise from the culture, society, or neighborhood one is in. Some dramas arise from the family microcosm. Some dramas arise from inherited temperaments such as excitability, responsibility to others, impulsivity, and activeness (Buss & Plomin, 1975), in relation to the various contexts in which one grows up. For example, responsivity to others might be encouraged or discouraged in families, meaning different things. Whatever the source, singularly or in combination, persons experience a wide range of primitive dramas, any one of which could probably develop into a plot for life.

We experience primitive dramas from two standpoints, that of a participant and that of a spectator (Britton, 1970; Harding, 1937, 1963). As a participant, a person is seeking to get something done. One is immersed in affairs of the world, trying to bring various aims to fruition. In the participant role, one decides, plans, acts, and evaluates, all from the limited perspective of one who is taking an active part in the immediate situation or in an expected future situation. A participant uses his or her representation of the world to get something done. Or to use Polanyi's (1966) influential account of attention, one attends from a tacit fund of knowledge to a pragmatic focus. What we intend or have in mind is explicit. The knowledge basis for what we have in mind is tacit.

As a spectator, a person is withdrawn from the affairs of the world, not seeking to get anything done. A spectator might be extremely involved or engaged, but alleviated of the necessity to act. For example, a person at an excellent movie is withdrawn, in this sense, but still highly involved. The role of a spectator is autotelic, like an activity rather than an act. There is no extraneous reason prodding one to become a spectator. It is done out of enjoyment, curiosity, interest, and perhaps compulsion. In the spectator role, one interprets, savors or appreciates, elaborates, and recounts, all from the vastly broader perspective of one who is not taking part in the situation. This difference could not be more decisive. For example, as a participant, one could be terrified, yet as a spectator upon one's experience, a person could find it to be extremely humorous. We can laugh at our own folly, misery, and hardship, but not ordinarily as a participant. Similarly, we can be saddened by our own gaiety, exuberance, or venturesomeness, but not ordinarily as a participant. We need perspective to do this, and breadth of perspective is what the spectator role offers. A spectator can operate directly on his or her representation of the world. Of course, one is still attending from a tacit basis of knowledge, but the explicit focus is the way the world is represented by oneself or others.

As a participant, one's experience is limited. However, as a spectator, one's experience is practically unlimited. Through family, neighbors, friends, television, movies, novels, newspapers, and so on, there is the potential for vast exposure to forms of experience. Still, being a spectator is secondhand and offers a different quality in dramas experienced.

Britton (1970) regards spectatorship as a way to restore one's representation, to make it more coherent and harmonious, adjusting it to the shock of events. First, spectatorship is a way to try to incorporate novelty within a whole. Second, it is a way to explore the range and possibilities of experience, consolidating one's ability to anticipate events (Kelly, 1955). Third, it is a way to create a livable worldview. Spectatorship is more concerned with a total worldview, one that calls for evaluation as much as anticipation.

Very like Piaget's (1968) cycle of assimilation and accommodation or Kelly's (1955) elaboration and revision. Britton conceives of a movement from the participant to the spectator role. From the limited perspective of a participant, we participate in affairs, experiencing harmony and disharmony, confirmation and disconfirmation, the familiar and novel. Later, from the broader perspective of a spectator, we imaginatively reenact the experience, interpreting, adjusting expectation, altering vision, savoring potential, and gaining insights. Indeed, difficult experiences create, in Britton's terms, a positive need to go over the experience again in order to adjust one's construction of reality in a way that is both valid and fruitful, that corresponds to reality yet is livable.

Experiences might be repeated due to external constraints and regulations. For example, Yehudi Menuhin (1978) was taken to many concerts and other sorts of performances during infancy. The contexts in which one grows up, to the extent that they are intelligible, are given to repetition. However, if Piaget, Kelly, and Britton are correct, we are also built to experience repetition by our need to develop constancy. Through concreteness, we build visions of the world that make one experience the same as another experience.

The work of Piaget, Kelly, and others who espouse a constructivist account of child development are well known and do not need elaboration here. While few would agree that they have offered a complete or wholly adequate account, there is little controversy over the basic movement from the chaos of the concrete to a more constant representation of forms. Without some degree of constancy, we cannot anticipate, plan, or act. From a dramaturgical perspective, the necessary repetition of experience in this movement toward constancy has three functions.

First, as a pattern of experience is repeated in different circumstances, more and more of life is bound into a certain kind of drama. It does not make sense any longer to just focus upon a concrete experience itself, but rather on experience as an instance of a pattern. Concrete experiences transform into a dramatic unit, an abstract or symbolic form that encompasses experience. This function of repetition is compositional; a world of experience is composed.

A significant part of this elaboration into dramatic form involves metaphoring (Cochran, 1986). It is as if one experience becomes a metaphor for another experience, seeing one in terms of the other. At least initially, there seems to be no conscious or deliberate use of metaphor. Rather, an experience has such significance that it is tacitly introduced and reexperienced in other events. For example, before his horse racing experience, Steffens had already had similar experiences. He continually found that adults made promises that they failed to fulfill. In horse racing, he did not consciously think at the time that horse racing was just like adult promises, all bogus. Rather, as the experience unfolded, he came to see and experience one in similar terms as the other, as if the prior experience were a metaphor for the other, even though he might not have consciously linked the experiences at the time. As a metaphor, concrete experiences are capable of being generalized broadly to make sense of life.

In the role of a spectator, a person might use metaphor more explicitly. On the basis of a variety of experiences, a person can seek a metaphor to sum them up, name their outstanding ingredients. For Steffens, the bogus nature of events became prominent. He might well have summed up life as a sham. Others might sum up life as a struggle, a test, or a business. Explicit metaphoring allows one to grasp the nature of life more definitely and to engage in more of a dialectic, with both oneself and others. For example, in disillusion-ment, Steffens became a spectator of his experience at the racing track. His friend, the bridge-tender, tried to help him to understand the world. "There's something to hang on to in racing, as in everything. This railroad, for instance. It's a crook in politics, but—there's some of us keeps it going straight enough to carry freight and passengers" (p. 39).

Symbolic elaboration is compositional, a matter of a personal construction of reality. As a dramatic unit forms, roles are clarified and situations are defined. Types of gaps are noted as unit boundaries. And in metaphor, the unit is given a character, capable of a broad structuring of the life world. The obvious reason metaphor is so important in the construction of reality as drama is that no other vehicle is capable of allowing us to make a coherent statement about the nature of life (Lakoff & Johnson, 1980; Pepper, 1942). No other form of statement has the capacity to structure experience with breadth and coherence. Once a metaphor is explicitly framed, it helps to fix the dramatic unit from which it was inspired.

A dramatic unit is extended, refined, and revised in a host of experiences, some of which are prototypical and consolidate the pattern, and some of which are deviant, calling for elaboration and adjustment of pattern. One of the most important aspects of development is that a separation emerges between ostensive roles and situations of concrete experience and dramatic roles and situations. For example, in horse racing, there is a jockey and an audience and the situation is defined as a competition. In the California Legislature, there is a representative and those he or she represents, and the situation is defined as a democratic process. Concrete situations tend to have their own definitions of roles and situation. However, as these experiences become encompassed within a dramatic unit, they are defined according to the nature of the drama. For example, Steffens began to view persons as innocents and suckers (those who take things as they seem, like his father), those who take things as they really are, those who pull the strings and really know, those who are fronts and go along with things for their own benefit, and those who strive to understand. And a situation might be defined as a sham, or a show for suckers, rather than as a competition or a democratic process. There are ostensive roles, role organizations, situations, and gaps. There are dramatic roles, role organizations, situations, and gaps. And as a dramatic form is used to make sense of a concrete experience, the ostensive gives way to the dramatic reality.

Another important development is that a dramatic unit can be viewed as a dramatic context, incorporating a variety of individual dramas. The personal gap that motivates an innocent or sucker is different from the gap that motivates a front, for instance. Any drama involves many different roles and each involves a story. Picture *Hamlet* as told from the perspective of Hamlet, Ophelia, Polonius, the King, the Queen, or Laertes. All would change, yet the whole would remain the same. In a dramatic unit, a person defines and populates a world with a cast of characters, each with his or her own life-defining gap spun from one's place in the drama.

The second function of repetition is role mastery. Certainly, mastery need not be limited to a role within a drama, but it comfortably bounds what is intended here. Repetition is practice, and practice fosters mastery. In ostensive roles, a person has the opportunity to develop abilities, interests, attitudes, and knowledge; in short, one develops toward what will allow one to act competently or even ideally in a particular role. Role competence not only includes what facilitates the active performances in role, but also includes less direct facilitators. One might become familiar with or control reactions, cultivate some emotions and not others. Role mastery is not concerned sheerly with duties, but more with a total way of being in role, and this involves a shaping of being. Steffens, for instance, practiced being a jockey; he did not limit himself to just trying to ride well.

The ostensive roles available to a person as a participant are typically quite limited, and generally perhaps are not the real roles that matter in the movement toward vocation. Menuhin (1978) began violin practice at age four and became one of premier violinist of this century. Certainly, there are others who practiced a way of being in an ostensive role that flowered directly into a vocation. However, ostensive roles remain limited, and for this reason, the relatively unlimited range available in dramatic roles should receive more weight as probable progenitors of a later vocation. Even Menuhin came to enrich and transform the ostensive role he developed early by a dramatic role he developed later. But for many, there is no obvious ostensive role that connects with one's vocation. For example, whatever mastery Steffens developed as a jockey remained unused in the rest of his life. It went nowhere.

We can understand dramatic roles only if we know the dramatic vision in which they have a place. Yet grasping the role alignment of a drama is apt to be indirect and difficult. Steffens, for instance, was focally aware of ostensive roles (such as jockey), but only subsidiarily aware of emerging dramatic roles. He had no sense of playing a role other than an apprentice jockey at the race track, but in devoting himself in this experience and becoming disillusioned, he practiced quite another role as part of his growing dramatic representation of the world. Steffens became a reporter, what at present would be called an investigative reporter, for both newspapers and magazines. Among other things, his experience at the race track provided him with relevant practice in talking with persons on a topic, striving to make something fully intelligible, persisting, managing reactions, weighing different viewpoints, and drawing out significance. He practiced many features of mastery that were used throughout his life, yet Steffens would never have thought, at the time, that being a disillusioned onlooker was preparation for anything, much less movement toward mastery.

From lives investigated for this book, progenitors for vocation tend to involve make-believe play, or what Britton (1970) terms imaginary spectatorship activities. In these activities, if done alone, a child is the author, director, stage manager, main character, and sometimes takes a turn at being other characters as well. If done with others, the dramatic performance is apt to be negotiated, but still the freedom for dramatic construction is enormous. As Britton emphasizes, a child seems to be directly composing a world, often taking a more satisfying role than one he or she has had in actual life. Children reenact problematic experiences, anticipated experiences, observed experiences, and created experiences drawn from models and material around them. In these vivid, dramatic productions, a person practices mastery of a given kind of part within a context that endows it with meaning. Sometimes, progenitive activities are indirectly linked to a later vocation. For example, Steffens playacted a romantic hero in an idealistic world. While he did incorporate aspects of these early dramas into his role as a muckraking reporter, they are subdued. Steffens's romantic imaginings functioned more as a setup for the piercing agony of disillusionment. His later role in life was largely to disillusion others from their make-believe views, to show them how things really were as necessary preparation for trying to make things better.

Often, progenitive activities are directly linked as a primitive model is to a more sophisticated model. Whether direct or indirect, imaginative activity is pronounced in incompletion, for the person typically has no outlet in actuality. With regard to reality, a person is apt to be rendered passive, incapable of getting much done. However, the dramatic sense of children is so powerful that I am inclined to believe imaginative activities would reign whether or not they were capable of effective action. Childhood and adolescence seem like a rehearsal of being.

The third function of repetition is inspiration. A certain spirit is invigorated over and over. In inspiration we reach the necessary complement of composition, without which composition would be a terribly dry affair. It was noted that symbolic elaboration is reality building, but by reality, I do not mean a scientific model of reality or a textbook version of things. These are just abstract, impersonal maps. We do not live them; we use them as maps in the way a traveler might use a map of California to drive from Sacramento to San Francisco. Unlike this kind of mapping, reality building in drama involves forms we can live. For instance, one can live vicariously and sometimes directly the sickening agony of Steffens watching a world turn sour. However, one cannot live the line on a map from Sacramento to San Francisco. This makes an immense difference not only in lives, but in how they are studied. A scientist could construct an impersonal map of a life. Or with an expanded view of science, one could build a structure that is capable of being lived; namely, a drama. Of necessity, the former model falsifies the subject from the beginning, for it involves a model and units that are not livable. The most essential feature of a career, its "livability," is left out. How can one offer an adequate model of something that leaves out such an essential part? The dramatic model might be fallible in many ways, which really only means that researchers can strive to improve it, but at least it offers the possibility of being true to its subject.

What is inspired in a person is a feeling about some state of affairs, a subjective judgment that matters. To be incomplete, to adopt a gap between what is and what ought to be, is to take a certain position or stance. This position is not a matter of conceiving or feeling in separation, but of a "feeling about" that is both conceiving and feeling. For example, we have feelings of pleasure and pain, but a "feeling of" is not a stance. More importantly, we have feelings about pleasure and pain, embryonic stances toward them that might evolve into a full position such as epicureanism. A stance can be described by varying shades and amounts of feeling, and by an organization of conceptions, but no analytic separation is possible. Without conception, a "feeling about" is just a "feeling of," a species-wide phenomenon that is about as impersonal as a cramp. Without feeling, a "feeling about" is a "conceiving of," a cognitive map that is about as impersonal as a computer program. In ordinary human judgment (not dispassionate judgment which requires lengthy practice to attain, if it is ever truly attained), there is no separation of conceiving and feeling, and no possibility for one (Cochran, 1985; also consult Solomon, 1977).

Over time, a stance waxes and wanes in vitality. For example, in a tale of revenge, we do not expect the hero to be burning with rage all the time. In a romance, the suitor does not have to be inflamed with love all the time. A stance varies from red-hot to cool. Sometimes, feeling is more prominent. Sometimes, conceiving is more prominent. The proportion varies, but a stance as a passionate judgment is always both.

In a way, passionate judgment could be regarded as the beginning of drama. When a stance comes alive, it tends to be regnant if only for the moment. The dramatic opposition is one's world, and that world matters. A person cares. Passionate judgment is dramatic in its very nature and it dramatizes one's world. In drama, the world is meaningful. In another way, however, passionate judgment emerges from drama. It is drama that is capable of bringing a stance alive. I take this claim to be so obvious as to scarcely need justification (however, see Cochran, 1986). It is as familiar as going to a movie. The same facts might be presented, but if one account is presented in dramatic form while another is presented as an official report, the dramatic account will be much more capable of moving us. Steffens, for instance, did not become disillusioned just because races were fixed. He became vividly and agonizingly disillusioned when those involved were known well enough to be dramatized.

The central difficulty with a stance is that we cannot directly take one any more than we can directly make ourselves like someone else. The stance seems to come over us, but as Solomon (1977) has argued, this is not quite true. We can be very active in indirectly doing things that will help to make a stance come alive. For example, to become angry, one can think angry thoughts, dwell on offenses, act angry, identify with wronged persons, listen to certain music, and so on, yet there still must be some response from within. A stance is partially something that we are responsible for and partially something beyond control.

As a stance is beyond direct control, the certainty of its recurrence is in doubt. For instance, one can exercise every day. That is within one's power. But one cannot be assured of being cheerful every day. One can influence cheerfulness, strive to cultivate it in various ways, but in the end, one must still just hope. It is within this context that the repetition of a drama gains considerable importance, for drama can move us, naturally and effortlessly. And if the drama is repeated in varying guises, a stance is reinspired, allowing life to be infused with a particular web of expanding meanings.

The Rise of a Regnant Dramatic Unit

Thus far, there are a variety of dramatic units, offering a fragmented constancy. There is yet no coherent organization of dramatic units capable of unifying a life. Rather, there are diverse dramatic units that are being symbolically elaborated, diverse roles that are being mastered, and diverse stances that are developing. There is no center for diversity to organize around, and the potential for conflict, instability, and scattered investment is considerable. Soon after his disillusionment with horse racing, Steffens was embarking on a new adventure, paying little heed to the rising conflict between his idealistic and heroic view of life, the view he playacted over and over, and his disillusioning experiences of life as he actually found it. He simply experienced one and then experienced another. With repetition, however, the two views, one idealistic and one disillusioning, would come into increasing conflict.

In a multitude of experiences, a child has built up some kind of picture of the world and his or her place in it. Within this context, a life-defining problem of existence is encountered (consult also, Csikszentmihalyi & Beattie, 1979). A problem of existence is both significant and engulfing. One cannot see beyond it and cannot ignore it as one's form of existence is at issue. A problem of existence is not something one has, but something one lives intensively and extensively (that is, it becomes pervasive). Consider some examples.

Steffens had built up a picture of the world that was idealistic. There were good persons and bad, and good persons were honest, brave, and moral, among other things. Through daring deeds and hardships, good persons displayed heroism in adversity. In this world, Steffens was special, different from others, someone to be indulged. He was the stuff of which heroes are made. Now, Steffens begins to endure a series of disillusioning experiences. Adults lie to him or break their promises. A horse track has fixed races. The California Legislature is fixed almost completely. At least the horse track did have fair races much of the time. The California Legislature apparently did not have fair races any of the time. In experience after experience, Steffens is left disillusioned at the end. Everything and everyone was a sham. There was another reality beneath the show, one Steffens could not quite penetrate or comprehend in any way that lasted. All he had were questions that no one could answer, or adults would not take seriously. "They don't seem to realize how painful your need is to find out just where you are at in a mixed-up world" (p. 60). Steffens yearned for answers. Why do supposedly bad men seem like good men to him? Why do good men put up with bad things? "I remember how I suffered; I wanted, I needed, to adjust the difference between what was and what seemed to be. There was something wrong somewhere, and I could not get it right. And nobody would help me" (p. 47). The development of an adequate understanding, one that was not subject to the pain of disillusionment, became the "main business of life" (p. 59).

Steffens's dilemma was that his picture of the world was continually undermined by things as they were. He could playact the world as it seemed, giving it an idealistic and heroic flavor in extended pretenses, but he had increasing difficulty living that world. That world was a sham, a front, not what it seemed, not what it was cracked up to be, and so on. He could not live the ostensive world, except in pretense, yet he could not live the world as it was, because he did not know it. Steffens was suspended in between, spending much of his time in vividly imagined fantasy and play, all the while yearning to understand.

Henry James (1983), the great novelist and brother of William James, was maddeningly passive. Overwhelmingly overshadowed by his brother at every turn, he could but look on to the roles William so firmly and confidently filled while he himself was forever dislodged, forever failing to secure a standing of his own. Inward, imaginative, timid, rarely participating in anything, Henry hung to and gaped, "a mere mite of observation" (p. 25). Like his brother William, others seemed at ease, accomplished, so superior that he, by contrast, appeared generally lacking if not odious. Without friends, dependent largely on William, Henry lived largely through others. Nearly always on the outside, a bystander rather than a participant, he gaped and gaped, like a disembodied eye with no life of his own. He longed to be other, not in particular, but in general.

Neither of these examples involves severe pain and agony. Although James more than Steffens experienced a negative appraisal of himself, each is distinguished not so much by agony in some form as by ambiguity and ambivalence. James, for instance, did not long to be someone else in a concrete instance. He probably would have recoiled at abandoning his imagination for some definite accomplishment. He longed to be indefinitely other, even while transported on occasion by the very richness of his growing artistic sensibility. However, there are problems of a more negative, but not more serious quality.

Gordon Liddy's (1980) childhood was dominated by unremitting fear. Within his family, there were real heroes and heroes his mother only told him of in stories. They were strong and fearless while Liddy was a sickly, cowardly, fearful weakling. Liddy was fearful of sounds, of others, of just about everything, but he was utterly terrified of the wrath of God, of being condemned to eternal pain with no hope of mercy.

Anthony Trollope (1978) was a pariah, a despised outcast, useless, joyless, and friendless. Never admitted to sports or the play of other, continually scorned and punished, forever slinking and skulking, Trollope lived as a useless burden, of whom Trollope imagined one could but feel shame. No one expected anything of him, nor did he receive favorable attention. What attention he did receive was intended to demonstrate his lack of character. He yearned to be a man of distinction while Liddy yearned to be a warrior.

Problems are not necessarily negative, or ambivalent and ambiguous. Problems can seem so positive as to be a blessing. In these cases, a person grows so naturally from a favorable environment that there is little sense of having had a problem.

Yehudi Menuhin (1978) recalled only the extraordinary harmony of his home. With stories, artifacts, and her approach to life, his mother cultivated a splendor of vision, exalted, mysterious, and utterly compelling. Menuhin was surrounded by beauty, the beauty of stories, of nature, of music, and of dance. With his mother and father, he attended concerts, theater, and ballet before he could talk. Moved by beauty, he yearned to produce it himself.

If Menuhin was surrounded by beauty, Conrad Hilton (1957) was surrounded by work. While prayer was his mother's answer to problems of living, work was his father's answer. And work meant business. In work, one made dreams real. It was the joy of work his father advocated, not the drudgery of it. His father was continually embarking on new ventures, new dreams, seeking opportunities everywhere. Hilton's youth was filled with diverse experiences in business, from trader to producer, and he yearned to fulfill his own dream in business. He did not begin with a definite dream, but with a yearning to have one that he could strive to realize.

In these positive cases, there is a smoothness of development, a congeniality of circumstance that, as Menuhin phrased it, "demands of me no more energetic act of will than compliance" (p. 15). The problem is how to continue, how to take a more active part in one's good fortune. For negative cases, the problem is how to discontinue one's existing life, how to take action to bring about everything one's life is not. However, for all cases, the situation is engulfing. There is no obvious escape. Certainly, in these lives, there were secondary themes, but there was also a central theme of situation that centered one's existence, and gave birth to yearning. More than anything else, Steffens wanted to understand the real world that fatally wounded his ideal picture. James wanted to be other. Liddy wanted to be strong and fearless. Trollope wanted to achieve distinction in place of disgrace. Menuhin wanted to be a vehicle of beauty. And Hilton wanted to succeed in business. Behind what persons become are not just abilities, interests, and values, but a history, a growing sense of meaning and a sense of what is required to be meaningful.

There is no one reason why a particular dramatic unit becomes regnant. Rather, there is a personal context or constellation in which a particular problem becomes pivotal. Steffens's world was upended. He could not live what was unreal, yet he did not know what the real was. In this situation, one is suspended and can only search for understanding. From the cradle, Menuhin was engulfed by beauty, or as he phrased it, ravished in soul and sense. On occasion, he was utterly transported and idolized those who could create such beauty. In particular, he learned to wait for a violin solo by Louis Persinger that entranced him more than any other. He identified with Persinger, wanted to be Persinger. Menuhin knew intuitively that to be able to play the violin was to be (p. 40), just as Steffens knew that to understand was to be. A problem of existence is a problem of being. It stems from a unique context, but when a problem is elevated to one of being, it necessarily assumes primacy and is utterly engulfing. Life stops, in a sense. There is no meaningful pattern of enactments in the future unless the central problem of existence is solved. That is what those who achieve vocation seem to have in common, a centering upon a problem that is so significant that it is as if their very existence were at stake.

Through repetition, a problematic dramatic unit develops, becoming a pervasive theme of life. It seems present everywhere one turns. One encounters it, imagines it, observes it, dreams it, enacts it, and in general, lives it. It becomes the dominant quality of life, continuously infusing a person with a gap between what is and what ought to be. A central yearning rises and takes on increasing definition. For some, the yearning is relatively ambiguous and clarification becomes an essential task. For others, the yearning is reasonably clear. Either way, a sense of one's incompleteness dominates experience.

The Way Out

A problem of existence requires as its solution an altered way of being, an altered role in drama. A person is attentive to anything bearing on this problem, searching for a way out, a way to realize a growing desire for change. In particular, a person begins to assume responsibility for change. Often, there is a model representing a solution, or at least an ideal to strive toward. One can now hope for change, anticipate being different. See Cochran (1986) for a fuller description of this movement toward positioning. Here, let us turn to the nature of solutions.

For some persons, discerning a solution is not problematic. For example, at age four, Yehudi Menuhin (1978) identified a model in Louis Persinger. He asked his parents for a violin and to take lessons from Persinger, both wishes that were eventually granted. Problems of being were channeled into the playing of music, given a focus for his movement into position. Menuhin's development seems so natural largely because his ostensive role was clarified early and became like a vessel into which he poured the meanings of his dramatic role of bringing harmony to the world. The mastery of his ostensive role coincided with that of his dramatic role, and as his technical competence increased, the expanding symbolic meanings found a vehicle of expression. Unlike other lives investigated, Menuhin emerged from incompletion with a clear ostensive role to practice, but with a dramatic role that was embryonic really, requiring great development in later phases of life.

Steffens's life is more typical. He continued to find actuality disillusioning. Even during a chance to be a hero, he discovered that heroism was not what it was cracked up to be. Indeed, he made the dreadful discovery that he, with all his heroic pretensions, was a sham. He became sensitive to his own poses as well as the poses of others, yet posing was nearly all he had. He had a sense that he was to be a great man, in short a hero, but eventually, in a quite negative experience, even this gave way. What he had left was a desire to penetrate sham to the reality of human society. Later in preparing for college, he discovered through vivid models the value of objectivity, of taking oneself out of the picture. Playacting and heroic dreams were over, he thought. He now had an intense desire to know and pursued knowledge at the University of California, and later at German and French universities. His vague general aim was to know, to be one who knows, and this aim was to shift from scientist to philosopher to writer to reporter. In growing up, he had written poetry and a novel, and had spoken of being a journalist, but he left the phase of incompletion with no ostensive role in mind. He had set aside heroism, seen the value of objectivity, and was ready to begin positioning himself for a quest of reality.

The shift from incompletion to positioning is a shift from passivity to activity. Certainly, the main character can be active in a variety of ways during incompletion. Steffens, for instance, was nothing if not exceedingly active. Rather one is passive in one respect, and this one respect comes to dominate life. In the face of a problem of existence, one is initially passive. One endures it. When a person becomes active regarding the problem is not a matter of age or general maturity. Menuhin was four when he became active; Anthony Trollope was twenty-six. Becoming active is more a matter of discerning a way to do something about an engulfing problem of existence. The conditions for moving into positioning are the conditions for taking any action whatever. These conditions could be drawn from philosophers who have examined the concept of action in considerable detail (Harré & Secord, 1973, have been most attentive in showing the relevance of this literature to psychological studies). However, for the present discussion, De Charms's (1968, 1976) theory of personal causation is quite appropriate. According to De Charms, a basic motive of human existence is to be effective in altering one's environment, to be a causal agent, an "origin" of action rather than a "pawn" of circumstance. De Charms's theory and research concern the development of powers of human agency. While the persons under investigation here do not need to be powerful human agents generally, they did have to acquire agency with regard to their difficulties. Following De Charms and apparent in life histories are the conditions below.

Goal-setting

Purpose, intention, aim, or any term indicating direction would suffice to characterize this condition. The essential feature of goal setting is that a goal has been made into something definite and realistic to strive toward. In passivity, one dreams, fantasizes, and wishes. One takes no action, nor is action expected. In activity, however, a goal is promissory. Action is expected to follow. There is probably no bigger gulf for one in a problematic situation than the gulf between a wish and a goal.

Persons move toward goal setting in several ways. First, the negative state of incompletion implies an opposing positive condition. Indeed, the regularity with which a person's later vocation is the direct opposite of an initial negative condition is so apparent that it is difficult to understand why Adler's (Ansbacher & Ansbacher, 1956) original work has been so neglected. For example, Norman Vincent Peale (1984), famous for his works on the power of positive thinking, has devoted his life to spreading a practical gospel from the New Testament, attempting to change lives, to help others become all that they can be through closeness to the being of Jesus Christ. It is difficult to think of anyone as positive as Peale is, or as industrious in communicating his message to others. Yet in growing up as the son of a preacher in small towns, he was made to feel different. The slightest misstep was exaggerated as a dreadful sin, no doubt to the amusement of other young persons. And if he did not misstep, he was probably regarded as a bit of a sissy. Peale, in short, developed an acute sense of inferiority, a strong self-consciousness, particularly if he had to speak to groups or strangers. He was timid, given to scenes of awkwardness and embarrassment. "In fact, I lived like a scared rabbit. I constantly told myself that I had no brains, no ability, that I didn't amount to anything and never would. I lived in a miserable world of self-deprecation" (p. 42–43). And others, Peale thought, agreed with his assessment. Peale is similar to Gordon Liddy, Anthony Trollope, and numerous others who became exactly the opposite of what they were in youth. However, if this were all, goal setting would be very simple, but it is not, not even in the lives of Peale and other who manifest opposition so strongly.

If the gaping Henry James were asked to imagine himself as an outgoing participant like his younger brother who took up friends and activities as naturally as Henry did not, he would probably have fainted on the spot. To suggest such an avenue of development, so beyond his capability (or what he perceived of it), would likely have condemned him to the situation of a pawn. Henry, like many others, had to struggle to make a negative into a positive. Unlike Menuhin, for instance, who was drawn by a positive, the task here is to reconstrue the possibilities of one's negative condition. Henry's adjustments and progress were so delicate, so hesitant, so groping, that it is difficult to convey in a manageable space, although it is obvious enough that gaping became a decided asset in the imaginative development of a novelist. His progress came in small insights, complex twists, and failed attempts, separated by years. He had to transform gaping into the positive vision of an artist, step by step. Slowly, he began to see not what he lacked but what he had and could develop. For example, while he yearned to be other, to have firsthand experience and to have important things happen to him, he learned a value in intense, imaginative empathy. Negatively, "whether or not they would prove to have had the time of their lives, it seemed that the only time I should have had would stand or fall by theirs" (p.461).

Positively, he was not limited to one life, but through his imaginative sensitivity, could live many lives, virtually without limit. What he lost in immediacy of participation, he gained in sweep and sensitivity of vision. Or as another example, rather than view his imaginative sensibility as a defeat, or softer, a secondary virtue, he could make "imaginative passion . . . the very interest of life" (p. 454), and he himself would be the foremost subject of study. Later, of course, imagination would be his vehicle of the discernment and representation of reality.

While those who leap from one pole to an obvious opposite offer a deceptively simple clarity, those who develop an opposition by transforming the nature of a negative, transcending it really, offer a subtlety and complexity of considerable magnitude. Loren Eiseley's (1975) home was as disharmonious as Menuhin's was harmonious. At age four, while Menuhin was confidently asking for a violin and lessons, Eiseley was begging his mother and father for peace, for sleep, and later for escape from the "terror, anxiety, ostracism, shame" (p. 24) that came to pervade his existence. His mother, deaf, on the fringe of sanity, spoke in a discordant jangle as she repressed young Eiseley at every turn, her strange behavior separating the home from the community as solidly as an asylum. His father, dignified and restrained, was on the downhill slide of life, suffering the chaos of home as well as his sinking prospects, yearning for rest, which he only found in occasional recitals of Shakespeare (for Loren) and in death.

Eiseley, the child of his father's second and unhappy marriage, was "a changeling, an autumn child surrounded by falling leaves" (p. 13). Although loved in a fierce sort of way, Eiseley had no home; like his father, he searched for one. Without peace, without belonging, without recognition, he was homeless, a wanderer in search of something lost or never had. Early in life as a part-time student in university, his father died and Eiseley became sick with tuberculosis, traveling west to recover by himself while his mother quarreled her way out of a refuge with her sister and went to work on farms. What home they had was a thing of the past. There really was nothing to come back to. He drifted across the country, hopping freights as he went, finding out more and more about the world that alienated him, making him a wanderer by conviction.

Like James, Eiseley slowly converted the agony of being a homeless vagabond into something much more meaningful. He did not reject his state. He accepted it and grew from it, elevating homelessness to a vision of life. An anthropological scholar of immense renown, one of Eiseley's last works (1969) is a virtual philosophy of life as journey, placed within the context of human evolution. For example, "man seeks his spiritual home and is denied it" (p. 4). Home is but a hope for peace. We are all homeless, searching, We are changelings whose "true face is no face" (p. 20);

"our identity is a dream" (p. 76). "Man was destined always to be a searcher" (p. 176). Eiseley made a home of wandering, in a sense, making it the very stuff of all human existence, in which he was no different from anyone else. While there was no place for Eiseley in his actual circumstances, he found a home of sorts among other wanderers within the broader context of human evolution. In the long view, he had a place and it was no place.

The immense sophistication, richness, and beauty of Eiseley's and James's elevation of a condition they could not escape into a way of being they avowed, I can only hint at here in brief illustration. However, enough should be apparent to sense the qualitative distinctiveness of this type of solution. James wanted to be other and heightened his imaginative powers as a novelist to do it. Eiseley yearned for home and became a wanderer to do it. Even these characterizations are too simple, yet convey the kind of opposition involved, which is more subtle, less blatant, than the kind exemplified by Peale, Liddy, Trollope, and others.

Second, goal setting is forwarded by models. In a way, the problem of existence polarizes the world. On one side are models; on the other side are opposing models. Often, the models a person observes are beyond his or her reach. For example, Trollope saw young aristocrats at his boarding schools who were everything he was not, but they were beyond his capacity to reach and he did not identify with them. Liddy became aware of heroes of stories and family members who were everything he was not, but they did not immediately serve as his model. A person seems to search in particular for a model that not only exemplifies a desired state but one whom the person identifies with as similar to oneself. Trollope identified with his mother's successful effort to meet overwhelming adversity with cheer and industry, as she became an author of standing. Liddy identified with Hitler and the German nation that had risen from fear and weakness to become the most powerful nation on earth. The model seems particularly effective if it models a movement from one's current state to a desirable end state. There are models that are like dreams and wishes; and there are realistic models that help to move from fantasy to goal setting. Realistic models inspire hope, a willingness to begin trying. Sometimes there is only one model such as this and sometimes there are numerous models or partial models, as was the case with Peale and Menuhin.

However, as with just about everything, the question of models becomes complicated in considering the lives of Steffens, James, and Eiseley. Steffens wanted not a hero of the illusory world, or a disillusioned person. He was in between and such models are complex and difficult to find. Indeed, the danger of a shadow model is keener. For instance, later after Steffens had been a reporter for some years, steadily digesting disillusionment in his effort to get a clear picture, he erupted angrily with an experienced newspaperman. To Steffens, the professional was cynical, contemptuous, alcoholic, and, in short, warped by the daily round of unsavory disclosures. Steffens dreaded these persons as he dreaded his own possible fate, the "ghost of my future" (p. 313). Steffens wanted to disillusion himself and others, to gain a true picture from which meaningful reforms might come, but he did not want to become a beaten-down cynic in the process. Steffens, James, Eiseley, and others who accept the initially negative condition find models certainly, but their models are more apt to be partial, incomplete. And the division between a good and bad model is much more ambiguous than is the case of those who strive to become the opposite of what they were.

Last, goal setting is facilitated by a foretaste or actual experience of what the end might be like at its best. Since such an experience is usually impossible in their actual circumstances, it occurs largely through imagination, stimulated by speeches, models, music, novels, dreams, daydreams, and the like. These experiences range from the joyous to the ecstatic, but when they come, the person knows experientially the end he or she seeks. Peale felt it first in prayer with his father. Liddy felt it in listening to German marital music and Hitler's speeches. James felt it when gaping elevated to visionary experiences. A sense of being comes alive in them, if only for a while, and it gives substance to their search, definition to their direction. They might not really be able to conceptualize yet what it is, but they know now that what they seek is real and that they will recognize it when they meet it later.

Goals might be clear or vague, very general or quite specific. Ordinarily, one does not vow to be a lawyer, engineer, or any ostensive role, although one might be able to make a clear, concrete identification as Menuhin did. The existential problem involves an "is" and "ought to be" within a dramatic reality. It is a problem of being that involves doing, not a matter of normative roles. Usually much later and after much groping will a person be able to name an ostensive role. The ostensive role is only really the housing for a dramatic role, and for a dramatic role, there might be a number of suitable houses. Steffens, for instance, was inclined to be a professor and this would probably have housed his dramatic role as well as journalism. His entrance into journalism was fortuitous, a matter of being cut off from financial support from his father and being instructed to earn a living. After failing to secure a job and failing as a freelance writer, he used his father's letter of introduction to get a job on a newspaper. This does not imply that ostensive roles are unimportant. They are of the utmost importance in actualizing a dramatic role. That is the value of housing: it provides an actual setting for the instantiation of drama.

However, foremost during incompletion is being, the nature of one's dramatic role in symbolic reality. A great diversity of ostensive role might be playacted, but the dramatic role is more stable. Within the drama Trollope learned, he was a pathetic outcast and he yearned to be a man of distinction. James was an onlooker and yearned to be a participant, the hero of his own tale. As they groped and progressed, the end would be formulated and reformulated, often developing into something that they had no conception of early on. Thus, in goal setting, it is better to think of a series, rather than an event. One requires enough direction to begin trying to position oneself more favorably, but more importantly; one requires a repeated experience of setting goals, pursuing them, and altering them in light of one's ventures in the world (Kelly, 1955).

Instrumental Activity

Plan, means, striving, or any term indicating action to reach a goal would suffice to characterize this condition. Actually, when the person begins taking action, he or she enters into the phase of positioning. Within the phase in incompletion, the stress is more on searching and planning. Menuhin planned to practice the violin. Liddy vowed to face and conquer his fears one by one. Trollope developed a plan of discipline to increase his industry in writing. Eiseley began to study the journey he was part of, conceiving of this as a journey really to understand journeying. In universities and as a reporter, Steffens began to seek a valid picture of human society as it actually was. Plans vary in realism and detail, but each person found some way to pursue his or her individual direction.

Confidence

Given the current popularity of this concept, it might be phrased as an internal locus of control (Rotter, 1966), self efficacy (Bandura, 1982), or as the opposite of Seligman's (1975) learned helplessness. Usually described as a belief that one can affect outcomes, confidence seems also to involve a certain optimism, or feeling of hope. For one who has been stuck in a negative condition, there is no dispassionate probability calculation. Rather, the rise of confidence is a more passionate affair, often involving vivid visions of progressing and of conquering. Perhaps it would be more accurate to regard this condition as hope that will transform into confidence later, but the basic sense that there is a way to strive, a way to change that is within one's power, remains the same.

Like other conditions, hope seems to arise most characteristically from models with whom a person can identify. Persons also draw from examples, insights, support, discussion, and the like. They are set for change, attentive to anything that might help. Of significance later, as persons begin to plan, weigh abilities, assess resources for the path ahead, they often recognize a special ability they have that can be cultivated and relied upon. James recognized his gaping as an imaginative capability. His life story was written as the history of a strong imaginative passion. Liddy had superior abilities, but what he highlighted was his will. It was his will that would allow him to face his fears. Steffens stressed his ability to think objectively. Within the dramatic context of their lives, these special abilities assumed great importance. Initially disregarded or downgraded, the special abilities became major vehicles for the way out, assurances of taking one dramatic role rather than another.

In the general plot of those who achieve a vocation, hope is a pivotal condition. Without hope, there is no basis for action. If a person believed that what he or she did would not make a difference, there would be no reason for trying. However, all those who progress from the passivity of incompletion to the activity of positioning come to believe, however haltingly, that what they do can indeed matter.

Responsibility

Responsibility is of obvious importance in two ways. First, a person must accept responsibility for taking action. An existential problem is not the kind that others can solve for one. If a child is sad for having lost a teddy bear, someone else can solve the problem by finding and returning it. However, if a child is sad because of what he or she is within a context that is the child's reality, others cannot solve the problem directly. Others can help, but when the solution involves a change in one's way of being, a person must assume some responsibility for self. And what one can assume responsibility for, one can also try to change.

Second, the assumption of responsibility is an important basis for a later evaluation of outcomes. In positioning, a person does not generally go through a series of sparkling successes. Rather there are shades of success and failure. To correctly assess what one contributed to the success or failure of a particular venture is to be able to alter one's contribution in later ventures with an increased probability of achievement. If a venture was unsuccessful due to extraneous and overwhelming circumstance, one can assess it properly and simply move to a new venture in a more favorable circumstance. However, if a venture was unsuccessful due to something one did or did not do, one can try to correct it. Without a more realistic sense of responsibility, a person is not placed well to benefit from experience and to progress. It would be farfetched to believe that this sharpened, more operational, sense of responsibility is acquired very fully in incompletion, but it begins here and how it begins can make a great difference.

There are other conditions such as reality perception, but this has been included under dramatic composition, and is apparent throughout. During incompletion, persons are very imaginative, but do not flee from reality for a make-believe world. As best they can, they seek a direction that involves actuality as they know it.

One other condition, vaguely termed 'internal control,' has been evident throughout the chapter. The term is essentially concerned with meaningfulness. For example, one could have a goal, a viable means, confidence, and responsibility, yet would still be a pawn if action did not arise from meaningful personal motives. One can act effectively as a pawn, but it is apt to be meaningless to do so.

While meaning has been characterized as a regnant gap that comes alive in a person, defining the structure of desire, it is such a central topic that it is explored further throughout the book.

3 Cultivation of Being: Rhythm of Positioning

The period of positioning is concerned with the composition of being. A person enters positioning with a plan, more or less, for bridging the gap between what is and ought to be. The desire for being and enactment of being is delayed, for one does not have the being desired and an enactment would be inauthentic. Positioning is a way to bridge the gap, a way to become in order to enact a desired way of being.

There are two interrelated facets of positioning. One involves the proper situation for enactment. To gain a proper situation, a person might seek certain circumstances, alter circumstances, qualify for circumstances, and in general overcome obstacles for attaining the appropriate setting. One is very like a stage manager who adjusts lighting, creates scenery, and introduces props to establish not only a functional setting for certain types of enactments but a certain atmosphere that supports these enactments. When Hamlet meets the ghost of his father, he does not do so on a bright, cheerful summer day. Burke (1969) refers to this facet as the scene-act ratio, a principle of drama "that the nature of acts and agents should be consistent with the nature of the scene . . . whereby the scene is a fit 'container' for the act, expressing in fixed properties the same quality that the action expresses in terms of development" (p. 3).

The second facet involves a cultivation of appropriate being. This is no more unfamiliar than, for instance, a professional athlete assuming an appropriate attitude or spirit to prepare and fortify himself or herself for the contest. Burke (1969) refers to this as the act-agent ratio, and it involves two movements. First, dramaturgically, a person is "author of his acts which are descended from him, being good progeny if he is good, or bad progeny if he is bad, wise progeny if he is wise, silly progeny if he is silly" (p. 16). For those without the fully developed being sought, what this means is that persons must center on or try to enhance what being they have to act

69

out of it. A football player might enhance hostility, for instance, to infuse his play with appropriate furor. Second, "his acts can make him or remake him in accordance with their nature" (p. 16). Acting with hostility is one way to cultivate hostility. Action restores or enhances being just as being is given to action.

The general proposition of positioning is that repeated action remakes being. Through repetition, action becomes enaction. Repetition is practice or rehearsal for the end sought. Liddy practiced courage by facing one fear after another. Trollope practiced a disciplined industry. Steffens practiced a pursuit of reality. Hilton practiced business ventures. Menuhin practiced music. As a way to anchor the discussion with a concrete instance, consider the life of Booker T. Washington (1956).

The Birth of an Educator

Washington was born into slavery and remained a slave for the first seven years of his life on a plantation in Virginia. From his reconstruction, there are two prominent scenes. In the first, he was busy trying to be of service. There were no sports or games. As soon as Washington could be of service, it was required of him. Thus, he cleaned yards, carried water to men in the fields, and did what he could. However, what stands out is that every week he had to carry corn to a mill to be ground. He would be seated on a horse to go the three miles through dense forests to the mill. Behind him, a large bag of corn would be set with weight balanced on either side. Filled with stories of how the woods were full of deserters who wanted nothing more than to cut the ears off any black boy they found. Washington set forth on his lonely journey in considerable fear. As the horse moved along, the corn bag would become imbalanced and fall off. Since Washington was not strong enough to reload the corn bag, he would have to wait for hours until someone passed by to help him. During this time he would cry, burdened by a task he could not do, afraid of what might be in the forest, anticipating a scolding or flogging when he got home late. Eventually, someone would come by and Washington would continue his journey, have the corn ground at the mill, reload the bag, and return through the forest at night, with all his fears heightened.

No doubt there are more vivid examples of helplessness, but they are difficult to come by. Washington was forced to overcome fear, but more importantly, he was forced to endure a situation in which he could not act effectively. Riding along on that horse, Washington could only hope and wish, all under the apparent expectation that he could do what he could not do. There was no one cause for this weekly predicament. Partially, he was inadequate for the task. Partially, he was provided with no adequate means or preparation. Partially, expectations were excessive. What he had was a vivid metaphor for being stuck.

In the second scene, repeated over and over, he carried his mistress's books to the schoolhouse door. There he saw dozens of boys and girls engaged in learning that was denied him. "I had a feeling that to get into a schoolhouse and study in this way would be about the same as getting into paradise" (p. 5). If the ride to the mill was the epitome of becoming mired in helplessness, education appeared as the epitome of progressing in character and capacity.

Like so many lives, Washington's early life emphasized opposing dramas, the carrot and the stick, as it were. On one hand was a negative situation that symbolized slavery as well as any for Washington. On the other hand was what seemed to be the exact opposite. In one, he was fearful, weak, and dependent. In the other, he was courageous, strong, and independent. As emancipation approached, education was generally viewed as a way out, a way to improve one's condition. Often enough in Washington's story, there were those who misunderstood education as merely a status symbol to flaunt. Thus, a person might study a book on the conjugation of French verbs, and with immense pride, point to the book presumably mastered. The bigger the book and the more esoteric the subject seemed, the more it rose as a symbol of status for one who had learned enough to give forth with a few comments no one else was likely to understand. The relevance of the subject for making one's way in the world was secondary to its impact upon one's immediate circle of acquaintances. Washington was aware of other views of education, but for him, it was the substance that drew him and its relevance to leading a constructive, useful life. The education he had in mind was more a remaking of himself.

After emancipation, Washington, his mother, and his brother walked to a salt-mining town several hundred miles away to join with the stepfather. There, Washington began what was to be a lengthy series of repeated efforts to become educated. Beginning as early as four in the morning, he worked in a salt furnace. In the evening, he studied a book on the alphabet to teach himself to read. When a new school opened, he was not allowed to attend, because the money he earned was needed by the impoverished family. He applied himself more diligently to the one book he had. Eventually, he arranged to have a teacher give him lessons at night, and after some time, was allowed to attend day school for a few months, provided that he worked until nine and came back to work as soon as school finished. For every avenue that opened, there were difficulties to overcome and setbacks. For example, school started at the same time he was let off work, but was some distance away. He had to stop attending day school, and took up night school again. Often, he had to walk several miles at night to recite his lessons to a teacher who knew no more than he did. It was very difficult to find a teacher who was satisfactory. Washington persisted, but his efforts only secured moments of progress. Most of his efforts led to disappointment and discouragement, yet his resolve to become educated remained fixed.

Then he was transferred from the salt furnace to a coal mine. The work was dirty and he could not easily clean his skin after work. A mile from the opening where he worked deep in the mine, there was no light at all. He did not know the complicated layout, and would often find himself lost. Sometimes his light would go off and he would wander in complete darkness until he chanced upon someone to give him a light. Aside form the terror of being lost, accidents were frequent. There were premature explosions and there was always the danger of falling slate that would crush him. Washington found that the experience of "hauling corn" was not limited to slavery, but was a kind of existential situation offered in life generally.

His experience in the mine fully repeated his experience in taking corn to the mill, but now Washington had an aim. Even returned to the helpless terror previously experienced, Washington could at least imagine, and he imagined what it would be like to be white and to have no limits placed upon his ambitions. With no obstacles, he pictured how he would begin at the bottom and rise through his effort until he had reached the highest success.

When Washington heard of Hampton, a school for black persons, his ambition took a more definite shape. Hampton appeared to him as a salvation, as attractive as heaven. He secured a position in the household of the owner of the town business. During the few years he stayed there, he developed his own small library and continued to study at night. While the idea of learning centered upon school and books, it was not unreasonably fixed to a location. In the delay between ambition and realization, he broadened his conception of learning to practical knowledge, lessons of life and character. And it is in this sense that he could later say that "the lessons I learned in the home of Mrs. Ruffner were as valuable to me as any education I have ever gotten anywhere since" (p. 30). He could learn from persons and practical things.

Yet there came a time, when if he were to go to Hampton, the effort had to be made. Even his mother who had supported all his efforts was afraid this venture was a "wild-goose chase." With a $1.50, he set out for Hampton Institute, some five-hundred miles away. From this point on, the story becomes more of a straight line. Hampton was a revelation, constantly introducing him to a new world. but there were still plenty of difficulties to overcome. Enough has been conveyed in this brief treatment of a selection of experiences to gain a sense of what positioning is about, its general spirit and problematic nature. One is not in position, neither in circumstance nor being, but striving toward it.

Positioning is analogous to a rite of passage. Van Gennep (1960) divided transitional rites or life crises into three major phases: separation, transition (liminality or marginality), and incorporation. In separation, one leaves (psychologically or physically) an established existence in which one has a definable place. In incorporation, one enters a new existence in which one has earned a place. As drama, separation and incorporation constitute the beginning and end. The transitional or liminal phase is the middle or means, characterized by a wavering back and forth as one progresses. One has no place and wavers, searchers, strives, and endures. For example, Washington was not a furnace worker, miner, or household help. These were but transient forms to pass through. Yet he was not an educated person either. Positioning is dominated by possibilities, not actualities. Washington was neither a helpless, terror-stricken boy, at one extreme, nor a competent, confident man of education, at the other extreme. He wavered in between in his experiences and passed through forms of existence that involved elements from both extremes, like a series of graded experience forms ranging from a clear bottom to an envisioned top. For all its defects, the most apt word for this phase is becoming. He neither was nor was not, but on the way to being. By its very indefiniteness, this phase is open, given to imaginative reworkings of the order of existence (see Turner, 1975), to an envisioning of and striving for imaginative possibilities. To bring out the nature of positioning in more detail, consider it in light of the three functions of repetition.

Composition

Through repeated enactments, a desirable dramatic unit develops and becomes more real. It is as if Washington, for instance, had walked through the door to the schoolhouse of his mistress and began to experience that salvational kind of activity he could only imagine in incompletion. The regnant drama of incompletion remains but the person begins, through his or her own efforts, to enact another drama, an opposing drama that is like a solution to the existential problem. As the desirable dramatic unit develops through repeated instances, life is polarized between two regnant dramas that organize one's world. One experiences the negative pole, experiences the positive pole, and experiences balances of each in experiences in between. Sometimes, one seems to be striving to avoid a negative. Sometimes, one seems to be striving to approach a positive. We waver, and some waver more than others according to the nature of their dramas. For those who have an extremely negative experience of a prolonged nature like Trollope or Liddy, it is a major step to be able to define the future as the presence of positives rather than merely an escape from negatives. For those who have more positive experiences of incompletion like Menuhin, the wavering seems much less. Yet even Menuhin faced his share of trials and disappointments, for instance, showing so little improvement after six months of instruction that his apparent ineptitude seemed fatal.

With regard to dramatic units, positioning is really a battle as if between a protagonist and an antagonist. The battle begins when the negative drama is strong and overwhelming, and the positive drama is weak and embryonic. It is no exaggeration to claim that the battle involves the nature of the world, for the regnant drama that achieves dominance will define the nature of the world for that person. As metaphors for life, consider Washington's ride through the woods and his imagined entrance to a schoolhouse. Given the first, life appears as a nightmarish trap, not too unlike the world portrayed in Franz Kafka's works. Given the second, life appears more as an unlimited opportunity.

Perhaps it is the momentous issue at stake that often endows this struggle with such seriousness. When Washington set forth to Hampton with $1.50, he had no clear means to cover five-hundred miles. He only had a will to do it. At the first stop in the mountains, Washington was denied food and lodging. To stay warm, he walked about throughout the night. By walking and begging rides, he finally made it to Richmond, Virginia, physically exhausted, half-starved, and penniless. He walked the streets until after midnight, not knowing what to do, and finally crept under a boardwalk to sleep for the night. In the morning, he was able to obtain temporary work unloading a vessel, enough to buy breakfast. Because he worked so well, he was allowed to work a number of days, which allowed him to recuperate. To save money for the remaining 72-mile trip to Hampton, he continued to sleep under the boardwalk. And when he did arrive at Hampton, he felt that he "had reached the promised land, and I resolved to let no obstacle prevent me from putting forth the highest effort to fit myself to accomplish the most good in the world" (p. 35). Washington's trip takes on an epic air of desperation in which he met and overcame several analogues of the ride through the woods and the coal mine. At the time, he was only sixteen years old.

Within the vicissitude of experience, the relation between the opposing dramatic units varies. First, one dramatic unit might compensate for the other. For example, Washington's imaginative experience of rising from his own efforts, unhindered by obstacles, partially compensated for the bleakness of his situation in the coal mine. Second, one unit might stimulate the other. For example, Washington's experience in the salt furnace stimulated his ambition to become educated. Third, one unit provides ground for the other. Without the stagnant traps of existence, the drive to plunge beyond limitations through education might lack grounding. Fourth, each unit might provide relief from the other. Manual labor provides relief from learning activities just as learning provides relief from labor. Fifth, one unit might serve as means for another. For example, at

Hampton, Washington learned the dignity and usefulness of labor through a more elaborated view of education and used labor as a means of becoming educated. Labor enabled him to attend Hampton, but labor was also a form of learning by doing. How many relations there are between two opposing units is difficult to estimate. As the units shift and develop, and circumstances change, the relation shifts. Even at one time, the relation is not fixed any more than the relation between two persons is fixed. It would be more accurate to think of two lived dramas that are engaged, and through this engagement oppositional descriptions arise, the life world is organized, and meanings are elaborated. In this way, the engagement offers the qualities of a dialectic.

Through the forms of opposition, two general movements can be discerned. First, the opposing dramas move from absolute opposition to relative, interpenetrating opposition, from conflict to complementarity. Certainly, in the extreme form of each pole, opposition remains strong. It never seems to be eliminated. However, a person learns softer forms of each pole, a middle ground of instances that combine elements of each. For example, labor is a way to learn. And if pushed, Washington would have agreed that even in the coal mine, he learned. Education was not just a matter of classrooms and books for Washington, and in his later philosophy of education implemented at Tuskegee Institute, constructive labor was required of students. Complementarity is facilitated by emerging goals. For example, in the beginning, learning appeared more as an end and, as Washington acquired an education, it became more of a means for living a constructive, useful life. Both labor and education can contribute to the good of others and oneself.

Second, there is a related movement from the regnancy of one dramatic unit to the other. In the beginning, the negative drama is vivid and actual while the positive drama is fledgling vision. Over the course of positioning, there is a gradual shift in balance until the negative is submerged, partially incorporated, and the positive assumes regnancy. A regnant dramatic unit is like the prototype of a category. It provides a central drama for other dramatic units to crystallize around, giving some importance and relevance, others not. Other dramatic units become parallels, means, extensions, and reliefs, and the like. Dramatic units also take on an order of prototypicality. Some seem like central enactments while others do not, and the person develops a sense of whether he or she is acting centrally or more peripherally, just as a social gathering is significant for one person and not another. As an anchor of influence, a regnant dramatic unit provides a perspective from which the features of other units are highlighted or ignored, altered or refined. As hopeless toil, manual labor is the antithesis of what education meant to Washington. But soften, alter, and reemphasize features and labor becomes compatible, indeed indispensable, for the role of education as Washington came to experience and conceive it.

As long as each dramatic unit develops independently, there is no possibility for a larger dramatic composition. However, from the perspective of one, others can be elaborated into a large composition. Even something as seemingly separate as marriage becomes an integral part. For example, Washington had two short-lived marriages and both ended in an early death of his spouse. While different in some ways, each was described as an inspiring, dedicated, and selfless worker on behalf of a shared mission in life, to help raise the southern blacks from slavery to useful and constructive participation through education. There is no reason why a romance, marriage, and love should resemble or become inextricable from a person's vocation. However, while the integration is apt to vary in lives, it is present. Dramatic units tend to be shaped to fit into a larger dramatic composition, centered by a regnant drama.

Were we all conceptual analysts, we could perhaps explicate features and create larger patterns on the basis of a central concept or drama. For example, through examining a number of uses of concepts such as freedom and obligation, one could emphasize senses of freedom congruent with obligation. Freedom, for instance, involves the freedom to enter into obligation, and in this sense, obligation becomes an expression of freedom. While one could do this regarding the dramatic units of life, the task is formidable and the results are somehow artificial or inauthentic. Persons achieve a similar effect by repeated experiences and enactments, struggling with conflicts and ambiguities, living out compromises and solutions. What an analyst merely analyzes, a person lives and adjusts experiences through enactment as well as environment.

Mastery

While incompletion involves a central drama that is repeatedly undergone, positioning, to a significant extent, involves a central drama that is repeatedly enacted. Sometimes the drama is the same, except that during incompletion, one is passive, while in positioning, one is becoming more active. Liddy faced fears in both places, but in positioning, he actively arranged to place himself in fearful situations in order to endure and master them. Sometimes, the enacted drama is different. For example, Washington's study of a book on the alphabet contrasted with his ride through the woods, although there was considerable overlap. For instance, he had no one to help him to master the book and it seemed as difficult as trying to get a bag of corn back on a horse in his younger days. However, Washington was so enthused, so excited to finally have a book that he approached it with immense thirst. He tried every way he could think of to learn the book, and within a few weeks, mastered most of the alphabet. The differences between the corn bag event and the alphabet incident involve positivity, confidence, and activeness. In one, he was more a patient. In the other, he was more an agent. For all persons I have studied, positioning involves the rise of agency as a central phenomenon, as might be expected given the way persons enter this phase.

Persons also differ in the amount of circumstantial positioning required. Menuhin, for instance, was able to obtain a violin. Certainly, there were difficulties. He was initially given an imitation violin, a toy, which he promptly threw on the ground, enraged, disappointed, and saddened. There were difficulties in obtaining a suitable instructor, and so on. But still, most of his life story in this phase involves an enactment of playing the violin, not striving to get a chance to play it. In contrast, Washington's efforts to arrange circumstances for becoming educated were so severe, constant, and pronounced that the actual learning experiences are, if not overshadowed, at least placed on an equal plane. And this matters a great deal in what comes later. Washington, for instance, did not become a noted scholar. He became an educator. The central enactment of vocation was not studying or learning, although he loved learning, but of striving to develop an educational institute, system, and national climate in order to educate others, giving them a better chance to lead fulfilling and constructive lives. What a large part of this central enactment involved was circumstantial position-ing. He had constantly to strive to simply have a place where others could become educated. All the striving to get into position to educate himself became part of his central enactment of vocation later!

In positioning, persons might engage in various ostensive roles, but the role of significance is only superficially an ostensive role. Like Menuhin, one might happily have an ostensive role that grounds the future, but it is still secondary to the dramatic role being formed in one enactment after the other, binding more and more meaning into it as one progresses. In the practice of a prototypical enactment, a person develops mastery of a particular dramatic role within a particular kind of drama, one that has emerged from the core dilemma of existence during the phase of incompletion.

Consider one of Steffens's first experiences in positioning. Bringing incompletion to a transition point were three experiences. First, through the help of a book that helped to crystallize his outlook, Steffens decided that adults were ignorant fools who could not answer his questions of disillusionment because they did not understand themselves. They lived in make-believe and did not even know that they did not understand how things were. Second, through an experience at military school, he became vividly aware of his own posings, which he could ignore or downplay no longer. He was all show, all appearance, just like the world, and with that realization, his heroic imaginings and boyish adventures dwindled as just one more disillusionment. Resolving to find teachers who knew the truth about things, he went to college. Third, he was tutored in preparation for college and attended intellectual discussions, which were a revelation to him. Not only were his questions encouraged and the absence of answers asserted, but this lack of agreement was strikingly evident in discussions. There were questions and no answers, and this was taken for granted!

But more importantly, these men in discussion seemed selfless. They questioned, debated, pursued issues, presented evidence, and the like, all without reference to themselves. Somehow, they were irrelevant to the questions at issue and were able to set themselves aside in seeking answers. In a word, they were objective, exemplars of a scientific attitude in which the world takes on more interest than oneself. Having so lately had his heroic vision of self shaken and thrown into an unflattering light, this objectivity was an inspiration, taking firm root as a basis for investigation. Armed with objectivity and an "intense desire to know" (p. 119), Steffens entered the University of California. He was ready to begin acting.

Much in his accustomed manner, Steffens became disillusioned with university education, a fraternity, and university administration. Now he engaged in his first significant act of positioning. In a class on American constitutional history, the professor mentioned references for those who wanted to dig deeper. Steffens got the list of references. He read the required chapters, noting how they differed. He read other authorities and found disagreement on the same points and others. He borrowed more books from his professors, drawn by the way the mystery deepened and the way authorities differed on both fact and opinion. He dreamed of writing a true history of the American Constitution while day by day he explored and formulated questions. He began to suspect that the founding fathers had never intended to establish a democracy, and that they had nor really done so. Quite different from his disillusioning experiences, Steffens began from curiosity and ended in fascination. With growing excitement, he cultivated his method and realized that here was something to do. Every work of history was "crying out to be rewritten" (p. 126). Nothing was settled; it was all still waiting to be done. For the questions he had, no one could teach him the answers. He would have to dig for himself.

In this episode, Steffens began to master the dramatic role of an investigator, or the equivalent, to master a kind of enactment. He practiced an objective attitude, persistence, conscientiousness, formulating questions, dwelling on questions, systematically comparing sources of evidence, framing hypothetical pictures or synthesizing, planning, and so on. He practiced a gestalt of features that make up a certain position. Such a gestalt is indefinitely analyzable. We could not confidently come to an end in describing it, nor could we isolate a feature for singular examination. For example, suppose we isolate questioning ability and regard it as a cognitive skill. Something might be gained in this way, but the distortion is severe. Questioning has a history in his disillusionments and it grounds an investigation. As lived, questioning involved an attitude of objective inquiry, a mood of curiosity and excitement, an activity in which it made sense, a focus for dwelling, and in general, a whole way of being. Without the proper attitude and mood, Steffens probably would not have posed the same questions or they would not have played a similar role in story. The enactment requires significant questions and these could hardly be posed if he lacked curiosity or involvement. Like other features, questioning is a focus within a whole. When we highlight this feature, we merely emphasize a particular perspective from which to view the whole. Mastery, then, has to do with including, shaping, organizing, and mastering a gestalt.

Over the course of multiple repetitions, persons add and cultivate new stances as part of a whole in formation. For example, objectivity does not spring full-blown into a composition. In Steffens's first enactment, for instance, he dreamed that he would write the true history of the American Constitution. But being a hero threatens objectivity. Instead of searching for the truth, one is also motivated to search for what would fire one's heroism in writing the truth. I do not believe Steffens ever fully vanquished his yearning for heroism in himself and others, but he certainly tried to curtail it. It did not fit within the emerging gestalt of an investigation. Washington envied and resented the advantages of white persons, but these emotions did not fit within his emerging gestalt of one who strives for education. Some parts must be cultivated, altered, and refined. Others must be deemphasized, adjusted to fit or contribute, neglected or subdued. The rejected or neglected parts were typically prominent in the phase of incompletion. One knows what they are like, and with them, there is no desirable future. The accepted parts assume prominence, for it is these parts that ground one's new future, the way out. During positioning, the self-importance of a characteristic becomes difficult to distinguish from its importance to one's perceived future (Raynor & Entin, 1982). Indeed, the esteem accorded oneself in adopting or attempting to adopt an emerging gestalt is difficult to distinguish from the enhancement of one's future that it promises (Melges, Anderson, Kraemer, Tinklenberg, & Weisz, 1971). In positioning, one practices a way of being, attempting to turn promise into actuality.

In acquiring mastery of a dramatic role, a person also develops a number of principles of living (Cochran, 1986), some that a person can explicitly state and some that are more like a tacit basis for action and reaction. Arnold (1962) has shown that principles of living can be drawn simply from the imaginative stories a person tells, and that they can be used to predict, for example, excellence in performance. A principle of living is like a proverb drawn from a fable, only a

person draws principles from his or her own experiences and those he
or she is a spectator of. Life stories tend to be filled with these
principles. For example, Washington (1956) scorned the role of luck
in human affairs. "Nothing ever comes to one, that is worth having,
except as a result of hard work" (p. 133). Similarly, he sympathized
with the evils of prejudice, but viewed it as an obstacle rather than an
excuse for lack of progress. "Say what we will, there is something in
human nature which we cannot blot out, which makes one man, in
the end, recognize and reward merit in another, regardless of colour
or race" (pp. 165–66). Merit will eventually be recognized and
rewarded. These and other principles of living were foundations of
Washington's participation in the world. He did not just state them;
he lived them over and over.

Many of these principles are individuating, reflecting an
individual's position in the world, but not others. And many of these
principles are profound, deserving much more study than can be
considered here. For example, Margaret Mead (1975) learned early
"an abiding faith that what was lost would be found again" (p. 65).
Such a person does not fear change, nor cling, nor romanticize the
past. Through elaborations such as new and old, security and
adventure, the principle spreads, and to fully understand it, we would
have to discern its thematic influence within her life. Quite in
contrast, Loren Eiseley (1975) learned that time's scythe was ever
busy, inexorably reaping loss in the affairs of humankind. Nothing
stays. All is lost eventually, just as we too are lost, forever laboring
with a shadow descending over our dreams. Principles such as these
reflect but one person in particular and perhaps some other persons.
They reflect the kind of world in which a person exists and the kind
of position he or she holds in it.

However, there are also many principles that seem to be held in
common, even if posed with an individualistic flavor. For example,
rather than simply state that achievements are made through effort or
hard work, Eiseley (1962) quoted approvingly a literal statement that
he used metaphorically: "Those as hunts treasure must go alone, at
night, and when they find it they have to leave a little of their blood
behind" (p. 56). Persons vary on how much meaning they pack into
a principle, but there are obvious commonalities as well. Common
principles concern achievement, worth in life, adversity, moral
conduct, and so on. Initially, the principles seemed to reflect De

Charms's (1976) concept of personal causation or Arnold's (1962) principles of constructive motivation. In this case, it could be asserted that the conditions that launch a person from incompletion into positioning (i.e., the conditions of action or the exercise of human agency) develop and diversify as principles of living. Or in short, a person becomes more of an origin (De Charms) or becomes more constructively motivated (Arnold). While this powerful development of human agency does seem characteristic of positioning, there are two qualifications to be made.

First, while broad commonality is evident, there are apparent exceptions. Unlike statistical investigations in which researchers seem to write off deviations with amazing ease as error, no such hiding place is possible here. If everyone does not manifest certain principles (such as, achievement is attained by active effort), then it alters how we take these principles. For instance, they would not be necessary for those who have a vocation in life. The exception is not dismissed, but made the subject of study to illumine reasons why the person is an exception, and what meaning it has. For example, Giacomo Casanova (1966–71, twelve volumes), far from scorning chance, cast his fate upon it. "Since I never aimed at a set goal, the only system I followed, if system it may be called, was to let myself go wherever the wind which was blowing drove me" (1966, p. 26). In discovering an exception such as Casanova, various courses are open. One might find the exception is not substantial or that it requires common principles to be altered somewhat to include the exception. For instance, given his view of fate in life and his apparent reliance upon it, Casanova did indeed develop a character to capitalize on the opportunities afforded him. Or one might examine the extent to which an exception really does manifest a vocation in life, and in this regard, Casanova is certainly questionable. Either way, the exception is welcomed and used to refine the subject of study.

Second, the principles of living evident in the lives of persons investigated for this book go beyond the work of De Charms. For example, whether an atheist or a saint, most persons seem to cultivate a transcendent relationship. There are various names used such as God, intuition, fate, fortune, destiny, humanity, and so on, but they function similarly as personifications one can rely on, relate to, or dialogue with. The frequency with which this relationship is prominent in lives of those with a vocation is striking. As a whole, this area of study lies waiting. It is at once startlingly new, and very old. In this century, for instance, Napoleon Hill (1960) interviewed hundreds of successful men to try to draw out the principles of living that made them successful. Nearly two thousand yeas ago, Plutarch wrote life histories to exemplify the principles of great men, pairing one Greek with one Roman, and offering a comparison. And before Plutarch was Aesop, who wrote fables to exemplify earthy principles of living. At present the scope of common principles for those who have achieved a vocation seems potentially quite broad. De Charms's concept of personal causation provides one important focus for a cluster of principles, but there are more.

Inspiration

The motivation for change is dual in accordance with the opposing dramas. For example, Peale was motivated by the negative condition of painful timidity, or more generally, by his continually negative appraisals that he acted out, and by the positive condition of what he summarizes as positive living or positive thinking. He never overcame completely the being of a "scared rabbit." Rather, it stands as an enduring reference point and is woven into his positive enactments. Before a speech, and Peale has made thousands of them, he might still feel some of the same feelings of inferiority. A sense of inferiority enters as a first step toward positive enactment, whereas during incompletion, it was the defining experience. While inferiority was an enduring character of life, it became an inspiration for living positively. In the same enactment, he would progress from the negative condition to the positive condition. In this way, the state of incompletion becomes a constant motivation in enactments, inspiring a person to overcome it in positive enactment.

Consider, for instance, how Peale might perform or be if somehow he could completely eliminate the possibility of negative living. It seems likely that it would undermine the sheer energy and vitality of his mission in life. If negative living is not a threat, not a possibility, not something one feels lurking, the positive is apt to lack the urgency it had and the significance it had. One can forget it. Yet as a reminder, so to speak, nothing so infused Peales' speeches and written works with vitality as a mild reexperience of inferiority.

Suddenly, the experience of positive living would appear all the more precious by contrast.

This duality is apparent in every life studied thus far, but the degree of tension varies. Trollope, even in old age, so dreaded the possibility of a return to degradation that he almost hoped his end were near. James never banished the pain of what he lost in not being more of an adequate participant. Eiseley's homelessness was never set aside. Liddy seldom mentioned fear and weakness in later life, but it was still evident in his efforts to fortify himself or "tune up" his will. No one attains an impregnable position. The negative is not banished, but subdued as a latent possibility.

During positioning, a person begins with the reality of the negative dominant. He or she ends positioning with the reality of the negative subordinate. Perhaps the best description stems from the figure-ground relation of Gestalt psychology. At the beginning, the negative is the figure. At the end, the negative is ground for the positive, which has become the figure. In positioning, incompletion is a general motivation for change and eventually becomes an inspiration for a positive way of being, built into positive enactments.

In this context, inspiration is concerned with an infusion of being. One is in potential and strives for actuality. The peculiarity of this state is analogous to imitation. For example, after seeing a play such as *Cyrano de Bergerac* (Rostand, 1959), one might yearn for the being of Cyrano, but there is no way to directly attain it. Practicing swordsmanship or practicing witty sayings might help, but they do not give one the way of being that is Cyrano. The way to practice being is imaginative role-taking, make-believe, acting as if one were Cyrano. At once, however, it becomes obvious that one cannot directly make this happen. To imaginatively take on the being of Cyrano, one must be swept away, so to speak, so involved that the phoniness or inauthenticity of one's play-acting is unnoticed. Partially, one can set the stage for involving pretense, but partially one must give himself or herself to it when the pretense sweeps in as reality. Inspiration is indirect, partially in control and partially out of control.

There is only one way that inspiration can be reliably produced and that is by drama. It is the dramatic that inspires, and this sense of drama is most prominent and natural in dramatic scenes. Persons also heighten a sense of drama by models and examples, by music or by art in all forms, but of most importance, drama is heightened by placing oneself in dramatic scenes. Over and over, the way out is enacted, reinspired, and developed.

After Steffens returned from European universities, from his quest for a sound basis for ethical conduct, he landed a job as a reporter. As a reporter, he had a chance to directly investigate realms of society. Initially, he was too fascinated to stop and think. He was learning too much. For example, he was assigned to the police department: "I went to police headquarters as I had gone to Wall Street, as I had gone to Europe, as I had come home to America, with the suppressed ardor of a young student and with the same throbbing anxiety that an orator feels just before he rises to speak" (p. 199). Yet soon, the fascination gave way to another experience he knew very well: "I seem to have had a conception, a diagram, of life which every new discovery wrecked, or if it held, had no place for new facts. Facts. It seems to me now that facts have had to beat their way into my head, banging on my brain like bullets from a machine gun to get in; and it was only by being hit over and over again that I could let my old ideal and college-made picture of life be blown up and let the new, truer picture be blown in" (p. 238). As the depth of corruption extended from the police to the city government, Steffens yearned for a valid picture of things as they were, "but nobody could help me paint one" (p. 249). He was overwhelmed. He was willing and even pretended to accept what he had discovered, but he could not. He was suspended, unable to assimilate what he "could neither doubt nor believe" (p. 251). And the old agony of disillusionment would rise as well as his yearning to get beyond it. "Would I never see through the appearance of things to the facts? Never get past the lie to the truth?" (p. 256). Similar to episodes in youth, Steffens experienced disillusionment and he also experienced fascination and excitement. But the major difference is that Steffens was now a participant. Day after day as a reporter, he was placed in dramatic scenes that inspired him, that made a certain kind of being come alive and elaborate.

With direct participation, there is a corresponding change in spectatorship, for in reflective moments that the difficulties of participation virtually require, what one is a spectator of is partially his or her own participation or role in drama. Steffens, for instance, did not just reflect upon the reality behind appearances, but upon his role in relation to this theme in his actual situation. From the broader perspective of a spectator, one's involvement in the world is told and retold to oneself. During positioning, a person's role as inspired in the positive drama is formulated and reformulated. The solution to the problem of incompletion is becoming transformed into a particular dramatic role (consult Bruner, 1987).

As one example, consider Washington. His early aim was to become educated. But after he becomes educated, then what? Washington had general ideas such as helping his mother and family, prospering in some way, and being of use in the world, but he did not have a definite vision of himself. As described at length elsewhere (Cochran, 1985), it is as if a person is searching for an apt metaphor that sums up one's history and brings it to a point, that agrees with models and influences, and that gives a name to one's dramatic role in the central enactment. During positioning, a person might go through a number of metaphors that eventually become integrated. For example, before Liddy fixed upon the metaphor of a warrior, he had also used the metaphor of a powerful machine. Through a series of transforms, a metaphor takes shape, and once it begins taking shape, practise is partially a matter of seeing oneself as one's metaphor, no different in form than a child's attempts to playact being Superman or Superwoman.

In Menuhin's case, an ostensive role was fixed early. As noted previously, a dramatic role need not correspond to any ostensive role. Similarly, a metaphor of self need not correspond to an ostensive role. If there is a correspondence, as in Menuhin, the ostensive role becomes a metaphor, a symbol into which one packs the meaning of one's life. In studying Menuhin's life, one cannot help wondering what being a violinist did not mean to him. However, a few instances will illustrate the movement.

Menuhin had talent. He could progress in technical mastery of the violin and was willing and eager to add a spirit to his play in his striving for sublimity, yet it is this spirit he did not have as yet. Partially, he sought more substance in music itself. "Here at last was a promise of authenticity! Playing Beethoven would lend substance to my empty bulk and legs to my unjustified altitude. He would make me massive, tall, real" (1978, p. 57). Through music and gifted mentors to interpret and bring the music alive, he continued to cultivate a certain spirit in playing, to move past imitation to being. Partially, he simply needed more experience in life to grasp what he sought to express in music.

His mother's exotic ideal of a Cherkessian warrior captured a splendor of vision that ignited Menuhin's imagination. For this exotic otherness he longed, and for the ideals of the Cherkessian way (freedom, courage, air, unrestricted assertion of nobility) he yearned. Partially, as a violinist, he conveyed the spirit of an Eastern vision of knighthood, embodied in his mother and elaborated in romantic stories. Yet Menuhin was raised in a virtual cocoon or haven of protectiveness, being educated at home and venturing out only with his parents. Dominated by his mother, home life was built around a schedule of activities that was so routine that any break in it had a capacity to thrill young Menuhin. Although his mother's dominance became excessive and grating at times, Menuhin's ongoing experience was hardly negative. It was comfortable, secure, and harmonious, but also, it was everything the Cherkessian way was not. Menuhin lived comfortably one way, yearning for another, which was expressed in his music. Minimally having contact with the world outside the home, he yearned for harmony among persons, contact. In the very security and dependence of his home, he was haunted by potential catastrophe and sought reassurances.

Between the unrestricted freedom of his mother's visionary splendor and the very restricted freedom of her home, Menuhin had several experiences in which he simultaneously existed and observed himself existing, a strange duality that made him feel that his life, and indeed, all lives were as meaningless as that of ants scurrying back and forth. From the epitome of meaning in music to the sense of utter meaninglessness in everything, Menuhin swayed, one invigorating the other by the sheer magnitude of contrast. He became an enormous success as a violinist before he was in position. He was profoundly unprepared, and his family's close-knit world was indeed a haven. He had to build his life, not from the ground up, but from the heights to the ground. It was not until he had been married and divorced, practically forced from home to a somewhat independent dwelling of his own, and had broken through the cocoon he adopted in violin performances, that he moved into position.

In positioning one can note the interrelated variety of polarities that Menuhin lived over and over in striving to perfect the being of a violinist. The literal role of a violinist was merely housing for a symbolic role charged with meaning. And it was his dramatic view of a violinist (a Cherkessian warrior, a peacemaker, an enchanter who transforms nihilism to sublime meaning) that had to come alive in him, being infused through one experience after the other from a life "full of holes" (p. 122), from a life filled with diversity of opposition to a "unity in diversity" (p. 177). While mastery of a dramatic role is involved, there is also this sense of being, a movement from what one is not to a sense that one is. No less than Washington, Menuhin had to move toward a metaphoric adoption, and to answer the question of what one shall do. Literally, of course, Menuhin would play the violin, but symbolically, what will he do in playing the violin?

There is such seeming inevitability in metaphors adopted that it is difficult to identify any one reason. There is more of a family of reasons. The metaphor seems to bring a dramatic role to a point, agrees with models, accords with special abilities, is evident in numerous early influences, and personifies the way out. In one way or another, the most striking aspect of a metaphor is that a major application involves treating others as oneself was in the negative condition. Thus, novels were Trollope's pulpit from which he preached character and in which virtue is eventually rewarded and evil punished. In his novels, he inculcated lessons of life, particularly lessons for improving one's circumstances. In one of Liddy's most significant experiences in later life, he was able to lead a powerless and fearful group of prisoners to victory just as Hitler had restored Germany and inspired Liddy. As an educator, Washington did all he could to make education possible for blacks who were just as he was. Eiseley's scholarly and practical works were largely for wanderers such as himself and about wandering. By enacting a metaphor, a person symbolically raises himself or herself from incompletion to position. This feature of metaphor is certainly not exhaustive, but it seems evident to a greater or lesser extent in those who achieve a vocation.

It is easier to state criteria for the acceptability of a metaphor than to identify any salient reason for how it comes to be. See Cochran (1985) for a more elaborate description of these criteria and their significance. First, the metaphor is regarded as good, not just as a means, but as an end in itself; to attain the being of a reformer, violinist, educator, or whatever constitutes an elevation, but also is a good in the world. Given the dramatic context that is one's world, the dramatic role is beneficial. Often, this goodness is strongly supported by one's actual context. For example, with the release of eight million slaves, ill prepared for earning a living or assuming the duties of citizenship, education was virtually synonymous with rising in the world. Education was the hope of the blacks during the reconstruction period, and Washington spared himself none to realize this good for as many as possible. His role was right for his times and situation. Liddy's metaphor of warrior was similarly appropriate, given the strong influence of World War II on him youth. Steffens discovered corruption rather than purity in the mainstream of American life, and that most persons were dupes, believing in an idealistic picture that did not exist. Just as he had to face disillusionment, he set out to paint an exact picture of society to others as a basis for reform. Certainly, not everyone would agree that the metaphoric position a person adopts is good, but the person believes it is.

Second, the metaphor is regarded as true or true in potential. In positioning, one desires and hopes. One simply is not as yet, but believes that one can become. The whole thrust of positioning is to make the metaphor true. To become united with the metaphor is to be in position, and that is what a person strives for, particularly toward the end when the metaphor is most clearly defined.

Third, the metaphor is beautiful. As applied to a work of art such as a novel, Saw (1971) has defined a test of excellence involving two interrelated parts. "The test of excellence in art, then, is in the number of related images that are evoked while still retaining their unity and harmony, and in the number of impulses that can be brought into harmonious play and satisfied" (p. 69). As Saw notes, this is hardly a scientific test, but rather an aesthetic test that partially involves our capacity to be swept away in aesthetic experience. An appropriate metaphor for self, one so fitting that a person frames his or her nature around it, involves precisely what Saw indicates for excellence in art. A suitable metaphor virtually sums up one's life in the most meaningful way conceivable, unifying divergent desires and giving them a central direction through which they can be satisfied.

Culminating Experiences

Positioning ends in a culminating experience. With the culminating experience, a person is no longer striving to get into position, but is in position and bent upon fulfilling his or her promise as a person. Often during positioning, there are many high experiences in which one temporarily attains the desired way of being, but it does not last. The person is not yet clear enough in orientation, confident enough to assume the dramatic role, or swept away enough by the vitality of its aesthetic fit. Even if experiences have the force and nature of a peak experience (Maslow, 1962), they do not necessarily culminate the series of repetitive enactments that characterize positioning. Culmination seems to require some sign or evidence that one is rather than striving to be.

Toward the end of positioning, the situation is analogous to that of the tin woodsman in Baum's (1979) *The Wizard of Oz*. Because the tin woodsman did not have a heart, he sought one. In the meantime, given that he was not like others, he would have to be especially careful that he did not harm anything. Of course, the tin woodsman was already more sensitive, more feeling than any of the others. The one who sought a heart had the biggest heart of them all. And so it seems with those who are about to assume a vocation. Washington was already passionately devoted to education before he became convinced he was an educator. Menuhin was already a world-renowed violinist before he was convinced of it. Peale was already an exemplar of positive living when he became convinced that he could be a preacher of it to others. Through an extensive series of enactments, each had transformed a drama of incompletion into a drama of completion that applied to actual circumstances, and when elevated, defined the nature of life. Each had practiced endlessly to take mastery of a dramatic role, a metaphor of selfhood, shaping one's being by addition, elimination, elaboration, refinement, and adjustment. Each had inflamed over and over a passionate judgment that developed into a fuller position. Now what is required is an experience that convinces, that dispels uncertainty and instills confidence.

Initially, it appeared that the culminating experience would be a very powerful one, perhaps like the high point of a vision quest or a pilgrimage. The rationale for this expectation is that being cannot be directly compelled, as noted previously. I cannot directly infuse myself with kindness. I can act kind, but acting is different than a sense of being. Rather, one can indirectly foster being and be prepared to accept it when it comes. The vitality of a feeling about is something we surrender to or give ourselves to. Now when the issue at stake is the central prototype of a person, an outward symbol or metaphor for inward formation that one has been yearning and striving for, the experience of finally adopting it, feeling at one with it, being swept away by it, is apt to be powerful. To be moved in this way requires dramatic power. However, as more lives were investigated, it became apparent that the culminating experience is not always distinguished by extraordinary power. Indeed, in an extensive series of enactments, it is sometimes very difficult to see when a transition has been made. All that can be identified is a gradual shift. On one side, the language, attitudes, and actions indicate uncertainty, a striving to inculcate a certain spirit. On the other side, the language, attitudes, and actions indicate confidence, a striving to diffuse a certain spirit outwardly. There are at least two major reasons why positioning does not always culminate in an extraordinarily powerful experience.

One reason is that the powerful experiences have come before and that all one needs is a last assurance or piece of evidence or simple ceremony. For Norman Vincent Peale, there was a rising series of experiences. As a newspaper reporter, he was present at a fire in which a young girl was trapped. To escape, she had to crawl over a plank to the next building, but was so fearful of the height, she could not. Peale shouted to her about faith in God and coaxed her across. When he denied being a preacher to a policeman nearby, the policeman said, "The hell you are not." Later, he prayed for an answer. Was he destined to be a minister or not? In answer, he experienced a sense of God's presence. Informing his parents, he then enrolled in the Boston University School of Theology. Even with this sense of presence, he was not yet convinced. During his stay at Boston, he had several significant experiences. He was a student minister for a troubled church and healed the divisions. This was like passing a test. He felt the power of preaching one Sunday when he was convinced that "the Holy Presence brushed every person" (p. 81). He helped transform a man filled with hate. He learned in a psychology class more about how one's way of thinking influenced being: "Through Dr. Vaughn's course I learned that a deeper commitment to the mind of Christ could turn my habits of thought from negative to positive, from self-centered to outgoing in nature, and would therefore increase both my well-being and my effectiveness" (p. 90). And during his ordination ceremony, he experienced a sense of peace, a sense of rightness. At least, given the detail Peale has provided, there is no one powerful experience, but several and it is quite possible that it was the simple ordination that culminated the series and that the more dramatic experiences merely consolidated it. In any case, what is less certain in Peale is more certain in others. Trollope, for instance, culminated his series when a novel was a modest success. While certainly important, it hardly has the power of previous experiences.

A second reason why a culmination is not necessarily powerful is that the metaphor of selfhood might not be an elevation of one's nature so much as a salvaging of it. For example, Steffens did not ascend as, for instance, Washington ascended from slavery to prominence as an educator. He descended, in a sense, from the noble world of heroes and lived ideals to a world of rampant corruption that belied every hope, every wish. His investigations were more compulsion than crusade. Certainly, he had to shape himself every bit as much as others, but with this difference. His vulnerabilities tended to be more ideal, more elevated than his existence. For example, he was vulnerable to heroism, its ideals and make-believe world. Certainly, he also had to adopt a metaphor of self, one shred of illusions, to make his way in a corrupt world, but his adoption was not elevating. it was his "illusions" that were elevating. Also, he had a number of highly dramatic experiences, but not powerful and transporting ones. He was not captivated, like Mill, by a vast vision of human improvement, but rather had to fortify himself always on the edge of hopelessness for improvement of any substance.

In the very determination with which Steffens punctured illusions about himself, there is at times a startling purity and innocence that shines forth, but that is not at issue. What is at issue is that his metaphor was not noble, not elevated, not heroic. And to adopt such a metaphor does not seem to require an elevating experience. For whatever reason of human nature, a person who has an elevated vision to attain requires an elevating experience, to go beyond oneself and become different or attain a new level of existence. But one who has no such vision requires only convincing in quite earthy experiences.

Whether a culminating experience is extraordinary, matching the extraordinariness of foretaste experiences long past, or more ordinary, it brings to fruition a gestalt of features that have moved in a swarm toward greater configuration. Typically, the person dreams, enacts, observes, and undergoes a particular pattern, consolidating it into a theme with variations or a prototype with deviations. It is no fragmented buildup of building blocks, but an holistic refinement of a whole in the making. But when it happens, one's life history is divided ;between preparation for position and acting out of position, between infusion within and diffusion without. One is ready to embark on his or her life's work.

4 Work of Life: Rhythm of Positing

The period of positing is concerned with the infusion and diffusion of being. Toward the end of positioning, a person adopts a regnant position that serves to unify a composition of stances. Usually, the regnant position can be characterized by a root metaphor for selfhood such as educator, apostle, artist, champion, warrior, investigator, and the like. With the adoption of this state and way of being, one consolidates a vision of what to do in life. Recall that a position is a unity of incompletion requiring actualization of direction for completion. In positioning, the direction is toward getting into position. In positing, one is in position psychologically, and acts to realize this position in deeds. A reformer reforms. An educator educates. And so on. During this phase of life, to be is to do.

Positing is dominated by a central or prototypical enactment of position. Over and over, the spirit of one's position is reinfused. Over and over, it is diffused without. In lives in which one has successfully molded circumstances in order to act out of position, a central enactment of life is obvious. It is so repetitive, so consuming of the person's energy and attention that one could only miss it by taking it for granted. Conrad Hilton purchased one hotel after the other. Booker T. Washington sought support for one educational project after another. Lincoln Steffens muckracked one institution, city, state, and country after the other. To summarize their deeds so baldy communicates nothing of the meaning of their work, but does indicate what they did. In lives in which one is not so successful in molding circumstances, more effort is required to discern a pattern, analogous to the difficulty a philosopher might face in working with many deviant instances of a concept and only a few paradigm cases. Yet the thrust of this phase is to enact a prototypical drama of existence, and persons show remarkable capacity to work even the most stubborn circumstances into a recurrent form.

Composition, mastery, and inspiration continue as important

functions of repetition, as in positioning. The dramatic context and one's individual drama within it continue to elaborate in positing, as one works new elements of the world into it. One's dramatic role might expand with success, leading to further developments of mastery. And one's position is inspirited in actual circumstances, consolidating a general stance in the world and on the world. Even St. Paul was not burning with apostolic fervor all the time. The vitality of position rises and falls in a rhythm of repetition. At one time with passions cold, position involves a stress on conceiving. At another time with passions red-hot, position involves a stress on feeling. Position as a developed "feeling-about" embodied in a metaphor is always both conceiving and feeling, but the balance varies over time and experience. The importance of a prototypical enactment is that it infuses and diffuses, allowing or stimulating the vitality of position to reach a peak. During these peaks, a person feels most alive, most himself or herself, and most meaningful. Accordingly, the first task of this chapter is to describe the nature of a central life enactment. The next task is to consider difficulties of being out of position.

The Nature of a Central Enactment

Based on previous work (Cochran, 1986) and confirmed in an investigation of other lives, there are seven levels of meaning in a central enactment. There might be more. With no claim to exhaustiveness, these levels are presented simply because they are evident and of considerable importance for an understanding of what a vocation means. The seven levels of meaning range from practical to symbolic.

Practical Achievement

An enactment is practical, an effort to get something done. For example, when Washington assumed leadership of Tuskegee Institute, he did not find buildings, apparatus, and a staff of exemplary teachers. Instead, he found no buildings, no apparatus, and no staff. He had an annual budget from the Alabama Legislature of two thousand dollars, which could be used only to pay the salaries of instructors. Students who wished to attend had little money, little preparation, and no place to stay. There was no strong basis of support for the school; indeed there was some distrust, a suspicion that it was folly. In addition, the black community often had unrealistically high expectations:

> I confess that what I saw during my month of travel and investigation left me with a very heavy heart. The work to be done in order to lift these people up seemed almost beyond accomplishing. I was only one person, and it seemed to me that the little effort which I could put forth could go such a short distance toward bringing about results. I wondered if I could accomplish anything, and if it were worthwhile for me to try [p. 83].

Yet Washington's mission in life was to uplift his race through education, just as he had been lifted up. Actually, while his own race was a focus for his efforts, Washington's desire to help expanded considerably beyond to poor whites, Amerindians, all who could benefit directly and indirectly. In those bleak, early days at Tuskegee, he vowed to build a school that was so constructive, of so much benefit to the country, that the president himself would recognize it with a visit. Although the scope of the problem was overwhelming, everywhere Washington saw the utter need for education to uplift society as a whole. Everywhere, Washington saw the practical importance of his mission. Through education, he would directly uplift members of his race, who would then return to communities as leaders, capable of fostering economic progress, ethical conduct, character, racial harmony, and respect. In this way, his school could play a prominent role in the reconstruction of the South.

It is within this practical context that his enactments assume one kind of meaning. School opened in a shanty and church in which he was the only teacher. Washington saw that he must establish a permanent location and build up, and when he found a run-down plantation for sale at only $500, he acted in a way that was to be repeated on a larger scale the rest of his life. To purchase the property for the school, he sought support for a down payment. He talked with others, trying to communicate his vision for education and the role of Tuskegee. He wrote letters. Internally, he strove for the integrity of Tuskegee as a school. Eventually, he was loaned enough for a down payment and he took possession of the plantation, having no idea where the remaining money would come from. There, he and his students cleaned out a stable and an old hen house, and school commenced in its new location. Soon, they launched commercial industries in which students not only learned by constructive doing, but earned money for themselves and for Tuskegee.

Washington's mission defines a gap between a downgraded people and an uplifted people. Education is both the vehicle and model of what uplifting means. Virtually any action taken to bridge this gap is a central enactment for Washington. More significant enactments tended to be those which accomplished the most, but still, it was the striving forward along a core dimension that makes an act central, whether the act is big or small. The immediate practical gain of Washington's action was a place upon which to build his educational institution. The larger practical gain was that he make progress along the core dimension.

Member of a Series of Practical Steps

An enactment does not exist as an isolated instance, but as a part of an entire series of instances that attempt to bridge a central gap. Each enactment is partially colored by instances that came before and instances that are envisioned after. The number of meaningful relations (or the ways past and future events endow meaning on an occurring event) are many.

One obvious relation is that one enactment is a means for another enactment. Once Washington obtained land, he and his students constructed a building. They planted crops. They experimented with and finally developed a brick-making industry. They built other academic facilities, added programs, and developed more industries, all the while Washington also worked to build a basis of financial support, to formulate and implement a philosophy of education, to establish credit and reputation, among other things. All of these enactments were connected with his buying a 100-acre plantation.

A second relation is that what one learns in one enactment is apt to be tested in another. At the peak of his career, Steffens investigated corruption in one city after another, striving for an accurate picture. What he learned in St. Louis was tested in Pittsburgh. What he learned in Pittsburgh was sought in Philadelphia. Very much like a scientist conducting one experiment after another, Steffens formulated questions and hypotheses, and tested them in different cities, which generated more questions and hypotheses. Eventually, Steffens was able to walk into a new city and describe its system of corruption before he knew anything about it.

A third relation is that memories, loyalties, grudges, and the like, are built along the way with other persons. As supporters showed their trust, staff shared his vision and worked selflessly, students progressed and helped as best they could, Washington partially worked with them in mind. His first wife died, having worked side by side with him to accomplish a shared dream. His mentor, General Samuel Armstrong, died still urging him on to the great cause of elevating the downtrodden of the South, both white and black. And so it goes, the aspirations, examples, betrayals, oppositions, and trust of others come to figure in an enactment.

There is no definite end to the relations among enactments in a series. When they are lined up and the question is posed, numerous relations become apparent. And even if these relations were not apparent, persons remark upon them. They often bring out the personal significance of a particular experience by linking it to other experiences. These relations come to constitute the historical context of a vocation, a forceful support for the path taken. Once a person has started on a particular mission in life, it is often not easy to backslide or change even if one wanted to.

Exercise of Mastery

The attainment of position is not absolute, but relative to the striving evident in positioning. There is nothing fixed about it, although it appears in life histories sometimes with the seeming inevitability of waves on a shore. As a person moves along his or her central dimension, there are moments of doubt, confusion, and just exhaustion. Sometimes persons wonder if they are worthy of their mission or wonder if they have been fooling themselves. Persons with a sense of vocation are hardly immune from rather perennial questions of human existence.

What these question, doubts, and concerns call for is a validation of revalidation of oneself as an educational leader, a preacher, or whatever. In this sense, enactments take on the quality of a test of one's worth. In a sense, each time one successfully enacts position, it parallels the culminating experience of positioning. When one fails, the enactment is more apt to parallel the helplessness of incompletion. For example, ten years after graduation, Norman Vincent Peale was asked to return for a speaking engagement connected with his alma mater. There before alumni, faculty, and students, Peale suddenly sensed a chill in the atmosphere. He felt disliked. While he strove to overcome these feelings to get through the speech, he apparently fumbled his way forward (from his perspective) and regarded this as his greatest speaking disaster. Far from confirming him as a communicator, he was unsettled, temporarily dislodged from position. As a powerful human agent, at least regarding his mission in life, he temporarily felt unworthy, pallid, a shadow without substance. In enactments, one confirms or disconfirms a certain character, a capability, or, in general, a suitability for one's dramatic role.

In most cases in which enactment involves participation, exercising powers of human agency, a test of worth is obvious. However, consider a more complicated case such as Henry James. Recall that James was a gaper, living his life largely through others. From this perspective, life was not an epic struggle to rise up, a prolonged effort to rid oneself of disillusionment, nor a striving to attain the mind of Christ. For James, life was a spectacle (1962). One can be part of a spectacle (which requires an activeness James did not seem to possess) or an onlooker. But as an onlooker, what opportunities are open? At the expense of simplifying the agony, peril, and delicacy of James's transformation from a gaper to an artist, being a novelist requires ideals and abilities, not the least of which is refined gaping:

> Experience is never limited, and it is never complete; it is an immense sensibility, a kind of huge spiderweb of the finest silken threads suspended in the chamber of consciousness and catching every air-borne particle in its tissue. It is the very atmosphere of the mind; and when the mind is imaginative—much more when it happens to be that of a man of genius—it takes to itself the faintest hints of life, it converts the very pulses of the air into revelations [H. James, 1962, p. 661].

For James, impressions were experience and it was the very business of his life to gather impressions and to shape them into an illusion of life that conveys their meaning. While a novelist might not have an extensive range of experience, one must strive to make the most of what one has. To experience with intensity is virtually equivalent to value, in this perspective. And a cardinal virtue is to not waste experience, or as James phrased it, "try to be one of the people on whom nothing is lost" (p. 662). Suddenly, gaping is elevated from an almost involuntary stupefaction into a peculiarly difficult and demanding way of being. One is required to experience with intensity, to be open to delicate and intricate reverberations on the web of consciousness, and to draw these impressions into a meaningful, revelatory pattern. These are at least some of the requirements of artistic vision, and the exercise of mastery in this type of enactment is uncertain. Like the other, James had to confirm and reconfirm his power as an artist.

Instantiation of Position

Closely related to the previous level of meaning, a central enactment is an instantiation of position in concrete circumstances. While the previous level is concerned mostly with power and worth as an agent, this level is concerned with the vitality or spirit of position. Persons do not act and experience in ways that are relevant to vocation all the time. Washington was not an educator all the time. Steffens was not a muckraking investigator all the time. Simply as a practical matter, each engaged in irrelevant action. For example, running an errand, shaving, chatting on a train, and so on, might all be done, but in constructing and reconstructing one's life story, they are edited out. While life histories contain few of these incidents, life contains a lot of them. What this means is that the vitality of one's position is not radiant all the time, nor is one enacting position centrally all the time. Vitality increases and decreases, and does so largely in accordance with the centrality of enactments.

Other names for vitality might be enlivening, inspiriting, or awakening, and in any case, the term used would be metaphorical. To clarify or refreshen the concept of vitality, consider a quality such as humility. One can act humbly, think humbly, seek examples of humility, and in other ways strive to be humble. One can directly act humbly or think humbly, but one can only indirectly foster the being of humility, and until that being comes alive, all those thoughts and actions are little more than pretense. Like Benjamin Franklin, who strove mightily and diligently to cultivate humility, one might never move past pretense: "I cannot boast of much success in acquiring the *reality* of this virtue, but I had a good deal with regard to the *appearance* of it" (Franklin, 1961, p. 104). One has no direct control over the qualities that are alive or dead, but one might have considerable indirect control (Solomon, 1977). In a way, they just seem to come over us. But in another way, they seem to be a result one is responsible for.

It is in this context that we experience a certain otherness to ourselves, part in control and part out of control, and in which it makes sense to speak of something being alive or dead in us. After considerable effort and yearning, suppose one day that one was not just acting or thinking humbly, but that humility seemed to come alive as a dominant quality of being. In that moment, one is naturally and effortlessly humble. What was a struggle before is a struggle no longer. Indeed, one would have to struggle to avoid being humble. With the rise of humility, different values seem apparent, different joys. The world looks different and one's reactions are different. What one might have done a moment before becomes unthinkable now. "All we know is that there are dead feelings, dead ideas, and cold beliefs, and there are hot and live ones; and when one grows hot and alive within us, everything has to re-crystallize about it" (W. James, 1958, p. 162).

One who has attained personhood and a sense of vocation differs from the example of humility in two ways. First, humility involves conceiving and feeling as a stance. In humility, what is prominent is a judgment or feeling about other persons, other things. The regnant position that constitutes personhood, however, involves a composition of stances. Second, in the example, humility was coming alive. However, in positing, the regnant position is already alive. It might increase and decrease in vitality, but it is not dead. Rather, the issue is one of rekindling rather than kindling from scratch. However, the effect is similar. When a person is fully in position, filled with the vitality of what has been brought fully alive, *one is* and is able to act from position in a full sense. Actions, reactions, perceptions, and the like are attuned, made indivisible in a unity of existence.

Certainly, in a way, the rise of vitality in a prototypical drama is validating, but validation is not a major concern of persons in this phase. They are much more concerned with validating their power to carry on their mission than to validate being. While the instantiation of regnant position might have a variety of functions, they are of no concern here. It is the state of being that is so meaningful, not necessarily any particular function. In a central enactment, when one is charged with the vitality of position, existence is fraught with meaning. One can act and think, plan and remember, but without this sense of being, there really is no meaning (see Cochran, 1985, 1986, for lengthy descriptions of vitality in central enactments). A central enactment, from this perspective, is a way to enact one's regnant position or dominant way of being.

Reenactment of Structure of One's Life

As noted previously, the structure of a drama is indifferent to length and complexity. The four phases of incompletion, positioning, positing, and completion apply to a momentary action as well as to a life story. Due to this structural commonality, it is possible to compare a central enactment of life with a life story. From the study of numerous lives, it appears that a central enactment is a mirror for one's life as a whole. In a central enactment, one enacts the very structure of one's life story in a condensed form. This is an incredible finding, yet it seems evident in the lives investigated, opening the meaning of an enactment for a rather awesome expansion. Not only do central enactments mirror one another in a series, but they are a virtual celebration or ritual instantiation of one's life.

Consider Washington's purchase of the plantation. In the beginning, he was overwhelmed with difficulties that confronted him. He felt nearly as helpless and trapped as he had in the coal mine or in taking corn to the mill. Yet in this phase of life, he had placed himself in the situation. The corn trip was forced upon him, but the task of building an educational institution was one he accepted as a part of his vocation in life. There is also a difference in agency. Unlike the coal mine where his powers of agency were so overwhelmed that he was more a pawn of circumstance, at Tuskegee he was more capable of being active, of taking effective action. He was indeed nearly overwhelmed with the task before him, and he experienced incompletion quite powerfully, but not as a helpless, frightened boy. He was an effective human agent, capable of seeking and acting on a way out more immediately. During incompletion, one endures, usually with feeble, ineffective actions. During the incompletion phase of an enactment in positing, one endures in preparation for effective action, and in striving for a way out, one is repeating the way out taken much earlier.

In the second and third phases of this enactment, Washington worked with great industry and faith to purchase the plantation and transform it into a school. From a friend at his alma mater, he received a personal loan for $250 and made a down payment. Immediately, he and his students set to work cleaning the hen house and stable, and clearing the land for agricultural programs. To raise money, they held festivals and suppers, soliciting items from white and black families to sell. And they sought direct contributions of money. These efforts continued unabated for several months until he could repay the loan and complete the purchase, at the same time striving vigorously to implement his vision of education within the school. To supplement classroom instruction, he started various industries. His plan was not to simply put students to work, but in giving them work, to teach them subjects in an applied manner, to provide them with solid knowledge of how to accomplish things with the latest advances in methods and to cultivate character and attitude. The opportunity to work also provided income for students and the school, but these benefits were integral parts of his view of a useful education, not sole purposes. Just as he had in growing up, he was continually striving to get into position as he was striving to posit or enact a way of being. His efforts to educate others parallel his efforts to educate himself.

In Washington's story, at least with the detail he provided, the completion phase of enactment is not notable. Partially, this is because one enactment was so intricately enwound with others that what is vivid is the sheer effort to make good on his mission. For example, over a period of nineteen years, forty buildings were erected. Thirty-six of those buildings were erected by staff and students. Partially, there is lack of emphasis because completion is overshadowed by the thrill, exhilaration, and meaningfulness of positing. No doubt Washington experienced satisfaction of some completion emotion such as this. And sometimes persons do experience completion much more strongly, but there is a tendency to stress the phase of enactment that matches one's phase of life. When in the positing phase of life, a person seems to stress the positing phase of enactment. So strong is this tendency at times that features of positioning are transformed into positing. For example,

Washington's efforts to raise funds for Tuskegee eventually transformed into a way to change attitudes and opinions to support education and the uplifting of people. One of his most significant actions was his electrifying address to the Atlanta Exposition.

When in the completion phase of life, a person tends to stress the completion phase of an enactment, and the sense of completion generally. For example, fifteen years after Tuskegee was started, Washington was offered an honorary degree from Harvard University. As he held the letter from the president of Harvard, tears filled his eyes:

> My whole former life—my life as a slave on the plantation, my work in the coal-mine, the times when I was without food and clothing, when I made my bed under a sidewalk, my struggles for an education, the trying days I had had at Tuskegee, days when I did not know where to turn for a dollar to continue the work there, the ostracism and sometimes oppression of my race—all this passed before me and nearly overcame me [1956, p. 209].

At this time Washington was still in the positing phase of life, but toward the end, experiences of completion seem to become stronger and more frequent, indicating a shift toward the final phase.

Some enactments reflect a life story better than others. There are no exact duplicates. Rather, there is a family resemblance among enactments, and between enactments and a life story. Some enactments seem like prototypes while others deviate in various ways. Circumstances always offer peculiar twists for enactment, but by observing enactments over a variety of circumstances, it becomes clear that persons move toward a prototypical form of enactment that also parallels their life stories.

Reenactment of Timeless Drama of the Human Spirit

There are no utterly unique positions, from the perspectives of persons who have them. Their positions emerged from dramatic roles within larger dramatic contexts that characterized what life was about. Individual constructions of the world are dramatic, and even for scholars who prefer to state their views in propositions, a more dramatic vision is apparent. As Pepper (1942) argued, one seeks a root metaphor to understand the world, and when that world involves the context for living, it is dramatic in nature. For example, a scientist might affirm a mechanistic metaphor, but this is not the metaphor he or she lives.

Recently, a psychiatrist with a mechanistic and materialistic worldview rather stridently proclaimed that soon we would diagnose depression with a throat culture. Naturally, it would be treated by drugs. And further, anyone who did not believe this was still living in the Dark Ages. While this psychiatrist's view would void any dramatic or human meaning to the experience of depression, putting it instead into the realm of material processes, it was quite clear that he was charging his own world with dramatic meaning. He was something of a valiant scientist courageously taking a stance among a pack of ignorant and superstitious primitives. Of course, this is one of our current myths, the myth of the scientist, although we are more apt to see this one as true while the myths of other ages are presumably false. Now it is this lived myth or drama that is under consideration here, not professed views like the mechanistic world picture.

Given the dramatic construction of reality a person has, there are a limited number of dramatic roles. For example, the psychiatrist included modern scientist in opposition to Dark Ages peasant. What this means is that the role one adopts has been played before. Certainly, one might fill the role with unique qualities or in unique circumstances, but as an enduring drama of human nature, it is a rather permanent role in human affairs, one that has been performed in the past and one that will be performed in the future. Exemplars of this role are a person's models, from whom he or she draws inspiration and toward whom he or she aspires. To enact one's role is to become consubstantial with these models in a timeless drama of human existence.

As with some other levels, persons vary in how much they stress this particular level of meaning. Some such as Liddy, have a number of models from the beginning. Others discover models as they go along. Sometimes the models are mentors and friends. Sometimes they are historical characters or even fictional characters. But the quality of meaning they involve for a person is similar. One is not an isolated actor, but a particular manifestation of the human spirit. One fuses with a quality of meaning that goes beyond self to a more timeless and general realm. In enactments, one makes a stand just as those who have come before and those who come after stood and will stand, and do honor to the part they have embraced since the world began.

While Steffens investigated corruption as the very fabric of a society that turns virtue to vice, he became increasingly pessimistic about reform. He had initiated reform, investigated reformers and reform movements, and all had ended in failure. His picture was adequate perhaps for conveying the nature of reality beyond illusions, but not yet broad and deep enough to understand how reforms could be successfully accomplished. It was at such a time that he reread the New Testament:

> The experience was an adventure so startling that I wanted everybody else to have it; I still recommend people to re-read the New Testament as I read it, without reverence, with feet up on a desk and a pipe in the mouth, as news. It is news. It made the stuff I was writing in the magazine, old stuff. All my stories of all the cities and States were one story; they had different names, dates, and location, but the essential facts were the same in them all, and these were all in the old story of Christ in the New Testament [1931, p. 525].

Even for Steffens, who had learned not to be too swept away in the disillusioning experiences of youth, the effect of a kindred spirit or fellow toiler is profound. Steffens did not emulate Christ like Saint Augustine, but he recognized Christ as someone who came before and saw what he saw and tried to offer a way out that ended on the cross. Steffens began to investigate much more the possibility of a way out, reform that would endure, gradually becoming weary of muckraking. The muck was endless and the latent purpose of his efforts rose to the foreground. What he really wanted was to restore a workable vision, ideals solidly grounded on facts. He wanted to restore the lost ideals of childhood with ideals that could endure, and that was partially what so excited Steffens about the New Testament.

Reenact the Nature of Life

This final level of meaning does not apply to everyone, but it applies enough to warrant consideration. If one believed that God is love, meaning that the ultimate nature of reality was love, then to enact love in drama is to reenact the very nature of things. In this sense, a person is at one with the deepest level of existence one can intuit, sense, or conceive. The paradigm case here, of course, is Jesus Christ. However, others ground their lives in the nature of life as well. For example, Carl Rogers (1963), therapist and personality theorist, viewed a self-actualizing tendency to be a characteristic of all life. It is what allowed him to empathize so strongly, for instance, with tiny palm trees struggling to live and grow on a rocklike extension into the Pacific Ocean, all the while being beaten and leveled almost flat by the powerful waves that surged upon them minute by minute for the whole of their existence. No doubt as well, when Rogers struggled to adapt, develop, and become more himself, he enacted the very nature of life. Similarly, Loren Eiseley (1975) was an outcast, doomed to journeying just as all living things have embarked on an evolutionary journey with no beginning and no end. For Eiseley, a striking feature of humans is an enormous and novel capacity to empathize, to heal in a way the breech among persons and living things. His life was punctuated by moments of often uncanny empathy. A bird, a fox, a dog, a skeleton, an escaped criminal who was shot by a posse, his father, his mother, his mentor, and so it goes, all cast as homeless journeyers with whom he identified. And as he journeyed himself, he was solitary but with the very spirit of all living things also cast adrift, eventually to be swallowed by time.

Certainly, some persons with a vocation do not mention this level of meaning. And some mention it in such a superficial way that it hardly seems to be a power in their lives. Yet for those who do not merely profess, but actually live the nature of life, at least in moments of central enactment, there is an added dimension of incredible depth. Such persons seem to be selfless and filled with self at the same time, perhaps since there is no longer a clear border between self and nonself. As Heraclitus (Wheelwright, 1959) stated regarding his inquiry into the nature of the world: "I have searched myself" (p. 19). And so it seems with these persons. To study and learn from them is a formidable task as a study of the person is so involved with a study of the nature of the world.

In summary, a central enactment has enormous symbolic sweep. The staggering expanse that opens in acting prototypically from a regnant position depends upon a unified orientation to living. No unrealistic requirements for unity are necessary or desirable here. Persons are more or less oriented; it is not a matter of either-or, but of more or less. Still, it is apparent that no such vehicle of meaning like a central enactment would be possible without reasonable unity. If the symbolic context or dramatic unit does not fit with practical circumstances, if the dramatic context is scattered, if the dramatic role does not fit the dramatic context, if there were no regnant position, if the regnant position did not emerge from one's life history in a direct and meaningful way, and so on, there would be no central enactment. A central enactment is a focus for a whole that in turn strengthens the unity of a whole in preparation for the next enactment.

Approached externally in the tradition of the "black box," the work of life in a vocation might be summed up by a few attributes. One might say that the work has intrinsic value rather than or in addition to extrinsic value. That is, one does not work just for a salary, for instance. Work is not solely a means, but an end in itself like an autotelic activity. Perhaps it is interesting, satisfying, and meaningful, and these qualifiers become like attributes of an object, just as we might say that gold is soft, malleable, and yellow. These statements would not be so much wholly wrong as just trivial and unilluminating. They convey little about what a vocation is and are so loose and abstract that one could not distinguish interesting work from the work of life. A person can leave interesting work for another job, but one cannot leave the work of life without a radical change in personhood. Whether Norman Vincent Peale went into the clergy, as he did, or went into clinical psychology, as Carl Rogers did, his work of life would be largely the same. Settings offer different contents, avenues of expansion, and ideals that color a work of life and influence it in many ways, but the work itself would merely be a variant of what it would be in another setting. With someone like Peale, it is difficult to conceive of his vocation outside the clergy, for the symbolic context and practical setting are so attuned, but communicating the joy of positive living and inspiring others to follow it through books, speeches, personal counseling, and example involve work that could be readily adapted to other settings. One can conceive of Peale in another setting, but one cannot conceive of Peale without his work of life.

Meaningful distinctions can be made between those who have a vocation and those who do not, and this will be attempted more fully in another chapter, but it requires subjects with meanings, persons with an inside rather than objects with attributes. There are few bald attributes that would not require extensive qualification. For example, is the work of life intrinsically or extrinsically rewarding? The only answer is both. Work is an end in itself and a means for other ends. Washington, for instance, found the building of his school to be tremendously meaningful work, but it was a practical means as well. The distinction simply does not fit well, nor do many others that are self-referenced. Washington (1956), for instance, phrases the peculiarity of self-reference in a way that is echoed in others. "I think the main thing is for one to grow to the point where he completely forgets himself; that is, to lose himself in a great cause. In proportion as one loses himself in this way, in the same degree does he get the highest happiness out of his work" (p. 128). For Richard Nixon (1962), political crises were his central enactments, and in these mountaintop experiences, one must lose oneself in order to find oneself. Personhood, as those with a vocation experience it, is self-giving (see Cochran, 1985, 1986) rather than self-centered. In the adoption of a metaphor of self, self-centeredness no longer apples well. One does not strive solely for oneself, but to realize the vision defined by a regnant gap. Indeed, many self-centered desires (e.g., I want X for myself) are regarded as threats to position and are actively combatted. However, for the present, let us skip these types of distinctions and concentrate instead upon the nature of a vocation, given the seven levels of meaning.

From the perspective of the person, his or her work has immediate and potentially great practical importance. Within the actual contexts and world in which a person lives, the practical effects are seen, in some sense, as vital for the well-being of others. Those others might include a neighborhood, a race, a region, a nation, the world, or some defined set of persons. One's work at any time is not bounded or isolated, but is seen as part of a series that is building. As one progresses, achieving more and more of what one set out to accomplish, old definitions of one's aim might appear too small and more expanded aims take its place. A vocation, if it is in the way of being successful, is experienced as progressing, developing, and expanding. Part of that progression and expansion is complemented by a sense of inward progression and expansion. Over and over in diverse contexts, one exercises mastery of one's dramatic role in life and validates one's worth as a powerful human agent regarding the work of life. In the work of a vocation, one enacts a dramatic position, infusing one's being with vitality and diffusing it without. One feels alive, at home, at one with oneself. There is a sense of inevitability to a vocation, as if one is destined for the role adopted. Partially, this sense of inevitability emerges from the exactness with which a central enactment reflects one's life story, relating somewhat like microcosm to macrocosm. The unifying fit of abilities, inspiration, reality building, and so on, that characterize positioning seem realized in a vocation, more naturally and effortlessly.

In reflecting on one's work of life and implicit in these enactments, a person is aware of a more timeless drama. What one does, avows, stands for, is not unique, but an essential part of the larger drama of human nature. Others have played the part, given themselves to the cause, and now it is one's own turn to take a stand in life and do what can be done. For some, this identification is even stronger. In a central enactment, one reenacts the very nature of the world. In this way, the personal is elevated to the cosmic and one's vocation is a particular expression of a universal.

Positioning

In lives, there are a wide variety of threats that might dislodge one from position or hinder the possibility of enacting position. When in position, a person is apt to experience a wide range of generally positive emotions or feelings such as involvement, enthusiasm, and exhilaration. When out of position for a period of time, a person is apt to experience restlessness, irritation, and deflation. One feels off-course. Certainly, circumstances are not always favorable for central enactments, leading to various deviations from prototype. However, of concern here are threats of more potency, capable of throwing one out of position, or at least capable of making one feel dislodged.

As argued elsewhere (Cochran, 1985), problems can be divided into two general categories. A problem is a departure if one is forced, in some way, to depart from position, due to circumstances or due to rival stances that are alive in a person (but not part of his or her position). For example, Peale was forced from position when speaking before an audience that did not like him (or so he thought). As another example, Saint Augustine (1961) was often forced from his fledgling position by carnal stances or desires. He could hardly maintain fervent piety when lust cloaked him from head to toe. A problem is an intrinsic upshot or outcome if it, in some way, arises from one's own position. For example, religion's call to love others might make one vulnerable to manipulation by others, giving rise to guardedness that hinders love of others. The major difference between these broad, overlapping categories is that the solution for an extrinsic departure does not necessarily require a change of position. The solution to an intrinsic consequence does require change.

Extrinsic Departures

When faced with a setting, influence, or event that threatens position, a person basically has three strategies. One can search for or create an appropriate setting. For example, Conrad Hilton was thirty years old before he became a hotel owner and knew that this form of business was right for him. It required considerable exploration and good fortune to finally achieve the right circumstances for central enactment. One can exclude, avoid, or get out of inappropriate situations. For example, one of Hilton's vulnerabilities as well as strengths was romanticism. He married Zsa Zsa Gabor who apparently spent her days pampering and primping herself, devoting attention largely to appearance and social occasions. For Hilton, as the romance wore thin, she came to represent an expensive oddity in his life that did not fit. She did not share in his life of faith and work, seeming more to be an unfathomable opposite. They were eventually divorced. Last, one can symbolically encompass and transform a situation from an inappropriate to an appropriate setting. For example, Washington had to depend upon people for financial support. Tuskegee needed money to grow and Washington had to approach a good many rich people and groups for donations, what some might construe as begging. By bringing the issue to the fore, Washington shows that he was quite aware of how his behavior might be viewed, but he could not continue if he viewed it in this way. On the contrary, he viewed himself as an agent for doing their work, providing these people with an opportunity to help a worthy cause. If they had the sense to earn a great deal of money, he reasoned, they have the sense to know how to give it away for the most worthy of projects. Given this construction, he was free to do his full duty in presenting the cause of education and in seeing that the money was well-used. More than one donor expressed appreciation, gratitude, and even a sense of privilege in being able to contribute to and share in the work of Tuskegee Institute. In supporting Tuskegee, they were supporting Washington's mission in life, and he strove very hard to fulfill their faith in him.

In lives, there are all manner of difficulties. In the phase of positing, one might search, exclude, and transform to create more unity in life, to bridge threatening divisions, or to enhance vitality, but what ultimately is at stake is a life's work. Until one is able to act centrally, being is separated from doing. For some persons, their vocation was never allowed to fully develop.

Gordon Liddy (1980) was never able to find an appropriate setting for the enactment of a warrior. He had shaped himself for battle, but he was never actually in one. Frustrated during the Korean war, he served his time in a stateside unit. Upon graduation from law school, he entered the FBI. Certainly, being an FBI agent is close, but it really is not a warrior in battle. When he was promoted to the rear echelon, he was promoted away from the possibility of a central enactment. He joined his father's law practice, but this did not work out. He became a prosecutor and construed his role in court as analogous to combat. With the country approaching crisis during the Viet Nam war, he entered politics and this led to an appointment in the federal government where he became involved in the Watergate crisis. If Liddy had developed in a way that reflected others with a vocation, he would have initially engaged in combat, and arisen from this experience as a leader. The fuller transformation of his early life would be to fearlessly and strongly lead a disheartened people from despair and weakness to power. He only accomplished this once, and then only temporarily, at Danbury Prison. Liddy seemed forever to be enacting position in border line circumstances or circumstances that had little meaning or did not build. Often his experiences consequently take on the flavor of a game of "chicken" rather than a central enactment with more enduring importance. This, of course, does not mean that he did not act constructively or contribute in his various jobs. Rather, he simply did not achieve favorable circumstances for his work and it did not build, at least as yet, into a life work. Behind the shifting circumstances is always, it seems, a nobler man, an explosive potential, a prospect for great deeds that have yet come to pass, never fully showed itself in action and never developed fully through action.

If Liddy struggled in unfavorable circumstances, Emily Carr (1966), the great Canadian painter, was overwhelmed by circumstance. Her life as an artist was put on hold for nearly twenty years. Incompletion for Carr was forceful obedience to convention and pretense. She was suffocated by the superficiality of outward show. Her father was stern and dictatorial, demanding absolute obedience and adoration. Carr rebelled as much as she could, becoming the contrary member of the home, subject to scolding and other forms of punishment. At age twelve, her mother died. At age fourteen, her father died, leaving her to the stern discipline of her oldest sister, who once whipped her until she fainted. In contrast to this tyranny of hypocritical decorum, Carr experienced a depth, sacredness, and beauty in the forest. She had also drawn since infancy, and when she combined art with the sacred woods she wished to express, her direction became fixed. Through art schools in San Francisco, London, France, and her own experiments, she sought a way to express the meaning of the forests, totems, and other scenes that so contrasted with the tiny pieties that continually threatened to enclose her. At forty years of age, she felt that she was beginning to achieve the expressions she wished, but her work was ridiculed and parents would not send their children to her art classes. Unable to support herself through art, she had to plan and it is here that she entered her years of misery.

The family estate was divided into lots, one for each sister. On her lot, Carr decided to build an apartment house. Victoria, British Columbia, was booming and with the shortage of housing, rents were high, but problems began immediately (Carr, 1967). Her plan for the house was "mutilated" by the dictatorial architect she consulted. His failure to comply with local bylaws cost her hundreds of dollars to correct, and she fell into debt. With World War I beginning, Victoria slumped. Rents came drastically down and taxes rose. The cost of living also rose. She had to supplement her income by pottery and weaving, and later, by raising bobtail sheepdogs. Ideally, being a landlady would give her time to paint. She had three apartments to rent and one for herself that included a big studio. However, she rarely had time. The work involved keeping the furnace going, tending her garden, and cleaning up after tenants left apartments in unbelievable messes; simply being exposed to tenant demands was consuming. She even rented her studio. During this time, she refused to paint pictures that would sell (essentially painted photographs), and could not give much time to paintings that would not sell. She was stuck catering to and struggling with renters who laughed at her and laughed at her work. In many ways, it was a twenty-year plunge back into the suffocating hypocrisy and propriety from which she had originally escaped. The agony, belittlement, and irritation seemed continual, and she seemed to accentuate her contrariness.

Under her older sister's rule in youth, she was regarded as the disturbing member. Others were "prim, orthodox, religious" (1966, p. 15). Home was dictatorial, hard, and she received the whip daily for her insubordinations. She could not or would not engage in sham, treating hypocrisy as piety, reacting to external form rather than to the underlying reality. "I would not sham, pretending that we were a nest of doves, knowing well that in our home bitterness and resentment writhed" (1966, p. 15). While differing in characters, setting, and Carr's own activeness and capability, her apartment house was like a return to the home of her older sister. There, renters tried to dictate to her, use her, and punish her. Out of place with the hypocritical airs of propriety, Carr was again the disturbing element for wanting such things as rents paid, rooms cleaned, pets cared for, and disturbing noise curtailed. In the stage of positing, when persons slide backward, it does not appear to be to an unfamiliar condition. Although her role as a landlady was novel and awkward, Carr understood the situation very well. Part of what is at stake in positioning, then, is not just a central enactment, but a return to an original state of incompletion. The major difference is that a person knows the direction out. Carr knew that she must return to her painting somehow, and she eventually did. With the support of a new school of Ontario artists, Carr emerged from what she termed the "house of all sorts" able to finally convey in painting the meaning of totems, of the deep northern woods, of shores and churches. Initially, her painting suggested majestic and mysterious ascents (as in *Big Raven*, 1928) and desolation amid approaching grandeur (as in *Vanquished*, 1928), and then she turned to the spiritual enchantment of the forests.

Generally or specifically, explicitly or implicitly, the movement toward prototypical rather than tangential enactment seems pervasive. Stall it in one way and it creeps out in another. If severe or prolonged setbacks occur, the person moves between an earlier drama of incompletion and an emergent drama of vocation. Certainly, there is no exact repetition. Deviant or contrasting settings cultivate elaboration or expansion more than refinement, but a family resemblance there appears to be, even in trauma. For example, C. S. Lewis (1963) married late in life, and his marriage was a belated experience of virtual paradise. Then his wife died painfully from cancer, and all too slowly. In his diary of grief, the devoted Christian regards God as a cosmic sadist, a being who "hurts us beyond our worst fears and beyond all we can imagine" (p. 31). Reality is cruel and unbearable. Earlier, Lewis (1959) had described his mother's death in a similar way. At age ten, alienated from father, Lewis and his brother came to rely exclusively "on each other for all that made life bearable" (p. 21), "two frightened urchins huddled for warmth in a bleak world" (p. 21). Security was gone. The possibility of enduring happiness was gone.

The children were enrolled in Wynyard School from 1908 to 1910. It was a boarding school run by Reverend Robert Capron, whom Lewis referred to as Oldie. He referred to the school as a concentration camp, a description that is not far off (Green & Hopper, 1976). Meaningless repetition was the daily work and terror was the atmosphere. Caning and other forms of punishment were incessant, as Oldie apparently descended into madness. In one incident, for example, he would run the length of a room to deliver each stroke of the cane.

Cruelty, torture, bleakness were contrasted with Lewis's experience of joy, connected usually with myths and with Christianity. In his grief, following the death of his wife, Lewis seemed to pivot from the drama of joy back to that of bleakness from which it arose. Yet, with seeming inevitability, he began to cycle back again. Later in his diary of grief, he comments that god made him realize that his "temple was a house of cards" (p. 61) by knocking it down. Slowly, his relation to God changes back as his vision of God changes back. Lewis never fully recovered from this trauma late in life, or perhaps I should say, he died before he fully recovered, if such a recovery is possible. In any case, his diary of the experience shows the descent into incompletion and the slow movement back. God as a cosmic version of Oldie was not a drama he could sustain; his life had been directed too long toward it opposite.

And so it seems with persons in this phase of life. They can be delayed, shocked, forced into poor circumstances, put through incredible hardship, and still they strive back. During incompletion, they were stuck. But during positing, they seem scarcely able to stay stuck. Partially, this perpetual movement toward central enactment is probably because the persons investigated are rather exemplary as human agents, manifesting De Charm's (1968) qualities of an origin quite strongly. However, partially too, they perhaps can do no other, so broad and unified is the way they endow meaning that there is but one real direction in life.

Intrinsic Outcomes

Over the phase of positing, an orientation vigorously develops. Dramatic units are elaborated, refined, and composed. One's position is shaped further and perhaps changed not into another position but into a transformation of one's established position. If change or development is coherent, there is such smoothness of extension that it is scarcely noticed. For example, after graduation from Hampton, Washington returned home to teach in the school he first attended. He was directly attempting to uplift persons through providing an education. Later at Tuskegee, his efforts were more indirect. He continued to teach and to be involved with students, but his major role was to build an institution. Later, this expanded to cultivating support for education in fund raising and speeches. Washington struggled to educate himself. Then he devoted his life to educating others, but in quite diverse ways. He was a teacher, educational administrator, innovator in educational practices, fund raiser, public figure, and so on.

The transitions were so fluid in Washington's life that they are scarcely recognized as transitions. This diversity is so composed and focused that one retains an immense sense of unity, overlooking perhaps the immense differences involved in the various roles he performed. However, it could have been otherwise, and indeed, it is apt to be common to falter. Fluid development does not just happen. As one achieves success and goals expand, adjustments have to be made. Sometimes a person can lose his or her way, requiring a major effort to get back on course. And sometimes, one meets intrinsic schisms that are capable of undermining position, and consequently, of destroying a sense of vocation. There are no perfect positions. Each is vulnerable in various ways, and some more so than others.

At nearly the height of his career, Lincoln Steffens began to wonder if muckraking, exposure of corruption, was useless. He had muckraked cities, states, institutions, management, and labor, and the country generally. Initially, he wanted to disillusion himself to gain an accurate picture of reality. Then he wanted to disillusion others. Only by an accurate picture, he thought, would persons have the motivation and clarity of vision to make lasting changes. But in his work, he found that the corrupt bosses were more honest and honorable than the reformers who backtracked when their interests were affected by reform. In his first experience with muckraking and reform, he commented that "victory was defeat for me" (p. 256). He did not find bosses to be evil men, but rather to be outstanding men, natural leaders of considerable strength. Gradually, he began to think that persons were not at fault, but the system in which they existed. Reform efforts always seemed to fail, with the heroic leader of reform downfallen and the system restored. And bosses continually told Steffens they acted from compulsion, not desire. For example, in order to have a railway that worked, one had to buy privilege or corrupt the government. His work seemed useless, and Steffens now wanted to stop muckraking. He could not continue in the same way, and here his life took a decisive turn.

No doubt, there are many reasons why Steffens's life reached such an impasse. For instance, his exposures became so repetitive that challenge diminished. However the most prominent reason seems to be that Steffens's way of seeing, his very position, involved a fatal flaw. He sought in corruption to disillusion himself, but this is not the same as straight seeing or an accurate picturing. He had virtually equated the two through much of his life, and it seems inevitable that one who continually seeks to be disillusioned will experience disillusionment. He sought muck, and not only is such a one-sided diet depressing after fascination has dwindled, but it involves a stress that is most apt to involve hopelessness. Or from another angle, in Steffens's stress upon the antiheroic qualities of persons caught in a determining environment, of persons merely as a product of environment, he erodes any basis for expecting persons to be self-determining or capable of change. So thoroughly are his characters ensnared in the muck of reality that he himself is ensnared and his vocation comes to appear as futile, if not a disillusionment.

Steffens was a naturalist, as that term is used in literature, and naturalism as a way of seeing and standing offers special problems generally. For example, as Burke (1969) has illustrated, to indict the brutalizing working conditions of, say, a factory, one must portray the brutalizing effect on persons. They become brutes, but when they become so, they scarcely look with saving. The more the thesis is established, the less there appears for one to do about it, or to want to do about it. Steffens was one of the most courageous, honest, and exacting naturalists who ever lived, so dauntless in following his investigations that even Upton Sinclair took on shades of romanticism (pp. 604–5), yet his position was vulnerable, like all positions, and he ended up at least temporarily out of position.

At a turning point, there are a number of models of options. Steffens could descend into his nightmare of a cynical professional. He could engage in yellow journalism, like other muckrakers, evoking the thrill of scandal without thought, without following through on implications. "Comfortable mental peace was their form of death" (p. 632). He could flee into a "settled creed" in order to have something to believe. Steffens rejected all these options. He would rather take the agony of what was real rather than escapist fantasy, even though he had come to an impossible situation.

Steffens resigned his job at the *American Magazine,* and became a free-lance reporter until he felt forced to rake muck. He quit again, retiring to New York, and then became a part-time editor for *Everybody's Magazine.* Steffens altered his situation, trying to gain distance and perspective. He would claim to be through with muckraking, then he would return to investigate Wall Street, for instance, where he found that "while men cried aloud for liberty they called secretly for a boss" (p. 590). He tried bringing in fresh talent (nonprofessional) such as Walter Lippmann, whom he recruited from Harvard. They muckraked together a little and at one point diagramed the chain of corruption in a town for a group before they had investigated, so certain was Steffens of the pattern. No one challenged the diagram. Upon invitation, he muckraked Boston, trying to establish a basis for reform. He recruited a "boss" and his organization to reform themselves. At the invitation of an owner, he tried to get workers to take control of the business, and they would not. The futility of his efforts was comic, and even before his efforts at reform, he laughed in anticipation. He experimented with philanthropy, wondering how to give money away without harming those he gave it to. He experimented with education at Harvard and experimented with himself to quench his hatreds and rid himself of prejudice to regain a mental balance. Over and over, he involved and withdrew himself, trying to extricate himself from the hopelessness of his situation. Through laughter (of the ironic sort), experimentation, perspective-taking, and floating, he searched for a way out. When his wife died, Steffens was free to roam, and roam he did in search of renewal. His life's work was dying in disillusionment and Steffens sought a basis for hope.

The story of Steffens's renewal would take too much space here. For a while he believed that revolution was the only answer and he went abroad, studying the Mexican and Russian revolutions firsthand. He married a young woman, had a child, and spent a few happy years in domestic retreat. However, what came from this trip abroad was a new way of seeing and thinking, one that emerged from his old position as naturally as Washington's administration emerged from teaching, and one that was hopeful, giving his life an enduring meaning. He came to see events and practices not as evidence of corruption or reform, but as experiments that led to gradual improvement. For example, President Hoover called together big businessmen to establish a national policy. Of course, this meant that government would partially represent big business interests. What was evidence of corruption, privilege, and misrepresentation in one era becomes accepted practice in the next!

From Steffens's old standpoint, there would have been considerable muck to rake. From his new standpoint, it was an open experiment. With this attitude, he began to notice many experiments, many signs of improvement that he had not noticed before. The experience had the shock of an earthquake, to use Steffens's metaphor. His life had not been futile. On the contrary, his work had generated an immense variety of social experiments. Most of his life, he had regarded himself as a scientist, much more than a muckraker, and it was late in life that he fully realized the meaning of a scientist and what it meant in his life.

Summary

The work of life depends upon a unifying basis of existence, involving being and acting. The attainment of personhood involves the adoption of a regnant position or root metaphor that centers a composition of stances or ways of being. Position is anchored in an intelligible and coherent family of dramatic units centered by a regnant drama. The unity of position is a unity of incompletion requiring direction to fulfill it. This gap between is and ought to be bounds a central enactment, which is the work of life. This work or vocation in life is a realization of one's being as a person and an enactment of a part in a dramatic vision of the world.

From a realist's view of science (Manicas & Secord, 1983), a position is a powerful particular (Harré, 1974), a real existent that is a formal cause of enactment. In Harré's example, a plan is a synchronic structure that is unfolded over time in a diachronic flow. In the study of lives, one must work backward. There are numerous diachronic flows or enactments. Similarly, one might observe numerous performances of Mozart's *The Magic Flute*, ranging from unskilled practices to polished productions of great musicians. The situation is analogous to a variety of diverse uses of a concept. From these performances, one could try to piece together the original composition that is the formal cause of the performances. The major difference is that we already have Mozart's composition, while in lives we do not have the composition of being. We must construct it.

Unlike other kinds of causes such as efficient causality, which in modern neopositivism involves external triggers or activators, a formal cause is concerned with form, the shape of something. The form of a central enactment depends upon the structure of a person's regnant position and composition of being. However, it must be unfolded in actual circumstances with demands of their own, giving rise to deviations and alterations, a person's efforts to reposition himself or herself. A person presses toward central enactment, toward an unfoldment of being in enaction, but it is not necessarily easy to accomplish.

5 Phases of Life in Work

Persons, whether ready or not, are required to work. A person might begin working during any of the phases of life. Indeed, a person might spend all or most of his or her career in incompletion, for instance. How does this matter? The aim of this chapter is to provide illustrative cases of persons who work while in different phases of life. By describing their lives and noting rather salient differences in the meaning of work, one can appreciate the significance of a vocation more clearly by the sheer contrast provided. Some of the lives are extreme, to say the least, but the very extremity of them will, I hope, make the contrast more understandable. There is no tacit assumption, however, that only those in a vocation can lead a happy life. Such is not the case. A person with a vocation might not be happy due to circumstances and the nature of the mission, but he or she knows what would make life fraught with meaning if one could but pursue the work fully. A person without a vocation might achieve happiness in other ways, but the deep satisfaction of life's work is denied them in whole or in part.

Incompletion in Work

There is no necessary reason why a person must ever develop past the phase of incompletion. Indeed, some or possibly even many persons spend their entire lives overwhelmed by circumstance, caught in an existential trap where hopes are rampant and unrealized. In literature, Weston (1970) regards this kind of person as a negative hero. The plot does not depend upon the hero's struggle to fulfill a powerful desire but upon the force of events that happen to a person. The negative hero is rendered passive by circumstances, hoping to avoid the worst and escape his or her fate. While some are nearly beyond hope, others are quite active in staving off the encirclement of circumstance. They are not necessarily passive persons, but passive in a critical way for the situation they are in. Seldom does hope become a definite intention that guides action. One might yearn to

123

be free, but there is little positive conception of what one would then be free to do. Usually in novels, the negative hero is used to explore the scope and variations of feelings that abound in an existential trap. Perhaps in life, a person might come to accept his or her fate with some tranquility, but in the cases I have studied, tranquility stems mostly from a respite from the forces of circumstance. As circumstances worsen, they once more are apt to become a cauldron of frustrated yearnings and hopes.

In Terkel's (1975) book, *Working*, there are several instances, one of which has been discussed more fully in Cochran (1985). In life stories, one of the most appalling examples is the life of Frances Farmer (1973), who escaped only briefly near the end of her life. The horror of her life would be difficult to describe briefly and I shall not attempt it here. Rather, a summary of events for the points I wish to make will be sufficient. With a weak father who was absent most of the time, home was governed by the mother. Farmer's mother was incredibly fierce, strong willed, domineering, and selfish. From the cradle, Farmer was dominated and manipulated. Safety lay in doing and being what mother wanted. Outside that narrow zone was danger. Apparently oblivious to the degenerate conditions at home, the mother sought publicity through one "crackpot" scheme after the other (e.g., trying to breed a red, white, and blue chicken to express her patriotism during World War I), generating commotion and embarrassment. Her manner was often wild and overwrought, excessive in nearly everything she set her mind to. Although Farmer developed many of her mother's qualities, she had less scope for them, yoked as she was to her mother's will.

During high school, her escape from family tumult was reading. She lived in the world of books, trying to ignore or shut the other reality out, but it proved impossible. There were only lulls between crises. Farmer won an essay contest with an essay that questioned the existence of God, for which she was castigated in churches, newspapers, and her school, but she was defenseless against the magnitude of her mother's public counterattack which had all the circus zeal of the early publicity attempts. And the next year, mother launched a public campaign to divorce her husband, reaching a peak when she went to his office and shot at him with blank bullets, while he hid under his desk. Defiance of mother could bring a serious impulsive attempt to kill (she once threw a pair of scissors at Frances that struck right beside her face) or an outlandish public campaign designed to make one wish one were dead.

Meanwhile, aspiring to be a writer, Farmer entered the University of Washington, later transferring into drama where she excelled. Also, for the first time in her life, she felt keenly alive. To continue after graduation, she had to get to New York. Through an arrangement of her drama professor, she won a trip to Russia from a communist newspaper, which would land her in New York on her return. Just as her mother launched a public campaign against father, mother now launched a vicious campaign against the daughter, gathering such flattering headlines as "Mother Uncovers Red Vice Ring" (p. 66). Unable to get into the inner circle of dramatic performers in New York, she secured a contract in Hollywood. Even as she rose to stardom, she loathed it. From her perspective, she escaped her mother's clutches only to receive a similar kind of experience in movies. Her life was not her own. She became even more biting and uncooperative, not allowing anyone to get very close to her.

From the time she joined a drama group in the university to her fall from Hollywood, a period of about ten years, she appeared to be seeking a protective refuge, a place where she belonged, a contrast to the world she knew. Mother's world was ruthless, loveless, scheming, and manipulating. In this world, Farmer was fearful, mistrustful, and vulnerable. Her strength in this world, so she thought, was anger that ranged from uncontrolled rage to a daily round of sarcasm and cynicism. The embryonic world of her drama teacher was, by contrast, real, dedicated, and supportive. There were the ideals of theater to believe in, skills to perfect, and a second family really to which she could belong. In one sense, she was no different than Anthony Trollope who also entered work during the phase of incompletion. In his first position as a postal clerk, he was regarded as useless and was not given much of a chance. He essentially re-created and reexperienced the degradation of his pariah existence in schools. However, he did find a more favorable position, one he was ready for. Within a year, he was regarded as a solid public servant and he was firmly launched into positioning. However, Farmer never found her setting from which she could grow.

In the midst of her "humiliating" experiences in Hollywood, she married. There was no particular reason for marriage except that the man was the only partially compatible element there, but he was uninteresting and unable to alleviate the growing pressures. She became depressed. After starring in a series of movies, she returned to New York, and this time she was welcomed into the group. While she did perform one meaningful role in a theater production, she was soundly exploited and abused. It was not the ideal alternative she had hoped for and she returned to Hollywood. There, the cycle of perceived domination or manipulation and hostile rebellion escalated, to a point of no return. Due to her mother's efforts, Farmer was deemed mentally incompetent and mother was appointed legal guardian. Although bizarre, the actions that landed her in trouble were rather subdued versions of her mother's extreme outbursts. The difference between Trollope's early misadventures and Farmer's aggressions is that Farmer's were magnified into consequences from which there was no escape.

Mother cared nothing for what Farmer wanted. Mother wanted Farmer to be a Hollywood star, a position that mother could take advantage of in money and, above all, in publicity. She held virtual life-and-death control over Farmer, who had no civil rights and could be committed to an asylum at will, yet Farmer continued her rebellion. She spent eight years in mental institutions, undergoing humiliations, degradations, exploitations, and horrors she could never have conceived of. Her very aggressiveness turned against her, singling her out for ill treatment and becoming an incontrovertible indication of madness. Through hydro therapy (restrained in a tub through which icy water flows, once for ten hours), violence, being chained, living nude in a pen with other nude women, being forced to eat her own excrement, and so on, she strove merely to survive. When not committed to an institution, she was forced to be like a lap dog for mother, always threatening to have her committed for keeps. Toward the end, mother and father needed her for care in old age and had her released. Apparently enjoying their power, she had to beg on her knees not to be sent back, and spent her days in constant work—cleaning up, fixing meals, and generally being subject to incessant demands and threats from her parents. Reality was the cage from which one might escape primarily by guile and solitude, but from which there was no real escape, only temporary reprieves.

Enough has been conveyed to give the general flavor of her life, her fight against total subjugation, first from mother and later through extensions of mother such as mental asylums, where she learned what total, merciless, unremitting terror really was. It is customary in psychology to look for some atomistic reduction to explain her difficulties. For example, her drinking exacerbated difficulties. Her ability to split off mentally as if she were a disembodied observer watching herself perform might be made much of. However, there is no isolated factor that even approaches plausibility. Rather, there is a whole dramatic unit that developed and enclosed. If there were no active mother force controlling the scene, she would be sensitive to and highlight what was available. Partially, for instance, the Hollywood atmosphere of the time might have been manipulative. But partially, Farmer was set to endow her circumstances with this kind of dramatic force and to provoke it through her own behavior. Only much later could she discern her contribution, but by then, life was nearly over. Meanwhile, things happened to her, so much in excess of what she provoked. She misjudged the evil power of her mother and her replicas, and that judgment was fateful.

Farmer's life might be excessive as a portrayal of incompletion in later life, but it is not different in nature. Whether the cage is malevolent or benevolent, it is still a cage. Some of the major differences between Farmer and one with a vocation would include the following. Farmer was unable to formulate a way out or cultivate a drama of salvation (although she found a kind of peace in her last few years through the friendship of an extraordinary family). Certainly, she imagined an alternative in serious drama and in belonging to a dedicated group, but her involvement was disillusioning and the alternative never developed. There was no model to follow, no end in view. Consequently, constraints appeared not as obstacles to get around in struggling to achieve a goal, but as continual oppressions to rebel against. There was little development of agency of De Charms's personal causation, no effort to shape her being as in positioning. Work (in theater, not movies, which she scorned) did not emerge from her life, giving it a meaningful direction. Rather, it was a respite, an enlivenment, a foretaste that did not develop. And work never pointed beyond herself. The functions of repetition were too curtailed.

As an illustration, the value of the comparison is that it offers such a strong contrast to those who pursue a vocation. Emily Carr resembles Farmer, at least during her occupation as a landlady, but Carr always knew what she wanted even if it were out of reach at the time. Such a striking case does not allow subtle distinctions to be made, but it does confirm by glaring contrast the major qualities of those with a vocation in life. The composition of life into a meaningful whole that can be enacted seems so inevitable in positive cases, but negative cases serve as a trenchant reminder that inevitability is an illusion. Things do not necessarily have to turn out very well, and yet in the very bleakness of existence, of one's future, which Farmer once described as an "open crematorium" (p. 51), there is a possible quickening of spirit that might not be easily found in another kind of life. Toward the end, Farmer transcended incompletion. She came to love selflessly, to find a joy in the life around her, and to sense God in the world. When she looked back, there was no work of life. There were only efforts to find a way out. Even her resurgence of spirit was cut short by cancer, and did not flower as it might, but she did leave a searing autobiography that she hoped would be of benefit to others, particularly those who are trapped as she was. In the last years, she did find a way out and it was partially for this reason that her book was written.

If some lives of incompletion are eventually ennobling, others descend into unbelievable degeneracy. Carl Panzram (Gaddis & Long, 1970) lived a cycle of crime and punishment. It is difficult to know which arose first, so intimate were they in growing up and in his movements in and out of prison. From Panzram's perspective, he was punished and punishment made him hate, yearn for revenge, which he took out on other persons and property. Punishment was extremely harsh, ranging from a whipping post to an electrical torture called the Humming Bird. His reactions increased in severity as well, ranging from burning buildings to killing persons. "I have confessed twenty-one different cold-blooded, pre-meditated murders, hundreds of cases of arson, burglaries, robberies, rapes and other crimes" (p. 251). He would make plans in prison about how to kill the most persons with the least risk. Such a life must seem odd in a book on vocation, but the reason for including Panzram is that he claimed to have a vocation of sorts and it was initially difficult to see how his worked differed from those who really have a vocation. Asked by a guard what his racket was, Panzram responded, "What I do is I reform people" (p. 144). To this he later added that the only way to reform people was to murder them. Another time, he responded that he was a fellow who "goes around doing people good" (p. 214) and the good he does is putting them out of their misery.

Committed to the Minnesota State Training School at age twelve, the aim of the institute was to reform character and inculcate religion. This the officials attempted largely through harsh punishment, severe discipline, and what Panzram perceived as phony pieties about loving Jesus and being a good boy. From inmates, he learned about sodomy, theft, arson, and so on. When Panzram later framed murder as reform, he was of course partially being ironic, but not entirely. From his multitude of rotten experiences, he believed the human race was no good, deserving of extermination. He hated everyone. No one acted except when it was to their advantage. There is no such thing as principle. There is no morality. Force makes right. Those who have the power are right, and life is an endless struggle to either have power or to avoid the power of others. From this perspective, no one could be trusted. Everyone was to be despised. And the more he was punished, the more he seethed with hatred and resolved to have his revenge, if not on those who abused him, then on those whom he could reach. He would give them the reform he had received. The question is why Panzram's reform efforts are not a work of life, a vocation. Without doubt, Panzram was a monster and what he did as well as what was done to him were monstrous, but does this matter regarding a vocation? Must a vocation be constructive, at least in intent?

Panzram's life is like a dark mockery of vocation in its similarity, but there are striking differences. For instance, he assumed no responsibility for murdering persons, for arson, or anything else. The blame was laid on those who had abused him, made him what he was. Never did he assume responsibility for himself or his life. It was all experienced as reaction rather than enaction. He was but a pawn of circumstance. He accepted the world as he found it, refusing to admit of any other possibility. This means that he never conceived of a solution to his problem of existence, never sought a way out, never shaped his being in positioning, and never fully became a person (never gave himself to a root metaphor to become inwardly composed). Except for his hatred and "mean disposition," his actions were not really an enactment of a full position he had formed, but of a reaction to brutality he experienced and did not assume responsibility for. Vengeance was not a way out, not a solution; it was simply a retaliation that made him feel good apparently. True to his dramatic vision of life, Panzram was selfish, self-centered rather than self-giving. Nothing extended beyond himself, and if anyone did something for him, it would be suspect. There was no empathy, perhaps stifled by his hate and mistrust.

Of more significance, however, Panzram's position is not substantial. For example, if the world is devoid of morality, and might makes it right, what basis is there for hate? Or if we are just products of environment with no responsibility, why hold others responsible for one's own lot in life? Most of Panzram's assertions presuppose another world rife with morals, values, and principles beyond sensory pleasure and pain, one that applies to others but apparently not to himself. Of course, if he really believed that we are all products of environment, he would have a basis for empathy or commonality with others, yet he had little that was evident. In this curious insubstantiality of position is the major difference between Panzram and those with a vocation.

For those with vocation, personhood is enacted in work. Initially, one sees good by contrast with one's own situation. For example, Trollope imagined a man of distinction in contrast to a pariah. The major problem is that one is not yet that which was envisioned. Thus, persons begin to shape themselves in anticipation of becoming a man of distinction, an educated person, a reformer, or whatever. The position one seeks is constructed, imagined, and later adopted in a culminating experience. With the adoption and perhaps success of enactment, vocation is clarified often as a way to lift up persons from the same kind of condition one was originally in. For example, Trollope preached character and its reward in his novels, the very thing he though he lacked. Menuhin wanted to move persons as he was moved. Washington wanted to lift up his people through education as he was lifted. Liddy, if he had ever been able to position himself, wanted to lead the fearful and weak to a position of strength. Not all manifest this symmetry, but all gave themselves to some cause or ideal that transcended personal interests. And for them, the position they attained and the work they did were good. As a good, they could adopt and avow.

Panzram differs in almost every way. Rather than conceive of a good in contrast to his own situation, he denied it. He did not envision a position he could strive to attain. Rather he accepted a position as it was in incompletion. Never could he avow the being he was, for one cannot avow a negative. If a position in life is regarded negatively, one is alienated from it rather than united to it. One can only accept and excuse, but not avow. Indeed, Panzram ended in self-hatred. His position scarcely rises above *lex talonis*, an eye for an eye, a tooth for a tooth. What he added to position has little substance of its own. Rather, it is in service of hatred. For example, might makes right is tacitly denied by his reaction to abuse but affirmed as a basis of position. It does little more than justify rather than frame action. In contrast, for instance, Washington believed that nothing comes without hard effort and his life manifested this constituent of position at every turn. Much of Panzram's professed position is a disguise for his enormous hatred and desire for revenge, to do to innocents what had been done to him. Due to the consistency he showed, he had a regnant position or became a unified person, however stunted, but his constitution as a person is deceptive and quite different than the formation in others. Others build from incompletion; Panzram built on incompletion. Others take over; Panzram was taken over.

Positioning in Work

During positioning, a person is concerned with becoming. One arises from incompletion with a greater sense of agency and some glimmerings of a way out. For some, much seems clear and definite, but this is not quite the case. Rather, there is perhaps one thing that is clear and definite, and this is a great advantage. For example, Menuhin emerged with a quite definite vision of playing the violin. However, he was as groping as everyone else on just what would be involved in playing. One of his major challenges was to augment his technical proficiency with an intangible spirit that infused his performance. It required a way of being and Menuhin sought to cultivate it through experience, through entering the minds of master composers in their work, through his mentors, through themes of his life (e.g., the reckless abandon of a Cherkessian warrior), and so on. Similarly, Washington sought to become educated, but his vision of education underwent considerable change. In positioning, little is fixed and certain. One finds anchors of clarity to pursue that in turn foster revised anchors to pursue. In such a period of development, any clear and definite goal is a great assistance. However, there are also some for whom there is little that might serve as an anchor. A person requires faith, a resolve to go one's own way, a search for goals of which one has but inklings. Perhaps there are a good many persons who enter work in the midst of positioning, and work takes on a different character than for those with a vocation. Christopher Milne's (1979, 1976) life is illustrative.

One ulterior reason to include Milne, as well as others in this chapter, is to become disabused of the notion that those with a vocation are at the top of some developmental order from which everyone else must suffer by comparison. A vocation is certainly a pinnacle of life, but it is not the only kind of pinnacle. And those with vocation strive to do some form of good, as noted in contrast to Panzram, but they are not the only ones who strive to do good. And so it goes. There are perhaps many exemplary ways to live, of which pursuing a vocation is but one.

Milne's first nine years were spent in happy attachment to and dependence on his nanny. At age five, his parents bought a farm, Cotchford Farm, and the play world of the nursery greatly expanded to woods and fields, streams and bogs. On weekends, holidays, and summer residences, he and his nanny would set out exploring and return excitedly with their adventures. While Milne invested the countryside with a vivid imagination, it would be wrong to suppose his enchantment was sheerly imaginary. For example, it was a real snipe's nest, not an imaginary one, he tracked down that provided enormous excitement. Undisturbed by strangers, who were trying for young Milne, particularly if he was expected to talk (he liked Nanny to talk for him), they spent unhurried days in friendship really with aspects of nature.

When Nanny left at age nine, Milne more or less transferred his dependence to his father. When home from boarding school, he continued to roam through the countryside in long solitary expeditions. However, new and disturbing elements entered his world. Milne was painfully shy and now he had to talk more, which he did in agonizing stutters. Added to his timidity, Milne was self-conscious of his appearance (he looked like a girl and had been allowed to have uncharacteristically long hair, perhaps like the daughter his mother had wanted). But above all, he was embarrassed by his name. His father, Alan Milne, was the author of the famous Pooh stories for children, many of which were inspired by Christopher's adventures at Cotchford Farm, and the main character of these stories was Christopher Robin, the same as Milne's first two names. From early on, Milne was identified with this character. When young, he delighted in it and continued to take a sort of pride, but as he says, he outgrew the part. Now he was teased endlessly by schoolmates, known almost sheerly by reference to the fictional character by adults. In one particularly enraging experience, a reporter who visited the farm had asked him if a watch was his, one that she had apparently found. He had responded that it probably belonged to the gardener's daughter, but when he read her article, she had forced him to say a line from one of his father's poems, "It's a good sort of watch but it doesn't quite go" (1976, p. 96). Initially, his nurse had spoken for him: "When people asked me simple questions like, did I want another piece of cake, I really ought to have known the answer and not turned to the hovering figure at my side and said 'Do I, Nanny?'" (p. 53). Now he found when others spoke for him, it was all wrong. Had he not been shy, unable to speak for himself (stuttering was an utter misery for him), perhaps the Pooh stories would not have cast such a shadow, but they did and still do. Much later, for instance, he found that his character and the nature of his activities were misrepresented by his father, who tended to be rather cynical about the virtues of childhood. Misrepresented, unable to speak, uncertain of what he would say or do anyway (for after all, who was he?), Milne endured, coming alive in solitary explorations of the countryside.

Milne loved literature but not as it was taught. He was good with his hands, good at fixing things. And he showed promise at mathematics. At nineteen, he entered Cambridge in mathematics. There he continued two kinds of dramas. In the first, he strove to be part of the human world. For example, when Milne was accepted onto a cricket team as Robin (not as Christopher Robin, not as a character in a story, but as himself), he reached an early zenith, so happy and proud to be among them. More negatively, his worst moment in life was being informed he was placed in Category C when he tried to enlist in the British Army at the start of World War II. In the prior physical examination, he had been so excited that he had trembled and this trembling was interpreted by physicians as a sign of something more serious. The error was corrected, but at the time of refusal, all Milne knew was that he had been rejected. Something really was wrong with him. He could hardly speak. "I blundered out blind with tears" (1979, p. 20). To repeat, this rejection, confirmation of wrongness, of not fitting, was not just a bad experience, but the worst experience of his life, this from a man who went through five years of war and four years of displacement after the war.

In the second kind of drama, Milne was alone and in nature. He would wander and feel. For example, while on Home Guard duty before enlistment into the regular army, he patrolled at night and came to love it. It was as though the night brought out another sense, a contact with another world. "On moonlit nights I like to climb out of my valley and stand on a hilltop and reach up to the stars and feel myself part of a larger world, a world that embraces moon and stars—and all Creation" (1979, p. 20). While Milne did not belong or belonged only with great unease in the social world, he did belong in a larger world of nature, in which the wind speaks in many voices and there is high drama round every turn of the path.

At war for five years as a sapper officer, Milne was thrilled and proud to be accepted and occasionally counted on, more secure in overcoming fear, and more able to act on his own authority. He regarded the war as a period of rapid maturation, a foundation for the future, for during the war he moved from the severe dependency of youth to a modicum of independence. He was more capable of deciding, planning, and acting. Through war, he emerged from incompletion, probably prematurely, for he had developed a greater sense of agency but still had not resolved a direction, one that was clear enough for definite action.

During the war, he continued to have strong experiences of nature. One experience in Italy was so strong that he likened it to an experience of God. The power and benevolence of the land swept over him like an "all-pervading presence" (p. 87). He also tried at times to write of his experiences at Cotchford Farm, but once he completed a description and read it, he would throw it away.

However, the daily round of practical affairs was geared more toward making progress in belonging to human society. But even after all he had shown and experienced, he still felt that he was but attempting and remained "a faintly ludicrous figure" (p. 82). After the war, this feeling intensified. He had to break off a love affair because he lacked the rather easy, superior confidence that she wanted. He was learning what he definitely was not. Shortly after returning to England, he married a woman much more like himself, completed a degree in English literature, and was ready to climb in the world, and any path would do. He wanted to be a writer, but could think of nothing to write. He found a job with the Ministry of Information, but work ran out. Rather than remain idle, he resigned and found another job as a trainee furniture buyer, which would hopefully use his carpentry skills. After about two years of work, he was fired. He did not fit for the same reasons he never seemed to fit. He was gauche, ill at ease, nervous, and very serious. He began to feel that no one wanted him and his newfound confidence dwindled as resentment rose.

Milne was at an early bottom and he tried new things. He wrote four talks for the British Broadcasting Company (little thinking at first that they would require him to read his own talk). His wife, shy as he, valiantly took his place for the first talk. Rallying, Milne did the next three. He grew a mustache and shaved it off (too idiotic even for one as desperate as he). He was turned down for job after job. The interviewers just seemed to know what he lacked. So overwhelming were his apparent lacks that his virtues could not be seen. Finally, getting an idea from an advertisement, he and his wife, Lesley, decided to become book sellers. In 1951 they bought a book shop in Dartmouth, and this was his occupation for the next twenty-one years.

The book shop involved many advantages. He was self-employed. He did not have to worry about impressing a superior, but he did have to make it a success. There was no other income. He enjoyed building things for the shop, dealing with customers (if they did not bring up Christopher Robin!), planning book and gift selections, and creating a unique identity for the shop, but work still remained a test of worth. Could he make his own way? Could he really escape from his perceived lacks, his father's fame, and the Pooh characterization of himself? More practically, could a book shop survive in a town of less than seven thousand persons? While the book shop did not thrive (how could it?), it did provide a modest success, one for which Milne felt great pride. They did it themselves. They became part of a community, with Milne overcoming his timidity to lead a fight to preserve its unique character against impersonal modern developments. They did not become famous, but they did achieve a sense of belonging and achievement, and this he cherished, even to the extent of being angry that when his mother died in 1971 (his father in 1956), part of his father's royalties would now come to him. He did not want royalties. He had made his own way. From nearly total dependence, he had risen through war, failure, and modest success to a certain kind of attainment he did not want spoiled, and certainly not by his father's achievements or by the Pooh books from which he had been escaping most of his life.

Over fifty years of age, Milne was still escaping. "There are two ways of navigating. You can take a bearing on something ahead of you and steer toward it. Or you can take a bearing on something behind you and steer away from it" (1979, p. 251). Steering away from rather than toward something requires some guidelines to avoid merely circling back. One guideline is to know what you are not and have the courage to steer away from situations that require you to be other. In life, there are pressures to conform, expectations, fantasy appeals, among other things, all inviting one to be different than one is, to strive to live up to some image that is a fiction. A more difficult guideline is to know what you are and have the courage to steer toward those situations, to find situations that fit, even if they seem more difficult because it required a knowledge Milne did not possess. Certainly, he knew that he was good at fixing things, willing to work hard and long, and so on, but he had no integrated conception. It was overshadowed by what he wished to avoid. In this situation, one steers into the unknown, and Milne did so with the resolve to stick to his own path wherever it might lead. His determination to make his way independently was almost fierce in its intensity, and perhaps such fierceness is required when one's life involves the tentativity or uncertainty of a journey with no map, no assurance of a destination, and not much confidence.

Milne's metaphor for his career is a walk he actually took. Setting along a path to climb a mountain, to attain the mountaintop, the path unexpectedly descended. He would have taken any path, but the one he chose was well worn by others and led downward into a forest, away from the sunshine. Plunging on, becoming more and more depressed, he eventually came to a glade, "a gleam of sunshine, offering a moment of pleasure and a ray of hope" (p. 116). He had now left the road and was on his own. Eventually he discovered a modest plain, offering freedom to follow his own inclinations, unexpected delights, and independence. Even if it was not what he had aimed for, at least initially, it was a happy discovery and he was content with it.

The groping uncertainty of Milne's career as a book seller is an obvious parallel of the phase of positioning. he found a suitable environment, and gradually over the next twenty-one years, his power of agency grew. He wavered, at one time fending off threats of incompletion, at another time enacting a better way of being. Gradually, as "freedom from" become more secure, it lost prominence or gave way to "freedom to." Now that one has secured an escape, what is one free to do? Book selling was a happy occupation, an appropriate setting for positioning himself. It involves more, for it was a livelihood for so many years, but it never rises to the vitality of what, for instance, investigation meant to Steffens. There is no vital relation such as to be is to do. Book selling had its own delights, to be sure, but its role in Milne's life was a means for independence, belonging, and confidence. When it had served its purpose, it could be left behind.

At age fifty two, he stopped book selling. His mother had died and royalties from his father's books were to come to him. After all these years of escaping his father's fame and the Pooh books, he did not want to now depend on them in any way. Yet he felt he had to in order to provide care for his invalid daughter when he and Lesley were no longer around. And this acceptance generated turmoil. He had to rethink his life, go back to origins to reconnect. He had to search for his father, not as a rival whose brilliance and ease in establishing himself so dwarfed young Milne, but as a father. And in searching for his father, he might discover himself. He might learn to represent himself, to weave through years of misrepresentation to a kind of truth.

For Milne, a cloud had covered the once bright plain. It had been explored anyway and there was a new path just ahead, one he had voiced when young and tried briefly after the military, but now he had something to say. In *The Enchanted Places* (1976), Milne explored his father and the setting for the Pooh stories, and he explored his happy childhood at Cotchford Farm, the reality behind many of Christopher Robin's adventures. He continued his exploration of his life in *The Path through the Trees* (1979). Through these explorations, finally facing it all, and a favorable reception that validated his talent as a professional writer, Milne felt that he had at last become his father's son, not a guilt-ridden failure. But more importantly, he achieved standing: "I could feel that I was myself" (p. 266).

In one way, writing his life history allowed him to piece a story together, to resolve issues or final issues of incompletion. In another more powerful way, it allowed him to reconnect with the dominant positive theme of his life. During most of his life, the sort of communion he had with nature had been secondary but sustaining. In childhood, it was primary, but later it was obscured through the pain of what he was not. As a book seller, he had set up shop in a small town, just right for long walks and slow living. He had fought to keep it that way, but when the bulldozers destroyed his enchanted place, he had moved four miles from town into the country. Nature was an avocation, one that was always there and perhaps never fully appreciated. And now, through his autobiographical efforts, he has restored the more positive existence of childhood. He finds sustenance in nature, not in society. There in the changing faces of life all around him, he feels truly a part of the great experiment in creation that arose from the primeval swamp and continues in a vole building its nest or the wild look in the eyes of an owl. What was once an occasional and deeply moving experience is becoming a way of being.

A sense of vocation has arisen in Milne, late but not less powerfully. Strands of existence have been proportioned, unified, and directed toward the benefit of others. In acting from a central way of being, Milne has found a solidity he had scarcely known for most of his life. For those of us who had followed him in his first two books, the question was what he would write next, not whether. It is remarkable to find someone still struggling as he writes, and his autobiography is very much a search. Quite likely, it constitutes the culminating experience that firmly launched him into a vocation, for it does not end with the sense that this is my *life*, but that this is my *beginning*. It gives one's expectations a certain tension. If the latter part of his biography is any indication, he might allow others to delight in nature through his writing. He might show us how we alienate ourselves and how a greater belonging can be restored.

Having lived in unease so long, he might focus directly upon how to live as square pegs with round holes all about us, to use his metaphor. Given a few years of anticipation, it was with some excitement that I found that his latest book is *Hollow on the Hill: The Search for a Personal Philosophy* (1985).

Positing in Work

A vocation is but one of perhaps many forms of unity. For example, perhaps there are major experiences, what Maslow (1962) termed peak experiences, that transform a person into a unity. For a more detailed example, suppose that one emerged from incompletion with no particular direction, implying that diverse desires had not been unified very well, or with a most general of directions such as rising as far as one can in a career. Incompletion and positioning provide a powerful grounding for orientation, but a rapid development of human agency might prematurely launch one forward. In a case such as this, a person might find a form of unity in an occupation. A vocation involves a dramatic role within a dramatic or symbolic structure. An occupation involves an ostensive role within an actual setting with its own ostensive role structure. One of the major differences is that one can leave an occupation, but one cannot leave a vocation without a radical change of personhood.

However, if a person invests so strongly in an occupation that he or she is virtually engulfed by it, a form of unity seems evident. For instance, Lee Iacocca (1984) seems to have unified his existence as an executive in the automobile industry. Even after nearly forty years, he seems to still be thrilled with developing a new line, involved with the car competition, and superbly competent in his work, but there is little evidence of a vocation, at least as considered here. In his dedication, he certainly resembles those with a sense of vocation, and resembles then in other ways as well, but there is still not the same sense of mission. There is no cause, for instance, in which he lost himself. For those with a vocation, the cause is a regnant drama or gap. Washington's cause, for instance, was the uplifting of his race through education, but for Iacocca, there is no apparent cause in this sense. As an executive in the automobile business, he strove to produce competitive lines of products. The sheer attractiveness of many professions (lawyer, doctor, engineer, etc.) invites acceptance and engulfment, a topic sociologists have studied much more than have psychologists (McCall & Simmons, 1978).

Csikszentmihalyi and Beattie (1979) have instigated the dominant life themes in the lives of thirty men, fifteen of whom were blue-collar workers and fifteen of whom were quite successful professionals. "A life theme consists of a problem or set of problems which a person wishes to solve above everything else and the means the person finds to achieve solution" (p. 48). They regard a life theme as an affective-cognitive gestalt that structures a significant portion of a person's life, which might be conscious or unconscious. Life themes are thought to arise in the following way. First, one encounters a major existential stress. Stresses are not some objective force, but rather, are in themselves interpreted. Thus, two members of the same family might endure the same conditions, but one might highlight poverty and another might highlight isolation. Second, a person attempts to find the problem and give it a label. The label allows a person to begin interpreting previously unrelated events as manifestations of a single phenomenon. Third, the person frames the problem in a way that allows for a solution. That is, one attributes a cause to the problem, and of course, different attributions suggest quite different solutions. Last, a person devises a solution or an approach to a solution that directs efforts.

Csikszentmihalyi and Beattie found two types of life themes, one kind that is evident for blue-collar workers and one kind that is evident for professionals. The comparison is flawed, however, because they selected outstanding professionals in comparison to blue-collar workers generally. Had they compared outstanding with ordinary professionals, the same split might have occurred. Or had they selected outstanding blue-collar workers, they might have resembled outstanding professionals. What is of interest here are the two kinds of themes, not attributions to the two kinds of work.

Harry was reared in extreme poverty, which he identified as the problem behind the many stresses he experienced (e.g., concern for food). The cause of the problem was lack of thrift and the solution accordingly became one of saving money. Harry spent the rest of his life saving money. To economize, he wears old clothes, drives an old car, and has never married. Although he has saved nearly a half million dollars and owns five apartment buildings, he continues to work at the steel mill and saves.

The son of recent immigrants, John was struck by a car while riding a bicycle. The driver was at fault: she disobeyed a traffic signal. A doctor, she rushed John to the hospital and cared for him, but did not let anyone know she was at fault, and convinced John's parents not to involve the authorities. The family ended up paying hospital fees and doctor fees. "They ended up paying a woman who almost killed me" (p. 53). The problem was the sheer wrongness of what had happened. The cause of the problem was the immigrant status of his parents. They were at a disadvantage, nearly defenseless. They could hardly speak English, knew nothing about liability, their rights, or whom they might turn to. The solution involved knowledge of law, particularly as it applied to minority groups. John received a degree in law, and later a degree in economics. He has held several positions in government where he defends the rights of minority groups. Upholding these rights became a life's work.

Following the authors, what are the differences between these two examples of the two kinds of life themes? First, John formulated the problem in a general way that included other persons, not just himself and his family. Harry's problem of poverty might have been framed generally, but it was instead framed as his poverty. The problem only incidentally extends beyond himself. Thus, while John was concerned with a general problem of relevance to others, Harry was concerned with a personal problem. Second, while Harry did identify a specific cause in lack of thrift, others who exemplify a more concrete life theme tend not to mention a specific cause. Those like John not only tend to identify a general cause, but that cause involves a condition of themselves that can be changed. For example, ignorance can be corrected by education perhaps. Third, for those like Harry, work is an external means for solving a personal problem such as acquiring money. However, for those like John, work is an essential part of their solution. In work, John defended the rights of minorities. It is an essential part of his solution. But for Harry, owning apartment houses is not essential. It was a means; another means might have done just as well. Perhaps it would be better to say that John's work was an end in itself and also a means for furthering his life work. John has a vocation while Harry does not.

While Csikszentmihalyi and Beattie's description is certainly compatible with the present book, it is extremely attenuated. When seen in a highly condensed way, a generalized problem appears like "nothing but a cognitive transformation" (p. 53), but offering a name such as this tends to direct attention to a cognitive manipulation rather than the reality behind it. For example, one might say that Milne's attainment of a vocation was only a cognitive transformation and this might be correct, but in such a limited way that it is wrong. It simply conveys nothing of the extensive developments that allowed a change to take place. Similarly, the idea of an affective-cognitive structure begs most questions work asking. For instance, it presumes rather than shows how affect and cognition are involved, or what kind of structure is formed. Nevertheless their study is extremely valuable, particularly in the way distinction is made between life themes.

Regarding work, what exactly is posited for cases such as Harry? First, the significance of deeds are largely self-referenced or self-centered. He keeps saving money for himself, not others. And there is no indication that he conceives of or invests in his means of acquiring money as a service or benefit for others. Second, the significance of work is largely practical and concrete with no vast symbolic implications as found in those with a vocation. What makes this odd is that while work is mostly self-centered, there is a relative impoverishment of self-definition. Harry has accepted a position or attained personhood, but it is a lower form than that of others such as Washington or Steffens. For example, being thrifty and economical do not require much self-definition, whereas becoming an educator required considerable positioning to attain. Perhaps the more self-centered a person is, the less self-definition is required. It appears plausible that the level of positing is scaled to the stature of position attained. Harry's level of work is impoverished in meaning alongside the rich compositions of those reviewed in the last chapter and the stature of position acquired seems stunted alongside the rich, self-giving metaphors of personhood others adopt (see Cochran, 1985, on levels of personhood).

Consider Harry's savings as a life's work and it seems odd. It is not as if a positive had been gained so much as a negative (i.e., poverty) had been avoided. He continues to stave off the horrors of incompletion, but no one with a vocation does this exclusively. Rather, they view themselves in a dramatic role that usually allows them to help others in one's prior state of incompletion. If Washington had had Harry's level of position, he would have continued educating himself the rest of his life with little thought to others or to a role in a larger drama. The difference is striking. Even if we expand Harry's work so that he does all manner of good, the difference would still be striking for all that good done would remain incidental. And even if we expand Harry's position into a richer portrait, he remains means-defined. He has not attained a position that is good in itself, but good as a means for saving money. What he is and what he does are incidental to having the security of money in the bank.

Harry resembles those in incompletion more than those with a vocation, but with this difference. He framed a concrete way out that he lives. His life is the living of a way out, not achieving a new way of living. The world of poverty remains virtually the only world, as if Washington had regarded slavery as really the only world. There is no contrasting drama. Rather, there are contrasting positions in a drama, one of having or not having. In contrast, those in incompletion either form a false solution (e.g., Panzram's solution is no solution at all) or falter in finding an adequate alternative. All manner of fallibility must simply be assumed.

Summary

Work appears to vary in meaning with the phase of life a person is in. During incompletion, work appears largely within a drama of entrapment. one might also seek and find contrasting dramas of a way out or try out defective solutions, but the general spirit of work is one of coercion, despair, or perhaps sad acceptance. A person reacts primarily to restraints, what one would like to avoid, rather than to what one can approach. Work is experienced primarily in terms of what it lacks or what is wrong with it. However, this characterization is based upon strong, negative cases and incompletion offers other possibilities. For example, if a person were engulfed in a positive drama with no way out (as Menuhin might have been if he were inept at music), work would pale beside the unattainable dream. Or suppose a person had yet to unify divergent desires. In this case, work might vary inconstantly depending upon the salience of momentary desires and their possibilities of satisfaction, or it might bear upon a subset of desires that seem peripheral to the person. Or work might achieve unity by external imposition of routine and situational constraints. Common to all cases would be a pervading sense of lack.

During positioning, work is largely promissory. One wavers, experiencing alternatively moments of incompletion and moments of positing. Work is primarily a means, although it wavers from senses of incompletion and completion. It involves a test of worth as one seeks to escape from the negative and to approach a more positive way of being. That is, a person reacts primarily to evidence of personal progress or regress, savoring opportunity and anguishing over old blocks.

During positing, work is an enactment of position, but only some positions involve a vocation. What is posited in work reflects the kind of position one has attained. A vocation is distinguished not so much by any one criterion, but by a gestalt of features that might serve as criteria. The difference between Iacocca's work, for instance, and the work of someone with a vocation is indefinitely analyzable. While detailed analysis might prove valuable later, it seems more important now to grasp the fullness of a vocation in relation to other forms of positing.

6 *Fulfillment of Being: Rhythm of Completion*

As a period of life, completion does not mean that one's work is over or that one has retired. Completion might come in mid-life as well as old age. In a concrete enactment, the sense of completion at the end might involve satisfaction, contentment, or even frustration. Completion is such because it somehow completes what was aroused in the beginning, and it need not be unambiguously positive. As a phase of life, a transient sense is elevated to an enduring quality of being. For example, instead of a momentary experience of contentment, life might seem pervaded by a powerful sense of contentment, peace, and well-being. Before describing the rather unique characteristics of this phase, it would be opportune to briefly review the grounding phases from which it arises.

Phases of Life

Recall that any completed experience involves four phases in order: incompletion, positioning, positing, and completion. However, in different periods of life, each phase takes on different qualities, analogous to the flow of seasons. Summer is active or decisive, energetic, a time of vibrant growth, of a powerful movement toward fruition. Winter is more passive in the sense of receptive, slow, heavy, more fixed in form (without growth and change), a time for incubation. Spring and fall are transitional offspring. Each manifests the beginnings of one and the endings of another. However, spring is a movement toward the infusion and diffusion of energy. Fall is a movement toward dwindling energy in one sense, but also toward openness, fertilization, and renewal. Below, each period of life will be characterized by the dominant pattern of enactment that is manifested within it.

145

Incompletion

The basic equations are: incompletion = spring, positioning = summer, positing = fall, completion = winter. Desires arise not in the depth of winter, but spring forth like new growths in a time of activity and perhaps optimism. There are many desires, new and without firm roots, which one pursues energetically. Positioning is undertaken with great zeal and often with vivid imagination, which contrasts glaringly with the decline of positing. With high spirit and enthusiasm, a person enters positioning, anticipating the realization of desire. But in positing, there is no realization. One is rendered relatively passive, subject to the posits of circumstances and other persons. If the posits are good, one experiences a positive completion. If bad, one experiences a negative completion. In wintry receptivity, one experiences the full force of that which was posited. In only one other condition is one so open to the impact of experience, so vulnerable to the potential of experience to foster fundamental changes. For Menuhin, the experience of beauty was sublime, transporting. For Steffens, the experience of disillusionment was profoundly unsettling. Whatever the experience, one is left enduring it, dwelling on it, being moved by it. Unable to act effectively, to close off in decisive action, this pattern is optimal for giving birth to desire, and giving birth to drama. It is essentially a pattern of incubation.

Positioning

The basic equations are: incompletion = summer, positioning = fall, positing = winter, completion = spring. Positioning is a one step progression from incompletion, beginning in summer rather than spring. The incompletion cycles fan incompletion into a summerlike zenith, which begin positioning cycles. Desires are unified and powerful when one's power of agency is low, forming the dominant contrast of this cycle. In short, one's desires are highest when the possibility of realization is the lowest. One's efforts to get into position suffer setbacks, disappointments, losses, a dwindling of enflamed desire into relatively exhausted efforts at realization. Where one desired a posit or deed of some magnitude, one must be content with a certain feebleness of action. During positioning, one endures more than acts effectively, focusing attention not on desire but on how one might realize it. In the midst of activity, one is most vulnerable and receptive, a spectator of one's own participation. While perhaps meager, results provide cause for hope. There is a possibility of change and development. Through this pattern, one endures yet acts, destroying some qualities and cultivating others, often in awe of or receptiveness to a higher way of being. This pattern is the movement of a rite of passage (Eliade, 1975; Van Gennep, 1960), of becoming.

Positing

The basic equations are: incompletion = winter, positioning = spring, positing = summer, and completion = fall. Positing is the exact opposite of positioning; it is no progression, but an inversion wrought by endless efforts to become. Over the course of positioning, one strives to strengthen what was initially lacking, and emerges from positioning when the opposites are in place. One feels aligned, in position, and stabilized. Desire is more fixed and less heated as one is able to focus on its realizations, on ends rather than motives. Through practice, it becomes more stable, less prone to rampant development, but open to a slower incubation. Positioning is conducted with more optimism, as one who is more confident, more effective, in need only of a proper setting in which to act forcefully. One's preparations are no longer merely wishful, but more certain vehicles for realizing desire. Positing now becomes energetic, productive, a powerful movement to bring aims to fruition and to build upon them. At last, positing is aligned with the vibrant growth of summer and one works with a will. Here, one is drawn toward building rather than contentment with what is built. One's sense of completion in work is subject to setbacks, losses, sudden reversals, and a dwindling of energy or attention. What one accomplishes is good perhaps, but never enough. One is thrilled in working more than in appreciating one's work. Spurred on by a sense of completion that is partially satisfying, partially dissatisfying, something but not quite sufficient, one is compelled by the work that needs to be done. This is the pattern of vigorous action upon which a life's work can develop.

Completion

Now we come to the primary subject of this chapter. The basic equations of completion are: incompletion = fall, positioning =

winter, positing = spring, and completion = summer. Completion is neither a progression, nor an inversion, but a one-step regression. Rather than begin in winter, as in positing, one begins in fall. Desire is not so much a fixed form or a slow incubation, but rather involves some withdrawal, openness to reversals and setbacks as one perhaps begins to take an enlarged perspective or to evaluate one's work of life. Positioning is more reflective, not requiring intense energy, yet still one is open to alternatives if they exist. To get into position, one is less likely to engage in feverish activity and more likely to simply be receptive, open to opportunities or invitations. The main differences are the relative reflectivity of the first half of the cycle in comparison with the struggle required previously and with the involvement and energy of the latter half of the cycle.1 The springlike quality of positing is to be understood in light of a life's work. One has stepped back, is no longer compelled as urgently, and seems able to approach work or life with a certain freshness. There are new growths yet and one might hope for a crowning work. André Maurois (1970), for instance, began his biography of Balzac at age seventy-seven. "For three years I was to lose myself delightfully in that existence at once trivial and sublime" (p. 409). It was his masterwork, complete with some novelties and a preface indicating that this would be his last biography. Although his power of agency had dwindled somewhat in old age, he could still exceed himself if he took his time. Yet, what makes this pattern most distinctive is the enormous involvement in the completing phase of enactments. Favorable reception might be cherished. Memories of similar deeds might be savored. Attention is drawn to what one has accomplished, coming to terms with a suitable ending. Maurois, for instance, wrote more on how his final biography was received and how he felt than upon how he came to want to write it, how he got ready to write it, and how he put it together. What might have received minute description in an earlier phase of life suddenly receives little. What was remarked upon with less emphasis before, suddenly becomes a focus. It is as if one were searching for a suitable end. All the qualities of summer are now bent upon the character of the end, an affirmation of meaning in one's existence.

This period of life is difficult to study in may ways. For example, accounts of this period tend to be sparse. Autobiographies tend to be written during this period, and consequently, tend to lack perspective on the immediate, or to treat it briefly. As another example, it is complicated by age and unsettling events, which often seem to go together. Upon his wife's death, the death of friends, and his own illnesses, Maurois felt that the "years of serenity were transforming themselves more and more into years of calamity" (p. 428). What is common to old age perhaps imposes upon what might be common to the period of completion. However, what in the end makes this period so difficult is that it is exceedingly difficult. Upon the basis of the accounts at hand, I intend to sketch a plausible story, an oversimplification, but one that I hope will clarify the pattern.

The pattern of completion is the exact opposite of that found in incompletion, and one ends each cycle of experience not with the slow incubation of desire, but with a spirited effort to complete desire. It is a product of the prior three phases, but it is also another quest or search. Persons do not just attain completion as sort of a natural upshot of positing. Rather, they are in pursuit of it and what they receive is scaled to the nature of their lives and the final venture. The pattern of enactment is partially a pattern that enhances the sense of an end and partially a pattern that enables one to search more effectively and to feel the results in the quality of one's being. Persons strive to experience a proper end to their lives, a proper completion.

If fully done, completion involves a different form of personhood. Recall that the person formed at the end of positioning is a unity of desire or incompletion. Desire, wish, hope, and the like are all states of incompleteness, requiring a gap to be bridged to fulfill one's desire, wish, or hope. A wholeness of incompletion aptly characterizes the nature of personhood during positing. One's life work is the striving to realize a pregnant desire. However, it seems apparent that a person who is incomplete or a unity of incompletion is not whole, in a stronger sense of wholeness. How could one be, always striving for what is not as yet? One might be wholehearted, but wholehearted about what has yet to be done. Now the potentially radical shift is from wholeness of incompletion to a wholeness of completion. One is complete, in some sense, and acts not from fullness of desire but from fullness of being. One who is full of love, for instance, acts from love. One who is full of joy acts from joy. There is no necessary desire in love, joy, or other qualities of completion, but more of an overflow of being like laughter. To be complete is to not lack, not be in want of or desirous of anything, a seemingly radical reversal of all that has come before. This kind of position will be more characterized later. For the present, it can be regarded as an outer limit of what might be achieved in this phase of life. If so, other attainments can be viewed as progressions along the way.

Flow of Completion

What happens during the completion phase of life can always be viewed from two complementary perspectives. First, what persons do and experience can be understood in light of their lives. To strive for the proper end requires attention to lacks that must be corrected, and these lacks might be idiosyncratic. For one person, the major lack might be a philosophy of life. For another, it might be a crowning work. For still others, it might be a thematic broadening of activities beyond the relatively narrow boundaries of one's work. Perhaps everyone manifests these lacks to some extent, but there is still a noticeable difference in emphasis. Second, what persons do and experience can be understood according to the level of progression toward full completion. Thus, one person might spend the whole of this phase upon one kind of topic while others plunge through to higher attainments. While I am reluctant to assert a graded series as any more than a tentative hypothesis, it does seem to make sense of the material.

Unlike other phases, these considerations suggest that not everyone will manifest the same characteristics. Persons strive; they do not necessarily attain. What all have in common is that they become absorbed in the sense of ending. Like Washington when he received an honorary degree from Harvard University, one is capable of being overwhelmed. Persons might begin to attend fully to honors or to how one's work is received. They might search for evidence of impact, of how their work matters. They might attend more to their own reactions of contentment and frustration, meaningfulness and meaninglessness. In various ways, the end comes to reign over one's existence.

Beginning

Completion begins when a person senses that the end is near. For some, awareness of approaching death signals a change. It is no longer a remote possibility, but a definite actuality taking shape, and one begins a kind of preparation. For others, one's work has hit a zenith beyond which one cannot go. For example, Hilton culminated positing with the purchase of the legendary Waldorf. From then on, life was divided into "before the Waldorf" and "after the Waldorf." After reaching such a high point, there were no more towering mountains on the same path. Certainly Hilton continued to expand his frontier, as he called it, but as one who had arrived. With this culmination at age sixty-two, he turned toward the end. If Hilton topped out of positing, Steffens bottomed out. In middle age, unable to continue muckraking, he began wandering to salvage his life. In different ways, each person was drawn back from the zeal of continued positing of a life's work to contemplate the end.

It is a sense of ending things (conclusion, completion, termination, etc.) that provides this phase of life with its distinctive tone:

> I can only put it that this is the human autumn before the snow . . . a vast mild autumn country strewn with broken seedpods, hurrying cloud wrack, abandoned farm machinery, and circling crows. A place where things were begun on too grand a scale to complete. Thomas Hardy speaks somewhere about the deep = - graven family countenance leaping from place to place across oblivion. Well, I am that face but here the journey ends [Eiseley, 1975, pp. 227–28].

One's ventures are initiated not with an upward spirit in which all yet lies ahead, but with a mood of denouement before the final fall.

Middle

Confronted with a sense of ending, a person turns toward the past. As the future runs out or takes on definite limits, the past seems to come alive. Memories occur in reflection, but also as accompaniments of current action. What was more tacitly involved in significant enactments, might now become more explicitly involved. Definite memories and whole strings of memories might come vividly into awareness as analogues of a current action. The past begins to pervade the present and some persons even dream of far-off days of youth. In one of Eiseley's (1975) dreams, the characters were himself when young and himself in old age. Others such as Carl Jung (1965) ritually or symbolically enacted analogues of the past, like a memorial service. There are no restrictions other than what a person might feel compelled to restrict. One's past comes alive in a general movement of being.

Although memories might cover a broad range, there is nothing particularly random about it. As Eiseley (1975) stated, "it is the individual's last attempt to order the meaning of his life before a spring breaks in the rusted heart and the dreams, the memories, and the elusive chemical domain that contains them fly apart in irreparable ruin" (pp. 227–28). The vividness of remembrance probably has a number of advantages. For example, it might anchor one as the present becomes less secure. However, most advantages appear as derivatives of an individual's attempt to order the meaning of his or her life. Certainly, one could approach the task more abstractly, but theory is not what is needed. That is required is a living order of meaning, not knowledge about such an order. Conceiving and feeling are united in the experience of something mattering (passionate judgment, feeling about, or stance taking), and this sense of mattering is enlivened by and embodied in memories. Perhaps it is more accurate to say that one does not just remember, but reenacts and reexperiences in memory. The sharpness of memories makes the past very close to the present. Trollope's (1978) memories of his earlier degradation were so graphic that he almost hoped the end were near for fear of returning to this state. Memories allow one to live an order of meaning, and to explore an order in all its infinite variety.

A memory need not be absorbing, vivid, lifelike, or in short, a virtual reliving of an experience. It might be vague, uninvolving, a mere bit of data. While persons can reflect on memories of any quality, the strong form is important in the completion phase of life, and the strong form seems to be facilitated by the sense of ending things. In this mood or state of mind, memories matter and seem to achieve a stunning vitality. Perhaps a personal example might clarify what is meant here. Like many students in high school, I had to read Charles Dickens's A Tale of Two Cities. It was an assignment, just something one had to do, and I treated it that way. Bored, uninvolved, I made my way through the book, and with that shabby effort, I recall being two-thirds of the way through the book, unable to remember very well what had come before. Nothing stood out. There was no coherent order, just fragments. I was bothered because there should have been more to show for the effort of reading and because there would surely be a test, yet apparently not bothered enough because I just continued reading. Unexpectedly, I became absorbed. Madame Defarge became loathsome. Mr. Cruncher and Miss Pross became sharp in character. When Sydney Carton replaced Charles Darnay in prison and later on the guillotine, memories of events came alive and came alive in a meaningful order. In the very last, unforgettable line of Carton, all seemed to fall into place. Not only could I remember what I could not remember before, but I remembered events so picturesquely that it was like a reliving of the novel. I wondered how I could have been so feeble in involvement before. In Dickens's story, the sense of ending things is very pronounced. Carton's life is ending on the guillotine, and through the genius of Dickens's prose, the meaning of it all comes to matter very much indeed. In this wistful, poignant, vulnerable state, memories leaped involuntarily into immense clarity, and the difference between weaker and stronger forms of memories that matter seemed as striking as the difference between a rose garden and a photograph of one.

In a stronger form of memory, an experience is more capable of being savored and explored. The past is made part of the present. One is absorbed, compelled, and effortlessly involved in a search for meaning. It is as if one were suddenly endowed with the capability to relive all of life's significant experiences in a short span. It is this strong form, in particular, that shapes the quality of completion.

First, one is pressed to complete one's life, but how? If one had merely a theoretical or cognitive understanding of one's life, how to complete it might have all the coldness of a deduction. One would merely follow a dictate of reason rather than a passion from within, and this would be futile. Completion is a matter of spirit or meaningfulness. If one is not infused with meaning in an enactment, it is hardly a proper enactment for drawing life to a close in a meaningful way. But with vivid memories, a reliving, we are able to intuit a far richer pattern than could ever be done by sheer calculation (Polanyi, 1966). One is not definite. Rather, one searches for clues. experiences a sense of rightness or wrongness to acts and possibilities, and approaches completion more tentatively. Like positioning, a person might have few clear goals. Goals emerge more clearly as one explores and tries out; the rightness of one's course might be judged only in retrospect. Completion is a search from the heart whose results are experienced in one's being, and this is the kind of existential search that the strong form of memory supports.

Second, memories strengthen a sense of personal continuity. Through memories, a person experiences himself or herself over time as a continuous subject. There is development and change, and there is also a rekindling of the same kind of position in experience after experience. For those with a vocation, Jung's (1965) statement seems appropriate:

> My life is what I have done, my scientific work; the one is inseparable from the other. The work is the expression of my inner development; for commitment to the contents of the unconscious forms the man and produces transformations. My works can be regarded as stations along my life's way [p. 222].

For those with a vocation, being is inseparable from significant doing.

There is an enormous series of doings that reflect one's way of being, a consistency that allows one to feel, like Jung, that "I consisted of my own history" (p. 291). One is one's vocation, or so it is felt. Eiseley is his journey. Washington is his effort to uplift his people. Peale is his mission to raise persons to the mind of Christ. Menuchin is his quest to transport persons beyond barriers and divisions, to unite them in common experiences of universal depth that music can ignite. While this function of memory seems like a consolidation, the prior function seems like an extension to unfinished business. It is as if one's life becomes an invocation for the final venture.

In dwelling upon one's life, a person becomes a spectator of his or her own existence. Recall that the spectator role, following Britton (1970), is ideal for evaluation with broad scope. One essentially fashions and rehearses a story, which is one's life. In contrast, the participant role is narrower in accordance with the perspective of one who is seeking to get something done. The life phase of positing gives maximal strength to the role of a participant, while the phase of completion gives selective strength to the role of a spectator (spectatorship is maximal in the positioning phase of life where agency is weak but growing). In particular, the positioning aspect of an enactment during the incompletion phase is wintry. A person positions himself or herself largely by memories, by spectatorship on one's life and much less by actual doings. This certainly does not mean that positioning is no longer active, but that as a characteristic aspect of enactments in this phase, spectatorship reigns like a pervading mood.

Behind the various preparations is a memorial preparation that gives an act significance as a partial completion of life. For example, when Eiseley's (1975) mother died, Eiseley made arrangements for the funeral, but more significantly, he had to prepare himself to finish his relation to the person who had made escape and wandering so dominant in his life. "Across my brain were scars which had left me walking under the street lamps of unnumbered nights. I had heard her speak words to my father on his deathbed that had left me circling the peripheries of a continent to escape her always constant presence" (p. 223). How he positioned himself for this last encounter was largely in the role of a spectator.

When Maurois (1970) began his final biography on Balzac, it required enormous study before he began to write. But Maurois had been studying Balzac for over sixty years. To write the life of Balzac had been one of his dreams and now was to become a capstone of his works, his final work of major importance. And he wrote it during a time when the textile mills closed; they had been his parents' and extended family's livelihood, and his own for many years. He prepared conscientiously to write Balzac's life, but overlapping this preparation was one of another kind, one concerned with completing his life in one last work.

Freed somewhat from the consuming effort of positing, persons step back or withdraw before reinvestment. But when they renew significant enactments, it is with an enlarged perspective that lends work a certain freshness and renewal of vitality. Over and over, one cycles from withdrawal in spectatorship to significant action as a participant. Often with the end near, there are novel ventures and a playfulness in working. For example, Maurois wrote a short "letter" for youth, not so much to give direct advice as to distill the wisdom of a long life from which they might benefit. With its publication, he reentered an active life of "round-tables, colloquiums, speeches" (p. 425), trying to "live each minute" (p. 425), hoping for death to catch him in stride. As one instance of a completing kind of investment, consider Conrad Hilton's (1957) late venture in the hotel business.

Hilton began to conceive of his growing string of foreign hotels as an invisible bond of hospitality spreading over the world, a bonding that contributed to world peace and freedom. Each hotel was conceived as a little America, "a friendly center where the men of many nations and of good will may speak the languages of peace" (p. 265). Each hotel was also a little America in the sense that "we joined hands in a business fellowship with foreign entrepreneurs" (p. 267). He began to write and to speak forcefully for his emergent dream of one world in which all are free to pray and work to make their dreams a reality. Late in life, Hilton turned more to the value of his life's work for others. Although it is not necessarily so, business tends to attenuate vocation by a too narrow focus upon profits rather than the value of products for others. Hilton certainly operated with the profit motive in mind, but it was more a sign of success than of greed. Hilton was not very self-indulgent, yet he had neglected what his frontier of hotels was for. Following the familiar pattern of those with vocation, Hilton turned more directly to the lifting of others as he had been lifted. Following his personal pattern, the link of prayer and work in the realization of dreams, he came to put work more in service of prayer than prayer in service of work. This late dream was a form of completion, shaping his life into an indivisible whole. Before, there had been a rather large gap. Life was unfinished or one-sided. Now, life was more balanced and holistic.

In his last dream, he was able to integrate the strands of his life into a project that was radiant with meaning. For example. it exemplified his code of living to dream big. It brought his religious convictions into full view. It fostered a sense of fellowship, and relations with others became prominent. There is no obvious end to the meaning of a significant completion; it just seems to vibrate along a symbolic web that constitutes a person's life.

Neither Hilton's late dream nor Maurois's biography of Balzac were radically different from what they had done before, yet there is a freshness and novelty in them. In the grounds of one's existence, it is as if there were buried seed or potentials that begin to bloom only in the completion phase of life. Life cannot be completed by the relative narrowness of positing. It is when one stands back and reflects on one's life with an enlarged perspective, toned by the sense of ending things, that these buried potentials begin to come alive. Their realization seems to balance the imbalances of one's earlier zeal, completing more fully what was aroused in the very beginnings. Reflection also seems to foster more objectivity, an ability to appreciate the world beyond one's desires in all its otherness and to appreciate one's own existence.

Ends

Adler (1985) has drawn a distinction between two kinds of ends that is of importance in clarifying levels of completion. The first kind of end is called a terminal goal. It is an achievement at a point in time. To use Adler's example, if one planned a trip to Vienna, arriving at Vienna is the termination. The goal has been reached. Similarly, if an architect planned a building, the completion of the building is a terminal goal. Once reached, it is over and one strives no more in its regard. One can rest in the attainment. If the attainment is good, completing, and satisfying, one is content. One feels at peace, if only for a while.

With regard to lives of those with a vocation, there are all sorts of completions of this kind. Maurois's biography was such a completion. It was a completion in itself and a completion of part of the pattern that made up his life. However, there are also a number of borderline instances. For example, when one symbolically extends or redefines the dramatic form of one's life, as Hilton did, it is partially a product that one can rest in and partially a frame for striving. As a lead-in to the second kind of end, consider a more detailed example.

Carl Jung (1965) spent most of his life exploring the contents of inner images, those fantasies that arise from the unconscious for which we can claim no conscious creation. The images arise in us unbidden as in a dream. Through these images, Jung strove to establish a meaningful relationship to the unconscious and to realize these meanings in life. For Jung, the unconscious is a synonym for God. In allowing certain archetypes (a primordial pattern of meaning) to come to realization in one's being and acting, a persons becomes an incarnation of God, or as Jung states, "I am a splinter of the infinite deity" (p. 4). This is an oversimplification. For instance, the unconscious is a dangerous, powerful, and mysterious realm, involving polarities that can destroy a person who approaches these forces with indiscriminate servitude. The ego must be strong and remain as a center of meaning and orientation within a swirl of potent forces that can overwhelm a person. With strength (and much else too lengthy to detail), one can affirm a destiny or personal mythology. One takes up a relation to rather than being devoured by inner images.

However, further qualifications are unnecessary to grasp the awesome power of the cosmic drama that can be enacted in human lives. One's work becomes divine. "I had to obey an inner law which was imposed on me and left me no freedom of choice" (p. 357). Yet Jung could also indicate "how important it is to affirm one's own destiny" (p. 297). One has control, yet only by placing control in service to one's unique mission from the unconscious does a person attain meaningful existence. One is caught with polarities that are superordinate to oneself. Dramatic and meaningful certainly, but there is something lacking that Jung came to recognize late in life.

The relation to the unconscious was conceived as a one-way influence rather than a reciprocal one, an impoverished relation rather than a full, mature one. Indeed, all sorts of questions about the relation could be posed. Why does God seem to need humans anyway? Why is the unconscious so treacherous, both sublime and devastating? Why are there so many contradictions or ambivalences, and how can one be said to have a relation to such an ambivalent domain? In short, the relation upon which he had built his life was incomplete, rife with questions.

Jung's dramatic solution might be summarized in the following way. God is not conscious of self or of creation, and the opposites of God are real and in need of reconciliation. Persons, then, can be of service to God in two complementary ways. First, through persons in relation to primordial sources of being, God can become conscious of self and of creation as a person becomes conscious of himself or herself. One's awareness contributes to God's awareness. Second, opposites can be reconciled in symbols. In creating and discovering a personal mythology, one becomes a symbol capable of uniting opposites, and the complementarily of opposites "gives meaningful shape to life" (p. 338). God needs us to develop and we need God to live meaningfully. The perilous undertaking into the unconscious realm is worth it, and upon such quests, the future of the world is apt to turn.

Jung's personal myth (his term) is a drama of great beauty. His addition, as described, is staggering, adding immense significance to the work Jung had already accomplished. For Jung, it was "the goal, or one goal, which fits man meaningfully into the scheme of creation, and at the same time confers meaning upon it" (p. 338). The goal was one he esteemed and found satisfying and meaningful. In one sense, the refinement of a personal drama is like refining an architectural structure. One can rest in the accomplishment and it might engender contentment. However, in another sense, one cannot rest in the accomplishment, for this vision requires continued efforts to become aware and to resolve contradictions in oneself and one's work.

Note that Jung regarded this symbolic elaboration as a formulation of a goal, not the achievement of one. Perhaps in old age with most of the work done, the symbolic addition is more one that Jung could rest in, but he still continued on his mission with this goal in mind. And since the formulation of the goal was part of Jung's ongoing effort to heighten consciousness of the unconscious and to realize it in his works, one would argue that this is not an instance of a terminal goal or completion, but of Adler's second kind. Dramatic developments seem like borderline cases, manifesting features of both kinds. In one way, Jung's symbolic elaboration is an achievement. In another way, it is a goal, a preparation for acting.

The second kind of end is called a normative goal. It is a achievement over time that can never be fully reached, and consequently, never rested in. In Adler's example, a symphony conductor prepares for a performance. The goal is musical excellence. Even if the performance is successful, the excellence aimed for is never fully or terminally reached. One cannot rest in but one performance that approaches excellence. It endures only as long as the performance, and afterwards, there is nothing to point to like a building. And during the performance, there is no one point where one can isolate excellence, for this involves an evaluation of the whole, which endures over time and cannot be reduced to a point in time (e.g., such as finishing a building). Even for terminals goals such as constructing a building, there is no point in construction where one can rest in satisfaction. One can anticipate a satisfying end, but the product cannot really be judged until it is finished. Normative goals never finish. Along the way, one strives to approach realization. Only at the end of striving can one judge properly, but striving diminishes rather than ceases. For those with a terminal goal, means really are means. But for those with a normative goal, "rightly directed means are the end aimed at in the process of becoming achieved or realized" (Adler, 1985, p. 139).

A vocation involves terminal goals of all sorts, completions along the way that one can rest in and look back on. However, a vocation is a normative goal. One cannot rest in a vocation. Rather one strives unceasingly to realize it. Persons can become confused certainly. We are not dealing with infallible beings. For example, Hilton tended to frame his hotel expansions as terminal goals and the purchase of the Waldorf was a major completion. However, Hilton did not stop and rest in the achievement. Rather, it seemed to release him to turn more properly to the central dimensions of meaning in his life. This distinction does not require a rigid separation. It would be unproductive to merely try to name the kind of goal under consideration. As we have seen with Jung's dramatic elaboration, there are borderline cases. Both terminal and normative goals are involved in a life. Understanding does not require separation so much as a relation between them. One's works are terminal goals, conceived in a bounded manner and accomplished. They are signposts along the way. And certainly, in the completion phase of life, one might enjoy a great contentment with what one has accomplished and with final efforts to bring life to fruition. However, terminal goals remain secondary. One's works are terminal, but the work of life is normative. One strives to shape it to the very end. In pursuing a work of life, one incorporates and manifests a way of being. This way of being is one's "rightly directed means."

Completion for those with vocation is nothing at all like the common stereotype. They do not retire, cease working, or devote themselves to amusements. In Super's (1957) theory of career development, the stage of decline involves deceleration (a slackening of work), disengagement from work, and retirement where one takes up new activities and assumes new roles. For those with vocation, this stage does not apply. It could only apply to those with a terminal goal or no particular goals, persons for whom work is capable of being finished. Such is not the case for those with a vocation. If one enters the completion phase in old age, declining agency is merely an obstacle to work around. It is hardly a reason to curtail effort. For the persons I have investigated, they continue to be quite productive. There is no disengagement whatever. Rather, they withdraw or stand back only to return with an enlarged perspective, renewed vigor, and a life perspective on the meaning of their work. And they do not retire. New roles and activities are part of the enlarged perspective and are woven into vocation. They do not amount to retirement as opposed to work. This incredible devotion alters how their completions are to be taken, for if they are not or not just terminal goals, what are they!

During the completion phase, one might achieve many terminal goals. After all, one is shaping the end, trying to bring all that has come before to a proper conclusion. In doing so, one might experience contentment. Actually, I have not found contentment to be nearly as prevalent as I expected. It is overruled at every turn by meaning, and the meaning of one's life might exclude contentment. Eiseley, for instance, could never be described as content. Nevertheless, suppose one did experience rich, sublime contentment. If focused on too narrowly, contentment is very misleading. Since persons do not rest in achievements, but continue to work, it is unlikely that it emerges sheerly from terminal achievements. And even if it did, it would remain secondary and must be understood as secondary. If considered central, it becomes very misleading for an understanding of this phase of life. Among other things, a focus upon a terminal point mistakes works for the work of life that is inseparable from a way of being. The lower level of completion involves works, but the higher level involves the activity of working and shaping one's life. Barring ill fortune or overwhelming circumstances, one does not stop pursuing a vocation. How, then, does the pursuit of a vocation during the completion phase of life differ significantly from the pursuit during the positing phase?

Consider the difference between an action and an activity. An action expresses what an agent has in mind, an intention and constellation of meanings. One is seeking to get something done, for which actions are means. Actions stop when something is accomplished. In short, one is a participant in Britton's (1970) use of the term. However, an activity is not directed toward some definite end. Ends might be involved, but if they govern what one is doing, activity becomes action. For example, dancing is ordinarily perhaps an activity. There is no purpose one is striving to accomplish. It would be odd to ask someone why he or she is dancing as it presumes an end in mind outside the dancing itself. However, if one were trying to impress others with one's skill, dancing becomes a means and would be properly regarded as an action. An activity does not express meanings an agent has so much as meanings the agent is.

That dancing is an activity for someone, or a favored activity as it was for Hilton, expresses the being of the person, what he or she is capable of becoming lost in or attuned with. And an activity does not cease because a goals has been attained, for there is no salient goal in mind. An activity is more apt to be set aside due to fatigue or extraneous reasons. The end of an action is a definite end. In taking actions, one acts and achieves some outcome. But there is no definite end to an activity unless set by convention (e.g., a chess game ends when the king is captured). It endures over time, and when lost in activity, the end dissolves as a significant feature. It appears open-ended.

What one achieves in completion is the transformation of action into activity. Pursuing a vocation during positing is largely dominated by actions. Pursuing a vocation during completion is dominated by activity. Adler's (1985) statement that "rightly directed means *are* the end" (p. 139) becomes a reality as activity. One is those means and what one does reflects what one is more than what one has in mind as intention or desire. The pattern of enactment from fall to summer is uniquely structured to enhance a sense of completion not just in deeds and reflection, but also in a transformation of one's way of being. As activity, one posits from fullness of being more than fullness of desire.

Gradually, the actions taken to complete one's life give way to activities in which one simply exists as the end. This does not involve two different types of work, but two structures of existence that contend in work. For example, suppose one were Norman Vincent Peale (1984) about the make another speech. For years, speeches were acts. One had been trying to inspire persons to the mind of Christ, to alter the quality of their lives. To do this, one had had to overcome shyness, inferiority feelings, and general awkwardness. One had to practice one's ability to speak well, using intonation, forceful gesturing, and the like. Now, suddenly, it resounds through one's mind that this could be the last speech. One is nearing the end. Partially, the speech becomes a little end, a completion, a way to round off or shape one's life as the end. Partially, also, with the end in view, one comes to notice the present more vividly, to appreciate what is in the immediate moment. As a parallel, a person could walk through a field for years, but once it occurs to the person that this might be the last walk, suddenly one might smell the fragrance, be moved by the beauty of wild flowers, or appreciate the wonders of this field. One could have appreciated the field for all those previous years, but the sense of ending seems to sharpen one's awareness of the present so much that it might seem as if one had been only half-awake to its wonders.

Now, as a little end, the last walk or speech becomes like a celebration, transforming action into activity. Certainly, Peale might still have a strong desire to help persons, but overpowering desire is, in his case, the joy of helping. Instead of striving to help, he can scarcely avoid helping. Desire, purpose, and the characteristics of action recede into the ground while perhaps delight, joy, or other characteristics of activity become the figure of existence.

Csikszentmihalyi (1975) has aptly described the experience of activity as a flow state. When totally involved, there is a sense of being in flow with the activity. Attention is undivided. Rather, one seems to be able to concentrate naturally or effortlessly. The activity virtually bounds one's scope of attention. All else seems to fade. One might be oblivious to surroundings and to the passage of time, giving the experience a sense of timelessness. One is the activity, in a sense. Self-consciousness is absent or minimal. Rather, one loses awareness of or transcends self, experiencing fusion with the immediate activity. There is a sense of control, but it is effortless, with little sense of actively monitoring or asserting control. One simply forgets about it and dwells in the activity. The activity seems to present clear, ongoing requirements for performing. As noted, there is no call to become self-conscious or to begin evaluating performance like an outside observer. Last, which seems redundant, the activity requires no goals or rewards beyond itself. One might experience flow in a purposeful act such as surgery, where the aim might be important, but in flow, what becomes prominent is a losing of oneself in the challenge of an activity.

To avoid awkwardness, we will stay with the term 'flow' rather than similar terms like 'intrinsic motivation' (Deci, 1975) or autotelic activities. These latter terms give rise to such muddled phrases as 'intrinsically motivated' activity, as if there were some other kind. And they tend toward excessive formulations. For example, both terms stress the absence of extrinsic aims or rewards. Presumably, "there is no apparent reward except the activity itself" (Deci, 1975, p. 23). However, this claim simply stresses the wrong feature. In real world situations, there might well be strong, meaningful aims, yet this does not exclude flow. It is just that when flow arises in actions taken toward a goal, they are transformed into activity. Aims are not excluded, but subordinated or coordinated. What one is doing is elevated to an end in itself rather than merely a means for something else. That what one does also has value as a means might be regarded as good fortune.

The sense of flow in activity ranges from rather mild to exceedingly deep. At present, there are no known boundaries. Strong flow is identical to numinous experiences (Jung, 1965) or peak experiences (Maslow, 1962). Indeed, Csikszentmihalyi's characteristics of flow are softer, more general variants of Maslow's characteristics of peak experiences. In peak experiences, perception is intense, objects are appreciated as unique wholes within a holistic or unified universe. Normal categories are burst as one seems able to perceive with incredible concreteness, yet holistically as well. During the experience, one is egoless. Normally, objects have relevance or irrelevance to our wants, but in this state, they are appreciated in themselves, as though one were at once absorbing and pouring into them. The experience is timeless, spaceless, evoking feelings of awe, reverence, humility, and love. One fuses with the world, an oceanic feeling of clarity and universality. Through such an experience, one is both humble as a part of the whole, yet elevated to Godlike stature as a whole. Fears, anxieties, and other disruptive emotions are vanquished. Polarities of existence such as selfish and unselfish are unified. One's cognition is more "passive and receptive than active" (Maslow, 1962, p. 81). About the experience, there is a sense of effortless ease. One is in total control, but by giving up active control. One flows as though at the center where the whole can be experienced and oppositions can be resolved.

In flow, a person can feel at one with the immediate or at one with all there is. It is as common as losing oneself in listening to music or as uncommon as a mystic experience of the unitive life. Without doubt, many of those covered in the present study had peak experiences, and during these experiences, they tended to feel fully complete. For example, in a visionary experience at age sixty-nine,

Jung (1965) felt "that there was no longer anything I wanted or desired . . . I had everything that I was, and that was everything" (p. 291). However, the experiences do not last; they offer a foretaste or partial realization of what might be. Perhaps there are some for whom normal experience approximates the quality of a peak experience (consult Underhill, 1974), but for those investigated thus far, there was no final arrival. They continued on their strivings to the very end, and this seems somehow more appropriate.

The goal of completion as a terminal goal seems misconceived. Certainly, persons pursue terminal goals or partial completions, but generally within the context of a normative goal that is never finished. Unlike a terminal goal, a normative goal involves continued uncertainty and tentativity. One can never be fully sure. Thus, near the end, person after person expresses an indefiniteness. Jung's statement seems to clarify many others'

> There is nothing I am quite sure about. I have no definite convictions—not about anything really. . . . In spite of all uncertainties, I feel a solidity underlying all existence and a continuity in my mode of being. . . . The more uncertain I have felt about myself, the more there has grown up in me a feeling of kinship with all things. In fact it seems to me as if that alienation which so long separated me from the world has become transferred into my own inner world, and has revealed to me an unexpected unfamiliarity with myself [pp. 358–89[.

Jung lived in a world of the mysterious and unexpected, and was forever in its pursuit. To finally be certain would eliminate the mysterious, and he would have been wrenched out of a meaningful position, a radical rupture of life in his last years. To achieve a terminal goal is terminating, and that is what makes it so ill conceived as a completion. As a superordinate, a terminal goal of life is a disaster. One ends the long struggle out of position rather than more wholly in position, and so it is with all of those studied. If there were no more point in uplifting his race, for instance, Washington would no longer have had a meaningful role in life. Terminal goals are meaningful, but only as secondary goals within a normative striving for realization. They function as focuses for bringing the past vividly into the present, shaping one's life into an experienced whole. In this way, they support normative striving. As a superordinate goal capable of being achieved fully, a terminal goal would undermine striving and would undermine activity, which is the real end.

During the completion phase of life, a person progressively transforms acts into activities. Previously, flow was experienced primarily at heightened moments of central enactments. Now, however, flow emerges as a potentially dominant quality of life, and there is no apparent end to the depths that can be reached. Flow in activities can pervade and elevate existence, offering endless levels of progression. Inasmuch as activity is dynamic rather than static, perhaps it would be better to speak of pervading and elevating rather than any terminal point.

In activity, story stops, and that is what makes it a fitting end. Gaps and oppositions are dissolved in flow, since desire is no longer the figure of existence. There is no dominant gap between what is and what ought to be in activity that shapes purpose; it has become the ground from which one engages in activity. The temporal becomes replaced by a sense of timelessness. Activity is open, without end. One engages in it, fully present to the moment without attending to a distant attainment. For those near the end, there is no more future, only the past and the present. One simply abides in activities until something external cuts them away. Peale (1984) conveys the general sense of this shift in being:

> Sometimes I am asked if I have any plans for retiring. In reply I have to ask, "From what?" Actually I have at least six jobs at which I work currently: *Guideposts* magazine, the Foundation for Christian Living, the church, writing books, radio programs, speaking engagements. Almost any one of them could be a full-time occupation. I enjoy work. It has always been my life. The idea of retirement has no attraction for me. I think perhaps I will go right on with my present activities as long as the Lord continues to give me health and energy [p. 284].

In meaningful activities that sum up a life, one feels complete. There are numerous paradoxical sounding phrases that can be applied to this sense of flow, and have been applied in great religious literature. For example, one attains control by giving up control. One discovers oneself by losing oneself. One accomplishes by letting be. One achieves harmony not by striving to realize desires, but by detachment from desire and doing what needs to be done. One becomes whole by becoming a subordinate part, at one with something outside oneself. Indeed, a great deal of classic religious works can be summarized by an advocation to transform acts into activities. For example, to pray in secret rather than in public where others can admire one's devotion is a way of saying that praying should be an activity. To pray without ceasing is to make prayer a timeless activity rather than a time-bound act. In activity, a person becomes whole not by struggling for completion but by embracing completion as a way of life, and the way is an endless exploration. Only in this manner do one's deeds express the fullness of being, a being that is endlessly developing. As Heraclitus (Wheelwright, 1959) phrased it long ago, "you could not discover the limits of soul, even if you traveled every road to do so; such is the depths of its meaning" (p. 58). Or as might be framed according to the analogue of seasons, completion becomes the summer of one's existence.

Balance and Imbalance

There appears to be a natural rhythm in the completion phase of life, which, if followed, seems capable of guiding a person to a way of being, not previously conceived. No one consciously sought to transform action into activity. Rather, it just seemed to emerge more or less strongly as persons repeated the dominant pattern of enactment for this phase. However, there are ways to go wrong and these ways might be summarized by imbalance.

Consider, for instance, the autumn quality of incompletion in the pattern of enactment. It sets the tone of an enactment, stressing the sense of ending things. If balanced with the other parts of the pattern, enactments lead to flow. However, if imbalanced, overstressed or understressed, the pattern is not apt to work as well or to work at all. Potentially, there are many kinds of deviations from pattern. As one example, Giacomo Casanova's (1966–71 or for an abridged edition, 1984) old age was one of progressive depletion. Due to a disease, Casanova was stupefied until about age nine, or as he phrased it, an imbecile. His mother and father were actors, and actors at that time were pariahs of society, a somewhat scandalous group who were both scorned and enchanting. Casanova rose from stupefaction to live by his wits. He wanted to impress others, have a place of distinction; but more powerfully, he continually engaged in adventures and comic misadventures in which he was both a stage director and the main character. He thrived on the excitement of working his way out of difficult situations in which no one knew the full truth but he. In short, he duped many "fool." According to Casanova, he lived to indulge his senses, largely in the pursuit of women, yet it was never just indulgence. It is also and probably more accurate to say that what drew him was the excitement of scheming, anticipating, hoping, deceiving, and impressing in the pursuit of indulgence. Casanova was a passionate adventurer. While dubious as an example of those with vocation, he does exemplify completion as depletion. As he grew older, all the features that had lit up his life began to go out, one by one. Pursuing women was over. Eating fine dishes was over; his health and digestion could not take them. Adventures were over. Instead of living on the edge of a precipice, in utter excitement, he was slowly being cast down into it. From cheerfulness, he turned to melancholy. It would be unfair to overemphasize his misery in later life. After all, the writing of his memoirs was a pleasure. It allowed him to relive old adventures; in setting them down, it was his last adventure really. However, it is also fair to note the striking contrast between positing and completion, a high and a low. He lived depletion, dwindling, falling, setback, disappointment, and catastrophe. For those with a vocation, completion was a continuance upon a different plane of existence, not a striking contrast.

Or consider the wintry quality of positioning in the pattern of enactment. It is characterized by spectatorship and, in particular, by participation in memories. Ideally, reminiscence is a natural, effortless activity, calling the past into the present and setting another tone for this phase of life as activity. It is part of whole-making. If underemphasized, the past is virtually denied and the sense of activity is diminished. The completion phase of life is apt to become a stunted form of the positing phase of life. If overemphasized, one might become lost in memory and curtail the full pattern of enactment, living in the past rather than living the past in the present. As Jung (1965) noted, the decisive difference for him was that he allowed his personal retrospections to be a preparation for fresh investments rather than a perhaps enchanting prison.

There are no doubt many reasons for imbalance, for the

attenuation and deviation of the pattern of enactment. For example, one might believe that reminiscence is somehow unhealthy and strive to avoid it. Or one might combat the sense of ending things. One of the major reasons is probably the force of circumstance. Calamitous events might well stress autumn qualities of incompletion too much. Nevertheless, persons in the completion phase of life seem extraordinarily resilient, perhaps because they have a lifetime of work behind them. For example, Emily Carr was overwhelmed by circumstance during the years she should have been vigorously producing her life's work. Yet in old age and ill health, when she was strongly advised by her physician to stop painting, she did not fall into the same despair. After wondering whether she wanted to get better if she could not paint, she decided to begin writing about "those things which during my painting life have touched me deeply" (1966, p. 265). While writing became a partial focus, she continued to go to the woods and sketch or paint. The longing was too great to stop completely. She could not scramble over logs anymore. Rather, she had to be taken out, sat down, and left. While her work slowed, her delight increased. She was able to marvel once more at the migration of geese, the power and beauty of her northern woods. Her outings became like an activity of communion with what had so moved her all her life. Persons seem more able, as Carr said, to adjust "themselves to life at different angles" (p. 264.

Perhaps, too, some vocations are simply more vulnerable to circumstances. For example, Eileen Garrett (1968) devoted her life to mediumship. She was an extraordinarily gifted psychic, capable of direct exploration of the "invisible world." She made herself available to numerous scientists and groups who wished to explore and gather evidence through her. She helped countless persons through her gifts. She initiated and supported conferences, publications, and groups to further psychic exploration. In nearly every sense, she was a medium between the ordinary world of existence and the invisible one. However, her life was filled with calamitous events. As one instance, she was seriously ill often, yet she would use illness for exploration. She endured great physical pain, fiercely holding on to grasp and understand it, to know the "full degree of suffering the body will maintain" (pp. 184–85). After studying her life, it is difficult to imagine what she would not have rewoven into her work as part of her vocation. Of all the persons studied for this book, she was probably the most delicate but unconquerable. Although some vocations might be more vulnerable to force of circumstance, it is greatly modified by a person's ability to transcend, conquer, or make use of the situation one is in.

The greatest threat is probably not circumstance, but narrowness of perspective. Given that the pattern of enactment functions as a whole in which, for instance, the autumn quality of incompletion is modified and made positive by its place in the whole, any part that is isolated, focused on too narrowly, or misemphasized would affect the whole as a hindrance. That is, the elements that evoke an autumn quality of incompletion (death of loved ones, illness, etc.) might be construed and experienced in too narrow and isolating a manner. The pattern works by a movement from incompletion to positioning to positing to completion. We desire, prepare, act, and evaluate. However, if one part is isolated from the natural flow of movement, the pattern becomes imbalanced. One essentially stops in that part, and it seems, at least hypothetically, rather easy to become stalled. As one's world comes to an end through gradual destruction or sudden calamities, it seems easy enough to be narrowly and excessively focused upon these kinds of events. It seems easy enough to dwell too much in memory, if the present seems hopeless. There are probably many variations on these types of difficulties. Focusing too narrowly on participation might weaken the ground for it. Focusing too much on spectatorship might enfeeble participation. While difficulties are relatively easy to conceive, and can be partially and temporarily identified in lives, I have not been able to find convincing and strong examples in the lives of those with a vocation.

Speculatively, it might be that the lifelong cultivation of a sense of vocation places one very advantageously for the last phase of life. But then, too, the pattern of enactment might be stronger and more resilient than imagined. For instance, it seems quite plausible that a sense of ending things leads one to dwell on past memories. It seems plausible that this would invigorate fresh efforts. In the context of ending, memory, and fresh efforts, it seems quite likely that one would savor more fully the completion. If so, the pattern is in operation and leads on to an unexpected transformation of the whole quality of life, with no end to the depths and heights that might be reached.

7 The Rhythm of Life

Even as those with a vocation are engaged in completing life, they seem keenly aware of the whole that life has been. In pursuing one's vocation, life is made whole. In retrospect, there is often a sense of destiny, so unified is the pattern they discern and feel:

> Looking back on the sixty years I have lived, I am struck most of all by the straightforwardness of the pattern. Everything that I am, or think, or do, almost everything that has happened to me, seems traceable to its origins with the simple clarity of geometrical proof. It is a curious, even a faintly disconcerting sensation to find oneself fulfilling what seems to have been a destiny [Menuhin, 1975, p. 15].

Jung's destiny was his daimon:

> There was a daimon in me, and in the end its presence proved decisive. It overpowered me, and if I was at times ruthless it was because I was in the grip of the daimon. I could never stop at anything once attained. I had to hasten on, to catch up with my vision [Jung, 1965, p. 365].

All those gropings, uncertainties, decisions, detours, setbacks, and efforts added up to something, after all. While good or ill fortune surely is apt to influence this sense of a whole life, it is not necessary that one's life be perfect or totally fulfilled. That is, the sense depends on acceptance as well as the pattern of deeds done or attempted. The Apostle Paul summarized this attitude most succinctly. "I have fought the good fight to the end; I have run the race to the finish; I have kept the faith" (2 Timothy 4:7–8)." He strove and a life of striving was the focus, not so much transient achievements.

However, even while persons express a solidity or wholeness to their lives, they often experience more uncertainty about themselves and the world. Recall that Jung experienced an unfamiliarity with himself. Eiseley (1975) stated that "I appear to know nothing of what I truly am" (p. 248). Uncertainty, in this context, is not necessarily painful in any way; it is more apt to be connected with novelty,

171

delight, curiosity, and freshness. Far from ending in certitudes, persons seem to experience or seek uncertainty as part of completion. "The unexpected and the incredible belong in this world. Only then is life whole. For me the world has from the beginning been infinite and ungraspable" (Jung, 1965, p. 356).

What is the whole that persons sense in their lives? What composes a whole? From the lives investigated, there appear to be two overlapping kinds of wholes that correspond to the two interweaving themes of completion. During completion, persons strive for a proper ending and they also come alive in activity. The first concerns a pattern of meaning, a "straight line" or destiny. The second concerns a metapattern that operates through the meanings of the first. The aim of this chapter is to characterize these two forms of wholeness in life, and then to briefly comment on their implications for research and practice.

Wholeness as a Unique Pattern of Meaning

A vocation is not so much something one has as a pattern of meaning one lives. Given a significant position, a person is centered within a regnant drama that endures over a lifetime. The unity of meaning discerned is dramatic unity. Looking back, one can identify origins of desire, preparation and development, enactments, and attempts to bring one's work and life to completion. Amid all the diversity life had to offer, there is still a coherent drama, capable of aesthetic judgment.

Like a novel, the unity of a life is indefinitely analyzable. Eventually, a fuller effort should be attempted just as literary scholars now attempt to explicate the meaning of a novel. For example, Parke (1955) explicated seven levels or layers of meaning in Melville's classic, *Moby Dick*. Here, however, it is only necessary to draw attention to the two complementary ways that excellence in art is judged (Saw, 1971).

First, as phrased most succinctly by Burke (1968), "form in literature is an arousing and fulfillment of desires" (p. 124). In looking back on the life one has lived, a person is a spectator just as if he or she were reading a novel. As a spectator, one is capable of being moved and transported. As a participant, one is capable of adding finishing touches to the drama of life. From this perspective, unity in life consists in seeing one's life in the form of a single act. Thus, there was an arousal of want and expectation that was satisfied. Owing to the tolerance and acceptance of the later phase, no exacting or unrealistic standard for satisfaction is evident. Since the productiveness of a person's life work partially involves good fortune, this realism is quite appropriate. Ambitions tend to outrun accomplishments, and at the end, a generous portion of acceptance is desirable. Note that the Apostle Paul did not say that he had won all his fights and races. Rather he fought and raced to the finish, keeping the faith. The stress falls more on the wholeheartedness of one's striving than upon the fruit of one's efforts. The feeling at the end is not like the satiation from a good meal, but more like the inspiration from a good example.

Second, form concerns the diversity of meanings and desires that are woven into s single pattern of movement. While the first aspect concerns the basic movement over time, the second aspect concerns the scope of what is integrated in a recurrent act. Aside from the levels noted in Chapter 4, what might be included is extensive. For example, Trollope's favorable recreation was fox hunting and "riding to hounds" exactly paralleled his central enactment of vocation (Cochran, 1986). To the extent that one's spouse is a central character, he or she is intimately involved in the central enactment. The sweep of integration is simply staggering, once one begins to look.

As a manageable example, a person might not only fulfill his or her own desires in life, but carry forward the aspirations of loved ones. "Much of my life's design was laid before I was born, and I sometimes feel that I have brought to consummation not just my own yearnings but also those of my parents" (Menuhin, 1978, p. 15). After stating that the meaning of his life was that a question had been addressed to him, Jung (1965) went further than Menuhin: "Perhaps it is a question which preoccupied my ancestors, and which they could not answer. . . . What I feel to be the resultant of my ancestors' lives, or a karma acquired in a previous personal life, might perhaps equally well be an impersonal archetype" (p. 318). In childhood, Eiseley (1975) identified with a criminal who escaped from the state penitentiary. Through the March snow he ran until the posse tracked him down and killed him. Eiseley could never forget this event near his home, and in his life of sensed wandering, he was partially making good on the failed escape of this prisoner. The prisoner became a personified symbol into which Eiseley had packed the meanings of his own existence. Whether ordinary or mystical, straightforward or deeply symbolic, many persons (actually, I cannot think of an exception) have a sense of realizing the ambitions and desires of others through their own lives, and in stronger cases, feel themselves to be a virtual community of others with similar yearnings. That is, Eiseley did not experience the prisoner as other, in strong moments, but as part of himself. Through completing one's own life, a person is able to complete the lives of others.

It would be a mistake to regard those with a vocation as narrow. In symbolic elaboration, a drama is bound to more and more of the world. In this dramatic encompassment, a "feeling about" or position is expanded to more and more of the world. Similarly, it would be a mistake to regard those with a vocation as imbalanced or the opposite of a well-balanced person. Unlike perhaps some, those with vocation have a focus with incredible depth. The early problem of existence was not set aside, neglected, or escaped from, but became a basis for positive development. It was faced and that confrontation made all the difference. Steffens could have denied his disillusionments. Trollope could have used his "castle-building" to flee from reality. Yet each person seems almost ruthless in his or her resolve to live what is real rather than fantasy, and it is this sense of reality that pervades their work. Their balance is manifested in drama rather than external ideals that might well lack a sense of reality to them.

Wholeness as Common Metapattern

Consider two difficulties of the first form of wholeness. A person becomes unified in a composition of desire, given a dramatic vision of the world. He or she prepares until a dramatic part can be truly adopted as a self-metaphor and then the person acts out of position to make good on the direction implicit within it. The first difficulty is that the position formed for the work of life is a wholeness of incompletion, dominated by a gap between what is and what ought to be. The decisive characteristics of this position are the depth and unity of desire, and by extension, of meaningful purpose. The obvious point about this kind of wholeness is that it is inherently incomplete. Wholeness suggests fulfillment or completion, but the wholeness of personhood is certainly not complete in this sense.

However, if we project ahead, we run into the second kind of difficulty. If a person fulfills the direction implicit in position and becomes fulfilled, he or she is out of position. Perhaps one can bask in contentment for a while, but then one must do something. However, what is it one could do? If a person is hungry and satisfies his or her hunger, then the gap has been bridged and the person can go on to other things. This is proper but only for subordinate and recurrent wants. For a regnant, enduring desire that stands behind vocation, that has invigorated life with a sense of meaning, one does not want to replace it with the satiety of a well-fed hog. To eliminate the desire would be to radically upend one's life, marking a cleavage between the meaningful and meaningless. With the termination of his desire to uplift his race and the south generally, Washington's life would have ended. Certainly, one might envision his going on to other things, but they would be different things and his life would be marked by discontinuity rather than wholeness.

To summarize these two difficulties, the wholeness of personhood seems incompatible with the wholeness of life. To become whole in the sense of fulfilled is not very desirable and the wholeness of incompletion looks wonderful by sheer contrast. That is, picture Washington filled with vitality in striving to accomplish his mission in life. Now picture Washington fulfilled, basking in contentment, and eventually having to turn to other things. In fulfillment as pictured in this way, there is an enormous loss and one would prefer incompletion. To resolve this difficulty between dramatic wholeness of a life and a personal wholeness of completion involves another movement in life that is not found in the meanings that a person lives but through them. This movement seems to emerge naturally in pursuing a vocation, but cannot be considered a part of vocation.

As an introduction to this movement, consider the basis for the problem. First, there is not one kind of personal wholeness, but perhaps several kinds appropriate for different phases of life. Second, wholeness has been unnaturally wedded to either activeness or passiveness. For decades, hedonically-minded psychologists conceived the end point of experience as a return to quiescence or equilibrium or just a passive state. The conception of need-reduction placed enormous stress upon the pleasure of a passive end and the disruption of an aroused need. Other psychologists eventually noted that humans are naturally active. Striving is not necessarily painful, but rather can be joyful, purposeful, and meaningful. More naturally, we are striving for meaningful goals rather than basking passively. After all, boredom is not restful. While striving seems more correct than the absence of need or want, both are incorrect in focusing too narrowly upon a part rather than a whole. In a complete pattern of experience, there is both. What seem incompatible as isolated phenomena are quite compatible, indeed mutually complementary and indispensable, within a whole enactment. It is to patterns of enactment we must turn to find a resolution to the difficulty, a resolution persons experienced rather than formulated.

Each phase of life is dominated by a characteristic pattern of enactment. In these patterns, the movement from incompletion through positioning and positing to completion is fixed. The seasonal stress of the movement is variable. The seasons serve as metaphors. For example, seeing incompletion as spring stresses springlike qualities and is clearly different than seeing incompletion as fall with fall like qualities. The reasons for using seasons as metaphors are that they are a natural cycle that parallels the cycle of stories, that they have been used for centuries as apt metaphors of human affairs, and more importantly, they are a model of interpenetrating opposition. Recall that stories are bounded by opposing poles and that a story involves a gradual shift from one pole to the other. The seasons model this shift with universal qualities such as active versus passive or receptive, participant versus spectator, and the like, and in this way, serve to illumine more enduring qualities of patterns beyond the particular meanings of the individuals involved. Now, consider each pattern of enactment in light of the problem discussed.

Incompletion is the winter of life, a time for incubating an organization of desire. The pattern of enactment moves from spring and summer to fall and winter. The energy of the initial phases is counterbalanced by receptivity in the later phases. If the pattern is followed, the result is a wholeness of yearning. one is a virtual container of desire and a spectator on it. A person moves forward by seeing a way out and beginning to develop enough sense of agency to act. The pattern of enactment not only broadens and deepens desire, but prepares for the movement out. That is, incompletion and positioning are imaginatively based, without long grounding in experience. One essentially is practicing becoming an agent, even as the feebleness of imaginative agency is revealed in confrontation with reality, where one is a spectator. Growth in one's capacity as a spectator is necessary to order desires drawn from experience and to envision a way out. Fresh desires, energetic preparation, dwindling initiative, and deep dwelling form the pattern.

Positioning is the spring of life, a time for preparing oneself to realize desire. The pattern of enactment moves from summer and fall to winter and spring. In this pattern, one is most energetic where only reflection is required and least energetic or capable where action is required. Or one is feverish in desire, but positioning is shadowed by imminent downfall. Another way to phrase this is that one is a spectator where participation is required and a participant where spectatorship is required. During the active phases, one is most receptive. This pattern is given to enduring trials and misfortunes as one strives to attain position. One endures and learns, culminating each cycle with hope or a little rebirth. As the cycle continues, there is a powerful development of agency, an infusion of spirit, and an elaboration of dramatic context. If followed, the result is a wholeness of personhood. The desire is not something one has, but something one is. Washington had a desire for education to be constructive and then he became a person centered in this desire. The natural upshot of this rite-of-passage pattern is that one attains a position to act from, becoming an agent of desire.

Positing is the summer of life, a time for realizing desire, producing one's life work. The pattern of enactment moves from winter and spring to summer and fall. This is the only pattern in which the seasons are fully aligned with the nature of the phases. That is, desire should be wintry, suggesting stable form and slow incubation. Positioning should be springlike, filled with the freshness of anticipation as buds begin to sprout or emerge from winter. Positing should be summerlike, charged with the vitality of bringing anticipations to fruition. And completion should be fall like, a time for reflection and evaluation as the vigor of summer lingers and dwindles. Overall, it is a stable form, leading to the production of a life work, to the realization of the desires and preparations of the prior two phases of life. If this pattern is followed, and barring ill fortune, it leads to fulfillment. One is filled with the realizations accomplished. Here we are back at the original problem. How can a wholeness of life be preserved with the wholeness of personhood?

Positing prepares for the transition into completion in at least two ways. First, as more and more works are realized, there are more and more partial completions. One moves toward being filled or completed, and attention is drawn somewhat from work to the completion or fulfillment of it. Second, as more and more is realized, there is less to realize. One becomes more aware of an end. The sense of ending things arises in many ways as indicated previously. Steffens was worn out. Aging drew Maurois's attention. Hilton felt that his biggest accomplishment was in the past. There is a sense in which the ending arises from positing, sometimes through deficiencies of this phase, and there is a sense in which it arises from external imposition such as aging. When these two shifts in emphasis and perspective occur, there is a change in the pattern of enaction.

Completion is the fall of life, a time for winding up and winding down, shaping the end of a life work. The pattern of enactment moves from fall and winter to spring and summer. The energy of the later phases is counterbalanced by the relative stability of the initial phases. If this pattern is followed, the result is a transformation of acts into activities. Certainly, there is also the possibility of a strong sense of fulfillment, but it is secondary and serves more to strengthen a sense of activity. It would probably be more accurate to speak of fulfilling rather than fulfillment, an activity rather than a state. In activity, the wholeness of personhood is a wholeness of completion. Desire or the regnant gap of life recedes to the ground while fullness of being emerges as the figure. In conjunction with the sense of ending things, fulfilling or shaping the last completions leads to fullness in which one acts less from desire and more from the fullness of a way of being attained. Kindness, for example, might be structured as a desire to be kind to those in want of it. However, kindness might also be intensified as a virtual overflowing of one's nature that transcends desire. One just is kindly, more wholly, indiscriminately, and pervasively. Kindness is a way of being in which one engages rather than an act one performs. Thus, one difficulty is resolved. Fulfillment is not a terminal state, but a prelude to activity in which one posits from fullness.

In activity, story is transcended. An outside observer could tell a story about someone's actions. From the outside, an act might not seem any different than an activity. However, from the standpoint of experience, story gives way to a timeless engagement in which one flows, to use Csikszentmihalyi's term. A person completes an act, but does not complete an activity. Activity is open, not something to complete, but to engage in, perhaps delight in, and give oneself to. In strong activity or deep flow, there is little sense of progress, of beginning and end, or of qualitative shifts in experience. One moment is like others. Past and future are now in one enduring moment. One completely is, yet is not. That is, one is fulfilled, but in activity, there is also an emptying of self to merge with elements of activity. As Csikszentmihalyi found, a rock climber feels at one with the cliff. In strong prayer, one is at one with God. A person takes on a sense of otherness in becoming himself for herself. Thus, the second problem is resolved. The story of one's life ends in activity. Activity dissolves or transcends the story mode of living as it culminates or concludes. The proper end of a life story is a movement beyond to a timeless engagement.

Beneath the unique dramatic pattern of meaning in a life, there is another pattern, what appears to be a natural cycle common for everyone who makes a vocation of life. This common pattern is not consciously followed. It is not something one resolves upon. Rather, a person tends to focus upon the meanings of his or her dramatic existence, trying to bring them to fruition. By devoting oneself to the realization of these meanings, another pattern unfolds and makes its presence known most fully only at the end.

The Nature of Movement

Most influential theories of global development are stage theories, or very like stage theories. The movement from one stage to another is conceived as a discontinuity, a radical qualitative leap from one context of meaning to another. The present description of vocation is not a stage theory. It is concerned with phases of life, not stages. There is no radical discontinuity between phases. One blends into another, is incorporated and transformed in another. Although phase and stage are different, they clearly have much in common as well.

Stage theories offer different views of how movements are attained. In Maslow's (1962) early formulation, a person progresses from physiological needs to higher order needs. When satisfied, lower order needs diminish in potency and a person is freed to become aware of and pursue higher ones. In Erikson's (1959) theory, persons develop according to a ground plan in which different parts arise at different times, contributing to the whole in the process of formation. These parts are framed as basic issues that arise in sequence. The first issue is trust versus mistrust. The way this issue is resolved and the degree to which it is resolved have enormous implications for the resolution of future issues in the hierarchy. Each issue, then, is a potential crisis one cannot avoid, and it calls for a radical change in perspective. In Loevinger's (1976) theory of ego development and Kohlberg's (1976) theory of moral development, a person progresses more by stimulation. In Piaget's (1968) terms, a person is confronted with experiences that cannot readily be assimilated to existing schemata; they require stretching as one alters schemata to accommodate the experiences. Loevinger and Kohlberg stress challenging experiences of this nature and models of functioning that are one stage higher. In this way, a person is stimulated to move forward both by the inadequacies of his or her current stage of development and by the promised adequacy of a more advanced stage. In Norton's (1976) theory, each stage constitutes a world governed by enduring principles. A stage exchange is a world exchange, a radical and instantaneous switch from one world to another governed by an incommensurably different set of principles.

The basis for this radical exchange is an illumination, revelation, or recognition that new requirements apply. As one fulfills the intrinsic requirements of a stage, the stage gradually relinquishes its hold, preparing a person for a sudden insight that alters the very conditions of living. For example, adolescence begins with the discovery of autonomy. Maturation begins with the discovery that one will eventually die, and one must make something of life while one can. Old age begins with the discovery that there no longer is a future. Each of these theories and others might ground the present effort in a more general view of human development. While there are supportive points of contact in all the theories, Norton's theory is probably the most compatible in general form.

Similarly, probably most of the material presented could be

framed in terms of these theories. For example, the problem of existence during incompletion seems to be precisely the kind of challenging experience that could stimulate development. The models used in formulating a way out do tend to model an advanced way of functioning. Erikson's issues are present to some degree. And there are certainly revelations in each phase. For example, the sense of ending things during completion is exactly the same as the illumination that Norton poses as the beginning of old age. Maslow's needs and general portrait of self-actualization are present, but there does not seem to be a progression from lower order needs to higher order ones.

Although there are impressive similarities, encouraging the possibility of further enrichment in drawing more directly from these theories, there are differences as well. Generally, those with a vocation could be characterized by advanced stages of development, but there is no correspondence between the phases and stages. For example, Menuhin entered positioning at age four while none of these theories would acknowledge much stage progression at so young an age.

The various needs, issues, and the like tend to be as intrusive as helpful in application to the lives investigated. Partially, this occurs because they are disembodied propositions that, when applied, collide with the proportions and interrelations of meanings in an integrated story. Partially, this occurs because the theories are intended to apply to everyone, and consequently are very abstract. If used as a basis for description, the theories (with the exception of Norton) would tell stories that do not adequately reflect the actual lives lived, and perhaps this is to be expected. They are concerned with human development in general, whereas this book is concerned only with the development of a particular kind of person. Nevertheless, consult McAdams (1985) for a fine study that fruitfully uses developmental theories to examine life stories.

Perhaps the biggest difference concerns the way persons progress. While the vehicles of change from these theories are present, at least in part, they are present as aspects of a holistic movement. Indeed, assuming that the whole of each phase has been plausibly sketched, future work might reconstruct each phase in much more detail. Yet these corrections, refinements, and extensions require a coherent context, and it is this larger movement that has been identified in the present study. The primary vehicles of change are four patterns of enactment that are repeated in phases. If a pattern of enactment is allowed to be repeated, one prepares for entry to the next phase.

The patterns of enactment are natural rather than human contrivances, but they are not mechanical. For example, the pattern of enactment during incompletion deepens and unifies yearning. It stimulates efforts to find a way out, but still, it is the person who must actually find a solution, and one's solution might be wrong or very limited. If one's solution is inadequate, the pattern continues, revealing one's error and stimulating fresh efforts. As the pattern is enacted over and over, it can also be perverted. For example, Francis Farmer never stopped trying to escape, but she also was so forcibly entrenched that she tended to bring on the very conditions of the entrapment. The ways she acted, for instance, called forth or invited contests of power and alienation. Still, the pattern churns on, calling for a more appropriate response.

If the patterns of enactment are followed and brought to a point, yearning gives way to positioning. Positioning leads to positing, and positing leads to completion. In retrospect, there is such seeming inevitability to these holistic movements that it can be deceiving, and one must be reminded that it could have been otherwise. Along the path, there are a variety of temptations, compensatory attractions, failures of courage, unfavorable circumstances, and the like, that might temporarily or permanently stall the movement of vocation. For example, as a young reporter covering Wall Street, Steffens was offered the presidency of a company. In contrast to his meager salary, he would have earned a large income, occupied a fine office, and become a man of distinction. As he learned to characterize these jobs later, he would have been paid to be front or dummy president for banker bosses. His real job would have been to take orders, accept punishment if necessary, and ask no questions. However, at the time, it was a flattering and tempting offer, but one that would have placed his emerging vocation in suspension. Probably positioning is the most vulnerable phase for the improper turn, but all phases have vulnerabilities.

To successfully follow patterns of enactment to a proper fruition requires certain virtues. For a brilliant study of virtues in relation to the intrinsic goods of activity, consult MacIntyre (1984). The pattern might exist, but without these virtues, it is unlikely that one will pass beyond. These virtues are supporting stances that must be cultivated within a composition around a regnant position. While I cannot enumerate all the virtues that might be involved, some seem quite apparent. The first virtue is wholeheartedness. This requires, among other things, an awareness of what one can be wholehearted about. Steffens could be wholehearted in reporting, but not in business. Once found, however vaguely, one must stick to it through doubts, temptations, dissuasions from others, or alternative versions of reality. Clearly, this is a tricky undertaking. Cynicism might prematurely arrest each birth. Doubts might undermine every effort. Peale's doubts were not subdued until he united the ministry with positive living. If one is steeped in doubt, negative thoughts, timidity, impending failure, feelings of always being out of place, what such a person could be wholehearted about is the eradication of these conditions and their replacement with positive thinking. Peale made doubt itself a condition for wholehearted involvement. Wholeheartedness is important to allow incompletion to pervade one's being, to undergo the trials of positioning, to produce a work of life, and to shape the end.

Wholeheartedness is one of the core virtues, one particularly stressed by Norton (1976), and it immediately draws in others. Actually, it matters little where we start, for others are immediately drawn in; there is no isolated virtue. However, wholeheartedness is an appropriate virtue to stress. To act wholeheartedly requires courage partially because one plunges into an unknown with no assurances and partially because one's existence is at stake. The whole is involved in an enactment, as Norton noted, and to hold back is a failure of courage, whereas to venture forth with oneself as a whole at stake demands courage. There is no requirement that one be courageous in a general sense, but courageous in venturing the whole in strivings. It is so much easier to engage in self-deception (Fingarette, 1969), to act perhaps as if something does not matter when it does, to tailor life with seams of prudence. It took enormous courage for Emily Carr to devote herself to painting amid ridicule and disparagement. It took enormous courage for Peale to become a minister, for Hilton to set forth in the world with his $5,000, for Washington to set forth for Hampton Institute with $1.50, and so on.

All the persons studied wavered on the edges of precipices and plunged onward.

Closely aligned with courage is faith. partially, faith is a distinctive quality of those with a vocation; they are other-centered. They have subordinated themselves for something greater, and in doing so, feel that they have become themselves. They come alive in forwarding some cause or dream. Partially, faith is a deeper form of hope. Irrationally perhaps and often in spite of evidence, they develop a faith in their destiny, and are willing to pursue it in circumstances that would incline most others to abandon it.

Industry—or more globally, individual power of agency—is required. A person does not go with the movement in the same way one floats on a stream that carries one somewhere. There is faith in one's vision, but only if one works to make it real. Menuhin (1978) captured this striving by an apt analogy:

> Laboriously the composer feels his way through the notes of his symphony to the last triumphant bar, only to discover that their choice and sequence were inevitable all along. The inevitability does not rob him of achievement, however, for only hindsight can preclude all other notes and only he could father these. So it is with my life. Once traveled, the route is clear, but prescience did not divine it and I am at least in part accountable for the turns it took [p. 15].

Along the way, persons plan, decide, act, and adjust. They strive and endure. And if this powerful development and exercise of human agency were not present, they could not follow the patterns of enactment.

Last, wholeheartedness requires excessive realism. This is perhaps a curious or questionable virtue, given that the sample of persons involves psychics and others who are supposedly inclined toward the unreal. However, realism, in this use, does not mean the nastier or more earthy side of life. One does not have to be cynical to be realistic. Nor does realism mean that one must follow the dictates of conventional wisdom. Indeed, one might shred conventional wisdom to pursue what is real. Wayne Burns (1982), for example, was a devoted teacher of English literature in universities. He used literature to penetrate through socially sanctioned lies and ideals to glimpses of reality. His life was and is dedicated to unmasking unrealities that he and his students might develop as individuals rather than as conventional platitudes. While he deemed himself "constitutionally incapable of accepting any faith" (p. 25), he had devout faith in his mission. During incompletion, each person discovers a reality that he or she cannot escape, but one that often collides with or is not supported by conventional ideas of reality as espoused by local influences. Each person is thrust back upon himself or herself to determine what is real, and this they do, often with ruthless zeal. For them, the unreal is usually portrayed as an evil.

Menuhin found music to be transporting. Jung found that his experiences of God were at odds with official doctrine. Carr found another reality in the deep woods. Burns found another picture of reality in contrast to convention. Garrett had experiences in which she knew more than was available to her by customary means. And so on. Although their individual versions of reality clash, their dedication to the reality of what they experience is common. They will not deny any experience because it does not fit that of others. They examine, question, doubt, and search. The question of what is real often becomes a special one to which they attend with extraordinary care. The connection to wholeheartedness is that one cannot live a lie, and each person seems to question whether he or she is self-deceived. Wholeheartedness requires a conviction that what one is and what one pursues is utterly real.

Realism enters in another way as well. Particularly for those who experienced incompletion quite negatively, compensatory fantasies are a threat. If ever one is to realize another condition of living, it must be real. Fantasy is an evil imprisonment that merely offers false hopes. Thus, there tends to be extraordinary effort and attention in sizing up oneself and one's situation exactly as it is. As Washington said of one of his many difficulties, "I determined to face the situation just as it was" (p. 46). In a way, the stakes are too high for deceits. In any case, those with a vocation are extraordinary in the extent to which they face realities. They might embark on projects with little chance of success, but they do so in full awareness of the risks and obstacles to overcome.

Whether an emerging sense of vocation calls forth better qualities, or better qualities facilitate a sense of vocation, it is difficult to say. One is inconceivable without the other in the common story. This certainly does not mean that they are exemplars of virtue in some general sense, although they generally are. We might well disagree with some of their decisions, principles, and actions. Rather, it means that character, the possession of virtues, supports personhood or a regnant position in life, just as this position calls for character. Character is not personhood, but becomes part of the larger composition of what makes up a person. In the end, we might question a person's priorities or standpoint, but we would not question that particular stances emerge in the role of virtues as one pursues a vocation. Character supports vocation as a means, but from a larger perspective, the means are little ends in themselves. Wholeheartedness is a means and an end. The claim, then, is that a certain quality of character is necessary to successfully follow patterns of enactment to fruition, or to pursue a vocation. Without these virtues of character, the insights, resolutions, decisions, models, and needs proposed in developmental theories count for little. Less antagonistically, the adoption of insight, resolution of a dilemma, nature of a decision, attraction to a model, and level of a need avowed are manifestations of character as well as vehicles for an improvement of it.

Holistic Construction

In teaching great ideas of the past twenty-five hundred years, Gregory Bateson (1979) would on occasion present an example from the nonliving world and the living world. His question was concerned with how one can tell the difference. How can one tell the difference between the world of forces and impacts, and the world of distinctions that matter? Regarding a crab, students noted that the claws were symmetrical despite a difference in size. The crab seemed "composed, like a painting" (p. 9). Regarding a disk, his daughter could tell that it was not a stone or a nonliving example because it had a spiral on the back. "A spiral is a figure that retains it shape (i.e., its proportions) as it grows in one dimension by addition at the open end" (p. 12). In Bateson's teaching, in his scholarly work ranging from schizophrenic communication and ethology to philosophy of science, and in his life really, he has drawn attention to what he calls the pattern that connects. Because established methods in psychology tend to draw attention away from pattern, in general by treating living beings as nonliving things, it is opportune to briefly reviews some issues involved in searching for the "pattern that connects" in lives of those with a vocation.

Events are events by virtue of interpretation. There are no brute facts that force themselves upon us outside our conception and experience of them (Hanson, 1969). For example, there is no fixed horse race outside a context of meanings that allows one to grasp what it is. Part of an event involves the interpretations of actors contributing to it and interpretation is always open, always subject to some indefiniteness. In pulling his horse, was Smoke obeying an instruction, earning money, fixing a race, breaking his own heart, ruining a horse, disillusioning a kid, safeguarding a livelihood, disgracing his profession, or opening himself to criminal charges? Can one really come to an end? Events cannot be bounded, for they are not discrete. "Our actions are offered to others as open sets of possibilities to be more closely defined should the need arise. There are no data, and *a fortiori* to attempt to formulate the descriptions of regularities in the sequence of human action as data, is a folly" (Harré, 1981, p. 17).

Not only are events open at a time, they are open over time. The meanings of an event or action cannot be absolutely fixed. As Dilthey (Rickman, 1976) noted some time ago, future constructions can radically alter the meaning of prior events. For example, in Trollope's stigmatized isolation, he created a fantasy world in which he associated with persons and did good deeds. Partially, in this "castle building," as he termed it, was an escape. Partially, it was a compensation. However, much later, it also proved to be essential practise in cultivating the imagination of a novelist. If Trollope's life had taken a different turn, we would not claim that his extended fantasies were practise for being a novelist, yet later events indicate that they were. Practise in heightening his imaginative sensitivity was partially there as a potential among an open set of potentials that might have been more fully realized later.

An event does not send us off reeling like Hume's collision of billiard balls. We interpret and reinterpret events that matter. We tell and retell the stories of events, and these interpretations and tellings are part of a larger story (see Bruner, 1987). The very concepts used in interpretation are open. Actors use meanings of ordinary language concepts such as devotedness and disillusionment. As noted previously, these concepts are not rigorously bounded containers (Wittgenstein, 1953; Rosch, 1977), but admit of degrees, shades, and proportions in experience and overlap with their opposite. The meanings of human actors frame and pervade events, without which there would be no significance, relevance, or understanding. Meaning depends upon context, or as Bateson (1979) phrased it, "without context, words and actions have no meaning at all" (p. 15).

The neopositivistic bent of psychological research is decidedly unsuited for illuminating a topic involving meaning and contexts of interpretation. For example, neopositivism requires the reduction of wholes to small bounded categories. The original idea was to create basic or elementary units that mirror the world. Understanding was limited to correspondent truth or the conditions under which a proposition can be said to be true. In short, this bypasses any serious consideration of what understanding is. Eventually, it was hoped that elementary units and elementary regularities would be placed within a hypothetico-deductive system, a systematic, abstract, and integrated statement of regularities. But how can presumably well-defined, bounded, elementary categories adequately represent a topic filled with categories or concepts that are ambiguous, open, and holistic? Meanings are not data, not discrete and stable facts, and to treat them as if they were imposes severe distortions. As William James (1958) commented on a similar subject, "the pretension, under such conditions, to be rigorously 'scientific' or 'exact' in our terms would only stamp us as lacking in understanding of our task" (p. 47).

Meaning depends upon context; neopositivism in practice tends to ignore context. Persons become objects with attributes, not subjects with intrinsic meanings that are lived. But to "thingify" a person makes the subject of vocation dissolve, for a vocation involves meanings lived. Without meaning, there is no way to distinguish a person with a vocation in life from someone who just likes his or her job. In his psychiatric apprenticeship, Jung (1965) confronted a similar situation. He entered psychiatry to study the meaning of "diseases" of human personalities, yet he found that it was regarded as unscientific and unprofessional to concern oneself with such matters:

> Psychiatry teachers were not interested in what the patient had to say, but rather in how to make a diagnosis or how to describe symptoms and to compile statistics . . . the human personality of the patient, his individuality, did not matter at all. Rather, the

doctor was confronted with Patient X, with a long list of cut-and-dried diagnoses and a detailing of symptoms. Patients were labeled, rubber-stamped with a diagnosis and, for the most part, that settled the matter. The psychology of the mental patient played no role whatsoever [p. 114].

The only admissible context for interpretation was psychiatric lore.

Similarly, neopositivism continues to presume that the only admissible context is the theory of some remote observer. This opens up the possibility of endless contexts of remote observers, for the subject lacks any intrinsic anchorage to limit what might be proposed. Of course, in human studies, meanings must be smuggled in through the back door to make any sense whatever. Consider, for instance, trying to understand a baseball game without assuming meanings and without the benefit of participants' accounts that would illumine what is going on. That persons act in accordance with meanings and that acts express meanings, radically alters how the topic can be profitably approached.

In contrast to rampant analysis, imposed and impoverished contexts, "thingification," absorption by quantity rather than quality, and reductionism, holistic construction requires attention to composition. For Bateson, the pattern that connects is a story, a fundamental basis for knowing. The very power of story is that it is uniquely capable of representing human meaning as lived. Story is a composition in which aspects are related in a context of relevance over time. We live in story and can be portrayed in story, and portrayal requires a continual alertness for distinctions that matter. Distinctions matter in forwarding or diverging from a pattern that connects. In story, it is never a matter of a thing in itself, but of its role or fit within an emerging or established composition. Menuhin was transported by music, Trollope by imagined dramas in which he participated, Steffens by objectivity, Jung by subjectivity, all quite different. However, each plays a similar role, meaning that each connects with other aspects of story in an analogous way that contributes to the pattern we would call a story.

For Bateson, stories were a manifestation immanent in the living world:

Thinking in terms of stories does not isolate human beings as something separate from the starfish and the sea anemones, the

coconut palms and the primroses. Rather, if the world be
connected, if I am at all fundamentally right in what I am
saying, then thinking in terms of stories must be shared by all
mind or minds, whether ours or those of redwood forests and sea
anemones [p. 13]

Story is a pattern or metapattern that connects all living beings:

Context and relevance must be characteristic not only of all
so-called behavior (those stories which are projected out into
"action"), but also of all those internal stories, the sequences of
the building up of the sea anemone. Its embryology must be
somehow made of the stuff of stories. And behind that, again,
the evolutionary process through millions of generations
whereby the sea anemone, like you and like me, came to
be—that process, too, must be of the stuff of stories [Bateson,
1979, p. 14].

Aside from story, it is well known that metaphor is our primary
vehicle for holistic construction (Pepper, 1942; Lakoff & Johnson,
1980). Particularly in attempting to make sense of a complex pattern,
metaphor provides a way to structure an unknown in terms of
something more known (Harré & Secord, 1973). In this sense,
seasonal flow is related to the life of those with vocation as a natural
cycle to a particular type of story. The seasons offer a basis for
discerning a whole more clearly, guiding discovery, and offering
perspective. However, if Bateson is correct, analogies and metaphors
are not just useful fictions. There is a valid analogue knowledge (see
Berman, 1984) for, as Holbrook (1981 phrased it in a surprisingly
similar appraisal of science, "the universe is, indeed, organized
analogically" (p. 216), and a metaphor is the way one captures its
wholeness.

Granted that the world is organized analogically, any cycle
might be used as a metaphor for other cycles or for the whole, but this
depends upon the nature of the organization. If the organization
resembles ordinary language concepts, there are paradigm cases and
deviant or borderline cases, and not every case would be a good
metaphor. Indeed, if the organization is like that of games
(Wittgenstein, 1953), there might not even be a paradigm case that
embodies core and enduring features. Rather, there might be a family
of prototypes. However, if there is a tighter organization with core

prototypes, Bateson's notion of mind immanent in nature or a basic logos of the world makes compelling sense.

Whether the seasonal analogue in this study is a useful fiction or an embodiment of a basic logos, I do not know. But in using it, I sought what Holbrook (1981) has termed a polar-complete paradigm to help illumine life stories rather than an absolutistic, fragmental one. A polar complete prardigm involves the unity of interpenetrating opposites. The unit stresses difference (e.g., idealism versus realism) and unity. Unity is impossible, in this view, without the interdependence of opposition. Stretched over time, an opposition is a story. Although it would be inappropriate to detour too far into this emerging view of science, it is important to characterize its nature, its relevance to the present study. In both, wholeness is intimately related to quality.

Wholeness and the Quality of Life

In the work of Bateson, Berman, Holbrook and others, there is a fundamental guiding principle. Stated most extremely, to unify is to sanctify. Wholeness is holiness. "Break the pattern which connects . . . and you necessarily destroy all quality (Bateson, 1979, p. 8). Stated less extremely, to unify is to enhance the quality of human existence. Wholeness only approaches holiness. If the pattern of meaning in a life is broken or fragmented, for instance, the quality of that life is diminished. If the pattern is established and maintained, the quality is enhanced.

Here, we are concerned with the weaker form of the principle, for we are concerned with a weaker form of wholeness. Personhood concerns what is common in the way persons become individuated. Human nature concerns a vast realm of potentials, only some of which are realized in any particular individuation. A strong form of wholeness would require a consideration of the potentials of human nature that must be realized in personhood. There are exemplars that seem to bring human nature to a peak, but those with a vocation are not necessarily such exemplars. In the unity they have attained, critical potentials and relations might have gone unrealized. Certainly there are some persons with a vocation who seem like a virtual fulfillment of human nature, but there are others who do not.

Those with a vocation are unified in two ways. They have

wholeheartedly incorporated a coherent position within a meaningful dramatic vision. Also, they have lived a unifying story. Position and story constitute the terms of unity for those with a vocation. To act centrally from position is to act centrally within one's life story. The relation of wholeness to quality can be framed in this limited way. To act centrally enhances the quality of life. To act peripherally or to be out of position for a sustained amount of time involves a deterioration of the quality of life.

Within the life histories investigated, the evidence is abundantly clear. A central enactment is vibrant with meaning, lighting up a person's life. Meanings are expansive and cannot be contained or definitely concluded. Everything in life seems to lead up to a central enactment and everything in one's future seems to lead from a central enactment. Even the anticipation of acting centrally as a whole person is profoundly enlivening. In medical school, still divided between his conventional personality and his mysterious, more cosmic personality, despairing that he must live in one world so antithetical to the world of the second personality, Jung (1965) began contemptuously to read a psychiatric text for a course. He wondered how psychiatrists might justify their existence, but as he began to read, all changed instantly:

> My heart began to pound. I had to stand up and draw a deep breath. My excitement was intense, for it had become clear to me, in a flash of illumination, that for me the only possible goal was psychiatry. Here alone the two currents of my interest could flow together and in a united stream dig their own bed. Here was the empirical field common to biological and spiritual facts, which I had everywhere sought and nowhere found. Here at last was the place where the collision of nature and spirit became a reality [pp. 108–9]

Over and over in lives, the promise and actualization of a whole from fragments and divisions is experienced as a kind of personal salvation, a flowering of immense quality.

In contrast, fragmentation attenuates meaning. From short incidents such as Peale's speech to alumni or Hilton's postwar restlessness in New Mexico to long episodes such as Carr's twenty years as a landlady, being out of position and off course casts a shadow on existence. This sense, that I have referred to as incompletion, is a necessary part of personhood and story, as a ground is necessary for a figure, but very dispiriting as a central experience.

Perhaps the most striking fruit of acting wholeheartedly or centrally is an extraordinary vitality. Vitality partially concerns energy, and the energy of those with a vocation is amazing. Even in old age, whether sick or enfeebled, they continued to produce what would be admirable in much younger persons. Trollope's prodigious output of novels continued. Mill's zeal for reform never diminished. Carr could not bring herself to stop. Hilton was always noted for his enormous energy. And so it goes. Vigor and energy are part of vitality, but what characterizes vitality best is aliveness. They are startlingly and awesomely alive. Except perhaps for love, vitality cannot be restricted to an emotion. Rather, it pervades and enlivens emotions and feelings. Ideally perhaps, vitality is most noticeable in joy, but Eiseley as one instance did not work in joy. The keenness of his experience was incredible, like a rose's last burst of beauty before it dies, but he could not be described as joyous. However, he and all those investigated can be described by the intense vitality of the meanings they live.

There is no absolute or perfect wholeness. Persons achieve more or less wholeness and approach wholeness in different ways with different hindrances. The relation between wholeness and quality can be conceived quantitatively, but this is a very limited conception. It is better to conceive of the relation more like a dance or friendship. One affects and adjusts to the other in a myriad of ways that might change over time. For example, Steffens' realism was unifying, but also it carried within it threats of helplessness and hopelessness. At the height of his career, Steffens began to feel worthless. Eiseley's isolation as a wanderer partially inspired the immense meaning of those moments when he achieved a form of empathic union with persons, creatures, and life generally. Yet it also seems prominent in what might be described as exquisite agony, an anguish so selfless and intense that it is beautiful and moving, endowing life with enormous preciousness.

Eiseley could appreciate what most of us perhaps take for granted. Both Mill and Menuhin were reared in extremely structured and sheltered circumstances. Both were profoundly unready for life on their own. Mill went through his famous mental crisis and Menuhin endured a failed first marriage before they emerged as more independent beings. Mill felt like a machine and Menuhin felt like his life was full of holes, even though united or on the way to uniting with a vocation. Part of the quality of their later lives involved the attainment of a complementary relationship to a woman. Both men were so enthusiastic in praising their mates, so lavish in what they attributed to them that it seems apparent that these women so filled what each lacked that they felt almost transformed or at least immeasurably enhanced. Without them, they would have no doubt have continued in their vocations, but life would have been greatly impoverished, or their work would have taken on vitality of a different shade and perhaps degree. As these examples suggest, the topic is complicated and diverse, requiring considerable investigation to make much progress. What the topic needs is not a correlation, but intensive case studies of the ways wholeness and quality of experience are mutually involved in lives.

In this sense, the principle is a promissory guide and perhaps the best one we have for exploring and perhaps helping persons to develop in a more individual fashion. At present, guides are almost all normative. For example, developmental counseling is concerned with helping persons to accomplish important developmental tasks that foster a more productive, meaningful life. The developmental tasks and developmental stages that guide counseling programs are normative (Erickson & Whiteley, 1980). For example, toward the end of adolescence, it might be assumed that persons must be able to specify an occupational preference, crystallize a sense of identity, or think more for themselves. Of the value of these conceptions and practices, there is no doubt. However, they are limited precisely because they are normative, offering guidance for everyone in general and no one in particular.

From an individual perspective, it is not so much that a general issue is resolved, but that a personal issue is resolved in a way that consolidates a more unified position or helps to further one's personal story. The task is aesthetic, similar to composing a novel. The principle that wholeness enhances quality directs attention to the personal context within which a resolved issue is to fit. Eventually, normative developmental theories might evolve into models of wholeness for human beings. Loevinger's (1976) theory of ego development is notable in this regard. With such a model, one could see the general potentials that must be developed and integrated if human nature is to be realized in a most fulfilling way. With such a theory, the strengths and weaknesses of individual forms of personhood could be assessed from a broader perspective. However, such a theory would not alter the requirements of shaping a personal drama and a significant part in it.

Consider the existential problem of the incompletion phase of life. From a sheerly remedial perspective that dominates much of psychiatry and clinical psychology, there is a problem or disease to get rid of. There is no person really, but a disease and it is this reification that is presumably treated. If one is depressed, get rid of the depression. If one has a conflict, get rid of it. If one is shy, rid oneself of it. The remedial vision is so conventional, so hedonistic in emphasis, so appalled by discomfort or anything unpleasurable that it is difficult to grant a vision at all. The contented pig vision is difficult to take seriously, yet it reigns undisputed. Whether a "cure" breaks the pattern that connects in a life, or whether it does not break it, could not be more relevant. The point is to get rid of whatever the immediate focus is with no consideration of personal context whatever.

The developmental perspective is a decisive advance. Whatever theory of development is used, the question is not automatically how to get rid of something, but a question of where it might lead. For instance, rather than cure Steffens of his disillusionment, one would consider where disillusionment might go. How will it foster or hinder development? From Kohlberg's (1976) theory of moral development, the dilemmas Steffens experienced are the very means by which he would progress to higher stages. His anguished questioning and search for answers were pivotal for the moral and personal stature he attained. Far from curing him, a developmental counselor might have helped him to pose more questions, to explore possible answers, and to determine how it all matters within the context of encouragement, warmth, and trust. A problem would not be viewed in a vacuum, but in terms of its potential for fostering those qualities of human nature most worth having.

From the present perspective, a problem of existence such as Steffens's disillusionment might stimulate development in general, but its entire personal significance is that it is a potential beginning of a life story, in whole or in part. Although this perspective is complementary to a developmental perspective, there are important differences. For example, if general moral development is the aim, it does not matter if the dilemmas are resolved. It is the challenge of dilemma, its capacity to stretch conceptions, that is pivotal for moral development, not solutions. However, from the present perspective, the solution is decisive. In the solution to a consuming problem of existence, in finding a way out, the future story of one's life is grounded.

The significance of a problem (event, issue, etc.) depends upon its potential role in story. How will a problem foster or hinder the dramatic development of a life? What virtues are required to maintain a pattern of enactment? What aspects of a person should be strengthened or weakened to fulfill a role? All these questions, and many others that could be drawn from the preceding chapters, are concerned with holistic construction of a dramatic nature. Dramatic form provides a basis for theory, research, and practice. A counselor, in this view, is like a consulting director of a movie who helps to determine which scenes should be kept and cut, what qualities should be emphasized or deemphasized in various roles, how roles are aligned, and what the movie is really about.

If a person is successful in discovering/inventing a whole from fragments and divisions, there is a gift of quality. One is enlivened, infused with a vitality that is diffused in work. If a person is able to establish a dramatic direction, achieve a significant position, enact position, and dwell in position, there seems at the end to be an open possibility for an elevation of one's nature. And for some, there appear to be glimpses of an illumination that, below the drama of one's life, a timeless cycle of human nature has also been realized. Through the personal, an impersonal or transpersonal cycle is completed that seems capable of startling elevation, but one that also creates a sense of unfamiliarity as though in preparation for a new story.

The whole of this book about persons who lived a vocation can be bound in one sentence: they lived in story. They made of life a single act. In one sense, a human being cannot avoid living in story. Dramatic form is our natural context of being. However, in many if not most lives, there are many divergent and episodic stories. There is no one story that makes a whole of life. Living a whole life is not given, but must be earned. There are difficult conditions to overcome before one can life a life story. For example, one must transcend self-centeredness and live for some vision greater than oneself. One must endure the pattern of incompletion until one is centered in a regnant desire. One must strive and endure the trial of making oneself a whole of incompletion, a self-metaphor. One might have to cling to the pattern that connects through circumstances that force one out of position. This is a book really about what it is to live in story, how it might be accomplished, and what counselors, clergy members, friends, and parents might do to help someone live his or her own story. If one can keep the faith to the end, as the Apostle Paul phrased it, there is a kind of dispersal of story into a more timeless sense that transcends both personhood and story.

References

Adler, M. 1985. *Ten philosophical mistakes*. New York: Macmillan.

Ansbacher, H., & Ansbacher, R. 1956. *The individual psychology of Alfred Adler*. New York: Basic Books.

Arnold, M. 1962. *Story sequence analysis*. New York: Columbia University Press.

Bandura, A. 1982. Self-efficacy mechanism in human agency. *American Psychologist*, 37, 122–47.

Bateson, G. 1979. *Mind and nature: A necessary unity*. New York: Dutton.

Baum, L. 1979. *The wizard of Oz*. New York: Ballantine Books.

Berman, M. 1984. *The reenchantment of the world*. New York: Bantam Books.

Bertaux, D. 1981. *Biography and society: The life history approach in the social sciences*. Beverly Hills: Sage Publications.

Blocher, D., & Schutz, R. 1961. Relationships among self-description, occupational stereotypes, and vocational preferences. *Journal of Counseling Psychology*, 8 314–17.

Britton, J. 1970. *Language and Learning*. Baltimore: Penguin Books.

Bruner, J. 1986. *Actual minds, possible worlds*. Cambridge: Cambridge University Press.

———. 1987. Life as narrative. *Social Research*, 54, 11–32.

Burke, K. 1968. *Counter-statement*. Berkeley: University of California Press.

———. 1969. *A grammar of motives*. Berkeley: University of California Press.

Burns, W. 1982. *Journey through the dark woods.* Seattle: Howe Street Press.

Buss, A., & Plomin, R. 1975. *A temperament theory of personality development.* New York: John Wiley.

Campbell, J. 1956. *The hero with a thousand faces.* Cleveland: Meridian.

Carr, D. 1986. *Time, narrative, and history.* Indianapolis: Indiana University press,

Carr, E. 1966. *Growing pains: The autobiography of Emily Carr.* Toronto: Clarke, Irvington.

_____ . 1967. *The house of all sorts.* Toronto: Clarke, Irwin.

Casanova, G. (translated by Willard Trask) 1966–71. *History of my life* (12 volumes). New York: Harcourt, Brace, Jovanovich.

_____ . (translated by A. Machen, edited by G. Gribble) 1984. *The life and memoirs of Casanova.* New York: Da Capo.

Chusid, H., Cochran, L. 1989. Meaning of career change from the perspective of family roles and dramas. *Journal of Counseling Psychology, 36,* 34–41.

Cochran, L. 1980. Client evaluation in psychotherapy: The role of contrast and alignment. *Journal of Psychiatric Treatment and Evaluation, 2,* 135–456.

_____ . 1986. *Portrait and story: Dramaturgical approaches to the study of persons.* Westport, Conn.: Greenwood Press.

_____ . 1985. *Position and the nature of personhood: An approach to the understanding of persons.* Westport, Conn.: Greenwood Press.

Csikszentmihalyi, M. 1975. *Beyond boredom and anxiety.* San Francisco: Jossey-Bass.

Csikszentmihalyi, M., & Beattie, O. 1979. Life themes: A theoretical and empirical exploration of their origins and affects. *Journal of Humanistic Psychology, 19,* 45–63.

Danto, A. 1968. *Analytical philosophy of history.* London: Cambridge University Press.

De Charms, R. 1976. *Enhancing motivation in the classroom.* New York: Irvington.

————. 1968. *Personal causation*. New York: Academic Press.

Deci, E. 1975. *Intrinsic motivation*. New York: Plenum Press.

De Waele, J.-P., & Harré, R. 1976. The personality of individuals in R. Harré, ed. *Personality*. Totowa, N.J.: Rowman and Littlefield.

Eiseley, L. 1975. *All the strange hours*. New York: Charles Scribner's Sons.

————. 1969. *The unexpected universe*. New York: Harcourt, Brace, & World.

————. 1962. *The mind as nature*. New York: Harper & Row.

Eliade, M. 1975. *Rites and symbols of initiation*. New York: Harper & Row.

Erickson, L., & Whiteley, J. 1980. *Developmental counseling and teaching*. Monterey, Calif.: Brooks/Cole.

Erikson, E. 1959. *Identity and the life cycle*. New York: International Universities Press.

Farmer, F. 1973. *Will there really be a morning?* New York: Dell

Feinberg, J. 1970. *Moral concepts*. London: Oxford University Press.

Fingarette, H. 1969. *Self-deception*. London: Routledge & Kegan Paul.

Franklin, B. (edited by L. Lemisch) 1961. *Benjamin Franklin: The autobiography and other writings*. New York: Signet.

Friedman, M. 1975. *Rational behavior*. Columbia: University of South Carolina Press.

Frye, N. 1957. *Anatomy of criticism*. Princeton: Princeton University Press.

Gaddis, T., & Long, L. 1970. *Killer: A journal of murder*. New York: Macmillan

Garrett, E. 1968. *Many voices: The autobiography of a medium*. New York: Putnam's Sons.

Green, R., & Hooper, W. 1976. *C.S. Lewis: A biography*. New York: Harcourt, Brace, Jovanovich.

Hanson, N. 1969. *Perception and discovery*. San Francisco: Freeman, Cooper.

Harding, D. 1963. *Experience into words*. London: Chatto & Windus.

––––––. 1937. The role of the onlooker. *Scrutiny*, 6, 247–58.

Harré, R. 1974. Blueprint for a new science. In N. Armistead, *Reconstructing social psychology*. Baltimore: Penguin Books.

––––––. 1981. The positivist-empiricist approach and its alternative. In P. Reason & J. Rowan, eds., *Human inquiry: A sourcebook of new paradigm research*. New York: John Wiley.

Harré, R., & Secord, P. 1973. *The explanation of social behavior*. Totowa, N.J.: Littlefield, Adams.

Healy, C. 1982. *Career development: Counseling through the life stages*. Boston: Allyn & Bacon.

Herr, E., & Cramer, S. 1979. *Career guidance through the life span*. Boston: Little, Brown.

Hill, N. 1960. *Think and grow rich*. New York: Fawcett Crest.

Hilton, C. 1957. *Be my guest*. Englewood Cliffs, N.J.: Prentice-Hall.

Holbrook, B. 1981. *The stone monkey: An alternative Chinese-scientific reality*. New York: William Morrow.

Holland, J. 1985. *Making vocational choices*. Englewood Cliffs, N.J.: Prentice Hall.

Iacocca, L. 1984. *Iacocca: An autobiography*. New York: Bantam.

James, H. 1962. The art of fiction. In S. Bradley, R. Beatty, & E. Long, eds., *The American tradition in literature*. Volume 2. New York: Norton.

––––––. 1983. *Autobiography: Henry James*. Princeton: Princeton University Press.

James, W. 1958. *The varieties of religious experience*. New York: Mentor.

Jung, C. 1965. *Memories, dreams, reflections.* New York: Random House.

Kelly, G. 1955. *The psychology of personal constructs.* New York: Norton.

Koch, S. 1959–63. *Psychology: A study of a science* (6 volumes). New York: McGraw-Hill.

Kohlberg, L. 1976. Moral stages and moralization: The cognitive-developmental approach. In T. Lickona, ed., *Moral development and behavior.* New York: Holt, Rinehart, & Winston.

Lakoff, G., Johnson, M. 1980. *Metaphors we live by.* Chicago: University of Chicago Press.

Leeper, R., & Madison, P. 1959. *Toward understanding human personalities.* New York: Appleton-Century-Crofts.

Levinson, D. 1978. *The seasons of a man's life.* New York: Ballantine.

Lewis, C.S. 1963. *A grief observed.* New York: Seabury Press.

————. 1959. *Surprised by joy.* Glasgow: Fontana.

Liddy, G. 1980. Will: The autobiography of G. Gordon Liddy. New York: Dell.

Loevinger, J. 1976. *Ego development.* San Francisco: Jossey-Bass.

McAdams, D. 1985. *Power, intimacy, and the life story.* Homewood, Illinois: Doarsey Press.

McAdams, D., & Ochberg, R. 1988. *Psychobiography and life narratives.* Durham: Duke University Press.

MacGregor, A., & Cochran, L. 1988. Work as enactment of family drama. *The Career Development Quarterly,* 37, 138–48.

MacIntyre, A. 1984. *After virtue.* Notre Dame: University of Notre Dame Press.

Manicas, P., & Secord, P. 1983. Implications for psychology of a new philosophy of science. *American Psychologist,* 38, 399–413.

Maslow, A. 1976. *Religious, values, and peak-experiences.* New York: Penguin.

————. 1962. *Toward a psychology of being.* Princeton, N.J.: Van Nostrand.

Maurois, A. 1970. *Memoirs.* New York: Harper & Row.

McCall, G., & Simmons, J. 1978. *Identities and interactions.* New York: Free Press.

Mead, M. 1975. *Blackberry winter: My earlier years.* New York: Pocket Books.

Menuhin, Y. 1978. *Unfinished journey.* London, Futura.

Melges, F., Anderson, R., Kraemer, H., Tinklenberg, J., & Weisz, A. 1971. The personal future and self-esteem. *Archives of General Psychiatry, 25,* 494–97.

Mill, J.S. (edited by J. Stillinger) 1969. *Autobiography and other writings.* Boston: Houghton Mifflin.

Milne, C. (1985). *Hollow on the hill: The search for a personal philosophy.* London: Methuen.

————. 1976. *The enchanted places.* New York: Penguin.

————. 1979. *The path through the trees.* New York: E.P. Dutton.

Murray, H. 1938. *Explorations in personality.* New York: Oxford University Press.

Nixon, R. 1962. *Six Crises.* Garden City, N.Y.: Doubleday.

Norris, W., Hatch, R., Engelkes, J., & Winborn, G. 1979. *The career information service.* Chicago: Rand McNally.

Norton, D. 1976. *Personal destinies.* Princeton: Princeton University Press.

Ochberg, R. 1987. *Middle-aged sons and the meaning of work.* Ann Arbor, Mich.: UMI Research Press.

Osherson, S. 1980. *Holding on and letting go.* New York: Free Press.

Palmer, R. 1969. *Hermeneutics.* Evanston: Northwestern University Press.

Parke, J. 1955. Seven Moby-Dicks. *New England Quarterly, 28,* 319–38.

Parsons, F. 1909. *Choosing a vocation.* Boston: Houghton Mifflin.

Peale, N. 1984. *The true joy of positive living: An autobiography.* New York: Morrow.

Pepper, S. 1942. *World hypothesis.* Berkeley: University of California Press.

Piaget, J. 1968. *Six psychological studies.* New York: Vintage.

Polanyi, M. 1966. *The tacit dimension.* Garden City, N.Y.: Doubleday.

Polkinghorne, D. 1988. *Narrative knowing and the human sciences.* Albany: State University of New York Press.

Raynor, J., & Entin, E. 1982. *Motivation, career striving, and aging.* New York: Hemisphere.

Rickman, H. 1976. *W. Dilthey: Selected writings.* Cambridge: Cambridge University press.

Rogers, C. 1963. Actualizing tendency in relation to "motives" and to consciousness. In M. Jones, ed., *Nebraska symposium on motivation.* Lincoln: University of Nebraska Press.

Rosch, E. 1977. Principles of categorization. In E. Rosch & B. Lloyd, eds., *Cognition and categorization.* Hillsdale, N.J.: Erlbaum Press.

Rostand, E. (translated by Brian Hooker) 1959. *Cyrano de Bergerac.* New York: Bantam.

Rotter, J. 1966. Generalized expectancies for internal vs. external control of reinforcement. *Psychological Monographs,* 80 (1).

Royce, J. 1914. *The philosophy of loyalty.* New York: Macmillan.

Runyan, W. 1982. *Life histories and psychobiography: Explorations in theory and method.* New York: Oxford University Press.

Saint Augustine (translated by R.S. Pine-Coffin). 1961. *Confessions.* Baltimore: Penguin.

Saint Ignatius (translated by Anthony Mottola). 1964. *The spiritual exercises of St. Ignatius.* Garden City, N.Y.: Image Books.

Sarbin, T. 1986. *Narrative psychology.* New York: Praeger.

Saw, R. 1971. *Aesthetics: An introduction.* Garden City, N.Y.: Doubleday.

Seligman, M. 1975. *Helplessness: On depression, development and death.* San Francisco: Freeman.

Sloan, T. 1987. *Deciding: Self-deception in life choices.* New York: Metheun.

Solomon, R. 1977. *The passions.* Garden City, N.Y.: Anchor.

Steffens, L. 1931. *The autobiography of Lincoln Steffens.* New York: Harcourt, Brace.

Super, D. 1976. *Career education and the meanings of work.* Washington, D.C.: U.S. Government Printing Office.

———. 1957. *The psychology of careers.* New York: Harper & Row.

Super, D., Starishevsky, R., Matlin, N., & Jordaan, J.-P. 2963. New York: College Entrance Examination Board.

Terkel, S. 1975. *Working.* New York: Avon.

Tolbert, E. 1980. *Counseling for career development.* Boston: Houghton Mifflin.

Trollope, A. 1978. *An autobiography.* Berkeley: University of California Press.

Turner, V. 1975. *Dramas, fields, and metaphors.* Ithaca: Cornell University Press.

Underhill, E. 1974. *Mysticism.* New York: New American Library.

Valle, R., & King, M. 1978. *Existential-phenomenological alternatives for psychology.* New York: Oxford University Press.

Van Gennep, a. 1960. *The rites of passage.* Chicago: University of Chicago Press.

Washington, B.T. 1956. *Up from slavery.* New York: Bantam.

Watson, L. & Watson-Franke, M. 1985. *Interpreting life histories.* New Brunswick: Rutgers University Press.

Weston, H. 1970. *Form in literature: A theory of technique and construction.* Edinburgh: Edinburgh Press.

Wheelwright, P. 1959. *Heraclitus.* New York: Atheneum.

White, A. 1967. *The philosophy of mind.* New York: Random House.

Whitehead, A. 1967. *Science and the modern world.* New York: Free Press.

Whitehead, A. 1957. *The function of reason.* Princeton: Princeton University Press.

Wilson, J. 1963. *Thinking with concepts.* London: Cambridge University Press.

Wittgenstein, L. 1953. *Philosophical investigation.* Oxford: Blackwell.

Index

209